THE HISTORY OF PHILOSOPHY

THE MIDDLE AGES AND
THE RENAISSANCE

THE MIDDLE AGES
AND THE
RENAISSANCE

BY ÉMILE BRÉHIER

TRANSLATED BY WADE BASKIN

THE UNIVERSITY OF CHICAGO PRESS

CHICAGO AND LONDON

Originally published in 1931 as Histoire de la philosophie:
L'Antiquité et le Moyen Age. III: Le Moyen Age
et la Renaissance. © *1931, Presses Universitaires de France*

*The present bibliography has been revised and enlarged to
include recent publications. These have been
supplied by the translator and Joseph Betz*

*The University of Chicago Press, Chicago 60637
The University of Chicago Press, Ltd., London W.C. 1
© 1965 by The University of Chicago
All rights reserved. Published 1965
Third Impression 1968
Printed in the United States of America*

CONTENTS

THE EARLY MIDDLE AGES

DURING THE FIFTH CENTURY the unity of the Mediterranean civilization was shattered just as its political unity was shattered. With the destruction of towns that marked the barbarian invasions came the disappearance of traditional centers of culture throughout the West, and with the destruction of urban civilization came the collapse of the sophistical instruction that had imposed its unity on the last part of the age of antiquity.

How was it possible for instruction to continue under the deplorable conditions that existed until the time of Charlemagne? Here we must recall one general characteristic of the late Roman age: attention was directed less toward intellectual training per se than toward the development of the spiritual life, and the universal need was met not by chairs of sophistry or of science, modeled on the Museum of Alexandria, but by spiritual conventicles that gradually became philosophical schools. They had sprung up among the Therapeutae of Lake Mareotis, described in the writings of Philo, and countless Pythagorean, Hermetic, and Platonic communities flourished even within pagan circles. Furthermore, although the spiritual life was still pre-eminently intellectual and the need for rational organization paramount in certain circles (for instance, among Plotinians), in others it tended to become in every respect a mystery cult with a set of formulas, rites, and sacraments.

Thus it was not by violent revolution but through natural inclination that all the remnants of intellectual life were preserved

I

in the Christian communities, particularly in monasteries, after the West had solidly embraced Christianity.

Almost imperceptibly, therefore, a remarkable change came about: intellectual life was completely subordinated to religious life; philosophical problems were studied against the background of man's destiny as conceived by Christianity. The period during which the religious life remained dominant marked the boundaries—which are naturally somewhat vague—of the intellectual Middle Ages. The modern age began with acceptance of the autonomy of intellectual methods and problems—a revolution so profound that even today we can scarcely comprehend all its consequences.

1 Orthodoxy and Heresies in the Fourth and Fifth Centuries

On this point we must carefully separate West from East. In the great religious controversies that marked the end of antiquity in the East we detect the same metaphysical preoccupation, the same concern with determining the intelligible structure of things as in Neo-Platonism of the same era. All of them concern either the Trinitarian question and the interrelations of hypostases or the Christological question—that is, the relation between the Word as a divine hypostasis and Jesus Christ as a man. And in spite of appeals to authority and to Scripture the divergences between theologians seem to be mainly philosophical.

On the one hand there were the heretics. Sabellius and the modalists feared that making the Word the Son of God would lead to polytheism, and Arius, in the same spirit, reversed the argument and accepted the Son of God as a person only on condition that he be made the first of all God's creatures "but without being eternal or coeternal with the Father, for God is his principle."[1] The whole Antioch school refused to see in Jesus Christ anything but a man perfected by divine grace, and it rejected metaphysical combinations of God and man, an idea that permeated Christianity

---

[1] Quoted by Harnack, *Lehrbuch der Dogmengeschichte* (3d ed.), II, 191, n. 2.

following Nestorius and spread even to the Far East. All such opinions bore the stamp of the same rationalistic inspiration directed toward classifying, avoiding confusion, making distinctions. Countering the heresies was orthodox dogma which sought to reconcile theocentrism (which eliminates any possibility of difference within divine unity) and the distinctions indispensable to the very existence of Christianity. Athanasius and the Council of Trent confronted Arius with the argument of the unity of substance in God together with the diversity of the three persons, and Cyril of Alexandria and the Council of Ephesus (433) condemned Nestorius by arguing that the duality of human and divine natures in Christ did not prevent Mary from being the Theotokos, the Mother of God.

Conflicts abounded in the West as well during the same era, but they were of a different order. All issued, directly or indirectly, from the need for the institution of the Church and its hierarchy. This was true of Donatism, which originated and almost prevailed in Africa, and which had been in existence for a century when the debate presided over by St. Augustine took place in 411. It was also true of Pelagianism, which St. Augustine combated all his life. The Church in its role as an institution necessary for the dispensation of divine grace was incompatible with both of these heresies. The Donatists held that the validity of a sacrament depended on the spiritual state of the priest who conferred it. This would have meant rejecting the Church as a society grounded on strict, practical, objective rules, and exposing it to all the hazards of a subjective appraisal of the morality of priests. Formalism is the prime requirement for stability, and it is no more necessary for the one who confers the sacraments to be a saint at heart than for the Roman jurist who decides what is right to be personally just.

As for Pelagianism, the starting point of the conflict was an attempt on the part of the monk Pelagius to promote monastic reform. To refute Christians who used the weakness of the flesh as an excuse for not complying with divine law, he preached that man has the strength to do good if he so wills and pointed to the powers of human nature. He insisted "that the soul should not be remiss or hesitant in the pursuit of virtue simply because it feels impotent and is ignorant of its own potential." [2] His view goes back to Stoicism with its confidence in virtue; but it is the negation of original sin transmitted by heredity, since God cannot impute to us the sin of another; it presents Christ's work as if it were the work of a model teacher or a model doctor, such as a saintly Cynic, and not as the work of a victim whose merits justify man; finally, it denies that the vehicles of grace, the sacraments which the Church provides for the faithful, are of any importance.

To counteract such notions St. Augustine cited the personal experience of his conversion and the effective reality of the Church. If Pelagius were right, man would not have to ask through prayer to be freed from temptation or to pray when he erred.[3] The Pelagians strove to identify our good with that part of us which is not of God; if they granted that good will came from God, this was only because they put it in the same class with existence; and in this case God would also be the author of evil will; or if we grant that he produces only will and that man himself makes it good, it follows that the good which comes from us is superior to that which comes from God. St. Augustine traced in detail the consequences of this attitude: good can enter the soul, corrupted by original sin, only through a special grace; salvation, which depends on merit acquired through grace, belongs only to those predestined by God throughout eternity; children who die without baptism are justly damned; the heathen, never having been touched by the grace of Christ, have never attained virtue.

This dual conflict, together with the solution proposed by St. Augustine, throws light on the setting in which Western thought was to evolve: a Church with full power thereafter to exercise full control over salvation. The work of Pope Gregory the Great was to be the final consolidation of the spiritual power of the Church.

The conflicts of the early Middle Ages have to do with ecclesiastical politics (in the highest sense of the term) rather than with

---

[2] *Ad Demetrium*, cited by Harnack, *Lehrbuch*, III, 161.

[3] Augustine *Ad Marcellinum* ii. 1.

dogma in the Eastern sense, that is, the metaphysical structure of the divinity. St. Augustine's thought, so rigid when brought to bear on the religious life of the human soul, is vague with respect to dogma in the strict sense. For instance, in the controversy over the origin of the soul (whose solution seems, moreover, to constitute an indispensable complement to his doctrine of grace), he hesitates without drawing a conclusion between traducianism, which holds that human souls are propagated by generation, and creationism, which holds that each soul is created *ex nihilo;* and he fiercely attacks those who believe that "man can discuss his own quality or his whole nature as if no part of himself escaped him." [4]

Furthermore, from the moment when they seized undisputed power with Gregory the Great until the twelfth century, the popes gave no encouragement to theological speculation. Politicians and jurists before all else, they were more concerned with establishing and insuring the rights drawn from their spiritual power over souls than with giving direction to an intellectual movement.

II *The Fifth and Sixth Centuries: Boethius*

It was still possible for the philosophical tradition to lend valuable support to the verities of faith. Such was the conviction of Claudianus Mamertus, a Provençal monk, who in *De statu animae* (*ca.* 468) drew together the views of the philosophical authorities on the spirituality of the soul. He cited St. Paul to prove that philosophers were not so ignorant of truth as their contemporaries accused them of being, and he took his colleagues to task for their intellectual indolence. He complained that Plato was treated with contempt even though "many centuries before the Incarnation," long before God had revealed the truth to men, Plato "discussed the one God and the three persons in him." [5] Through Claudianus, men of the late Middle Ages came to know the views on the incorporality of the soul expressed in the *Phaedrus,* the *Timaeus,* and

---

[4] *De anima et ejus origine* iv. 2.
[5] Migne, *Patrologia Latina,* LIII, 746d.

the *Phaedo*; his work also provided them with a model of a lamentable type of erudition, which consisted of disconnected extracts and was the last descendant of the doxographies in which the age of antiquity summed up its philosophical past as it was drawing to a close; in his work we find alongside the Greek philosophers (Pythagoreans and Platonists) the Roman philosophers (Sextius and Varro), then the barbarians (Zoroaster, the Brahmans, Anacharsis), and, of course, the Stoic Chrysippus, whimsically cited to prove the spirituality of the soul.

In the work of Anicius Manlius Severinus Boethius, "the last of the Romans," born in 480, named consul in 510, appointed to high office by Theodoric, and accused of magic practices and executed in 524, the late Middle Ages had a less comprehensive but more substantial account of ancient philosophy. Boethius had undertaken the staggering task of translating into Latin the works of Plato and Aristotle and those of several of their commentators. Had he succeeded, his project, which was not revived until the eighteenth century, would probably have changed radically the course of medieval philosophy. Actually, however, his accomplishment was limited to the translation of some of Aristotle's writings on logic: the *Categories,* followed by a commentary inspired by Porphyry's; *De interpretatione,* followed by two commentaries; Porphyry's *Isagoge,* followed by a commentary inspired by Ammonius. He prepared handbooks on categorical and hypothetical syllogisms and on topical differences, but he translated none of Aristotle's other works on logic.

Thus a portion of Aristotle's writings on logic stood as the sole cogent representative of antiquity! This fact is important. Aristotle's categories of substance, quality, quantity, and so forth, do not refer to things themselves, as Boethius indicated on the basis of Porphyry's work, but neither are they simple grammatical classes. Aristotle deals with words as signifiers of things and with things as signified by words. For him, therefore, language is a human institution and any name is first of all a name that serves to designate a particular corporeal thing. It follows that categories and, after them, the whole of logic are naturally adapted to corporeal things and made for them.

This is the crux of the problem posed at the beginning of the *Isagoge*: "As for genera and species (designated by words that no longer signify corporeal, concrete things), have they an existence or are they only in our thoughts? If they exist, are they bodies or incorporeal things? If they are incorporeal things, are they separate or do they exist only in sensible things?" Porphyry merely raised the questions; Boethius in commenting on them indicated but did not sanction the solution proposed by Aristotle. The proposed solution is patently drawn from the criticism of Plato's ideas: a genus exists simultaneously in several individuals and obviously cannot exist in itself; numerical unity of a being in itself is incompatible with dispersion of genus in species or of species in individuals.[6]

Boethius also completed some theological works which were widely read and annotated until the twelfth century. They are closely linked to his dialectical writings; for instance, his *De sancta Trinitate* is based on the question, "Are the rules of dialectic applicable to propositions enunciated by the theologian? What precautions are to be taken and what particular rules are to be followed in using discourse for subjects for which discourse was not designed?"

Boethius was also influential by virtue of his celebrated work, *The Consolation of Philosophy,* which he wrote in prison following his disgrace. There is hardly a trace of Christianity in the work.[7] Its literary form (a mixture of verse and prose) is modeled on the Roman diatribe and its substance is drawn from the Stoic and Platonic theodicy. His aim is to explain the injustice of which he is a victim: Is the course of human events, so disordered when compared with the perfect order of nature, in the hands of blind fortune? The old theme appears in Plato's *Gorgias* and *Laws* and in Plotinus' *Enneads.* His doubting and despair are dispelled by two types of

[6] *Ibid.,* LXIV, 82b–86a.
[7] Gilson (*Revue Critique,* 1928, p. 377) finds almost no trace of a distinction between purgatory and hell (*Patrologia Latina,* LXIII, 806).

remedies. First come the "milder cures": Fortune, in a diatribe similar to that of Teles, shows Boethius that he has no reason to complain, that true happiness accommodates all events, that even bad luck has its advantages. Then come "more violent cures": Philosophy shows that true happiness, which is independence, resides solely in God, who is the Good and perfect unity. God, who is the author of nature, can direct beings only toward the good; and evil, since it cannot be produced by God, is nothing. All that remains is to fit the affirmation of Providence to the fact that, as experience shows, the wicked prosper. Philosophy replies, through the *Gorgias* and the *Republic,* that their prosperity is only apparent, for all wicked men are actually unhappy. The fate of each being in reality depends on Providence, whose will is executed in detail through natural forces. The result is the realization of true justice, which is quite different from apparent justice. And if the objection is raised that such a view of destiny assumes the negation of freedom, which seems to be antithetical to divine prescience, Boethius at first answers with Cicero that prescience does not prove the necessity of events, and then that it is wrong for us to base our concept of the foreknowledge of God, who lives and perceives in an eternal present, on our own type of reasoning.

A moving book in spite of its factitious character, it long remained one of the few testaments to a moral life inspired by something other than the spiritual powers of the day. The only reason it cannot be classed as unique is that the works of Lucan, Vergil, and Cicero were also studied during the late Middle Ages.

If to these works we add his treatise *De institutions arithmetica,* based on Nicomachus of Gerasa, and his *De institutio musica,* we see the role that Boethius played in the Western world in the transmission of Hellenic culture to the Middle Ages.

After Boethius, who was not original but at least deserves credit for going to the sources and dealing with questions in depth, we find only humble compilers who devoted their attention to preparing extracts and summaries of ancient works for the instruction of clerics. One of their models was Martianus Capella the African, who, toward the end of the fifth century, under the title *The Wedding of Mercury and Philology,* had written a manual in which each book from the third through the ninth was devoted to one of the seven liberal arts. The author was himself a compiler who owed most of his knowledge to Varro. The fourth book (the *Dialectic*), which begins with a eulogy of the famous Latin scholar, acquainted men of the Middle Ages with the five terms—genus, species, difference, property, and accident; with the ten categories; and with oppositions, propositions, and syllogisms. The sixth book consists mainly of a long description of the earth, borrowed from Pliny the Elder, and a few details from Euclid's *Elements.* The seventh book juxtaposes a symbolic arithmetic and some positive theorems.

Cassiodorus (477-575), a friend of Boethius who spent a part of his long life in the monastery of Vivarium, took upon himself the task of assembling and transmitting the fragmentary knowledge to which he had access. He wrote an encyclopedia of theology called the *Institutiones divinae* and explained the liberal arts in *Saeculares lectiones.* In the first of the two works, however, he states that knowledge of the liberal arts is rooted in the Bible and must be put to the service of truth. He cites as basic the grammar of Donatus, the rhetoric of Cicero annotated by Marius Victor and Quintilian, a dialectic that does not go beyond that of Martianus Capella, and summaries of Boethius' arithmetic and Euclid's elements.

His treatise *De anima* was based on St. Augustine and Claudianus Mamertus. The author was aware of the duality of inspiration that sets philosophy against religion in the matter of the nature of the soul. The "masters of secular letters" define the soul as "a simple substance, a natural form, different from bodily matter, possessing the use of the organs and the potency of life." But "on the authority of veracious doctors" it is "created by God, spiritual, a true substance, the cause of life on the part of the body, rational and immortal, and capable of turning to good or evil." He was able to separate proofs of immortality offered by secular men of letters (mainly the proofs found in the *Phaedo*) from the much easier proof offered by the "veracious authorities" (that the soul is created in the image of God). Finally, in discussing the knowledge of evil among men, he mentioned philosophers "who follow human error rather than the law of the creator." [8]

III *Reason and Faith*

Under such conditions the question of the relation between reason and faith was not easy to resolve. An institution like the Church is not a set of speculative verities that can serve as a basis for agreement or conflict. It is first imposed in the same way that political constitutions or rules of law are imposed: it is a spiritual city, one that Augustinianism intended to establish definitively. This city implies two kinds of knowledge: secular and divine. Secular knowledge embraces the totality of propaedeutics, or the liberal arts that men like Philo and Seneca posited as the starting point of philosophy. It embraces the trivium—grammar, rhetoric, and dialectic—which includes all the arts of speaking and discourse; and the quadrivium, which includes the four subjects posited by Plato as the starting point of philosophy—arithmetic, geometry, astronomy, and music. Here as in the philosophy of Philo and Seneca, the liberal arts are not ends in themselves; the cleric who teaches them to other clerics is justified in doing so only to the degree that they advance knowledge of divine things. The trivium finds its justification in the necessity of reading and explaining Scripture and the writings of the Church Fathers and of teaching dogma. The quadrivium is indispensable in liturgy and ecclesiastical computation. Such restricted applications do not focus attention on the need for enlarging upon acquired knowledge and promoting these fields of learning for their own sake; emphasis is placed instead on providing, through encyclopedias that vary in scope, an inventory of the heritage of the past. The result is that all such knowledge is purely rational and lacking in autonomy, for all that is retained is that which has been inherited and can be of service to the Church.

It is not surprising, therefore, that before the time of Charlemagne

[8] Migne, LXX, 1279, especially chaps. i, ii, and x.

encyclopedias were written in the regions of Europe where traces of the intellectual life still subsisted, namely in Spain and in Ireland. Isidore, Bishop of Seville (570–636), wrote his *Etymologies* dealing with "the origin of certain things as recalled in ancient books": three books on the trivium and the quadrivium, in which chapters on dialectic taken from Apuleius and Martianus Capella contain some of the elements of logic as well as the divisions of philosophy; then seventeen books on everything that might interest a cleric in matters of the calendar, history, natural history, and geography. Later the Venerable Bede (672–735) of the monastery of Jarrow wrote a *De natura rerum* of the same quality. In it he copied Isidore, but more often he relied on Pliny the Elder.

Knowledge of divine things, which rests on authority, is different. Authority is not something simple; even the heretics based their arguments on authority, and the Arians cited Scripture to support their view. St. Vincent of Lérins tried in his *Commonitorium*, written in 354, to resolve the difficulties raised by arguments based on authority. He laid bare the thought of the Middle Ages as he formulated standards for identifying the true tradition in matters of faith: one should show preference for the opinion of the majority and look with distrust on private opinions; if heresy threatens to spread, however, one should cling to the opinions of the ancients; if these opinions are found to contain errors, one should follow the decisions of an ecumenical council or, if no council has been held, question and compare orthodox teachers and hold to the opinions common to all. Tradition does indeed grow, but its growth is organic; it never proceeds through addition or innovation but rather through development and elucidation. Thus from the beginning of the Middle Ages standards were set up to allow spiritual unity to be preserved without any intervention of philosophical thought.

In contrast, medieval thought concerning divine things was influenced by St. Augustine and the Neo-Platonic tradition. God is intelligence in the highest sense, the source of the intelligible; and knowledge or contemplation of God is the highest limit of intellectual knowledge. Like Plotinus, St. Augustine thought that "when the soul has been put in order, made harmonious and beautiful, and communes with itself, then it will dare to see God, the source from which all verities flow and the father of all truth." Beneath this vision, reserved for the few, "the intelligent soul united naturally with intelligibles perceives truths in a certain incorporeal light identical in nature with itself." [9]

The two themes are unrelated: on the one hand, a set of formulas discussed by councils and synods as if they were rules of law; and on the other hand, a free spirituality in which knowledge is not limited by faith but is directed toward complete knowledge of God. The great paradox of the Middle Ages is the affirmation of their solidarity: to understand the truth about God is to understand the truths of faith; reason, viewed as enlightened intelligence, must consummate faith.

The spirit of the age is revealed particularly in works on the instruction of clerics, such as the *De clericorum institutione,* by Hrabanus Maurus (776–856), Abbot of the monastery of Fulda in 822. The third book in the *De clericorum institutione* is a compilation of the last three books in St. Augustine's *On Christian Doctrine*. It relates all wisdom, directly or indirectly, to knowledge of the truths of religion revealed in Scripture. "The foundation and perfection of wisdom," Hrabanus Maurus wrote in the second chapter of the third book, "is the study of the Holy Scripture." And the literary production of the period consists mainly of countless commentaries of the Old Testament (especially of the work of the six days), the Gospels, and the Epistles. For the most part these commentaries merely repeat and amplify the commentaries of the great scholars of the preceding century, St. Hilary and St. Augustine.

The rules for writing commentaries were drawn, through the intermediary of the Greek and Latin Fathers, from Philo's allegorical commentaries. The commentator has a right to make use of all knowledge, whether scientific or philosophical. Hrabanus Maurus requires the cleric to have knowledge of *pura veritas historiarum*

[9] Cf. Boyer, *De l'Idée de Vérité chez saint Augustin* (Paris, 1880), pp. 190, 199.

and of *modi tropicorum locutionum*—in other words, to be able to distinguish between Scripture that must be taken literally and Scripture that must be interpreted allegorically. He also provides a lengthy dictionary of all the allegorical interpretations of the names of biblical people, thus assembling materials for commentaries.

But the commentators go further. All disciplines must serve their end, even the *doctrinae gentilium* which include the "liberal arts" and philosophy. From Boethius to Hrabanus Maurus we detect in doctrinal writings an intellectual tradition wholly alien to Christianity and the Church. But our concern is not so much the enumeration of all the remnants of ancient culture preserved in the old encyclopedias as the assessment of the attitude of Christian commentators toward the mass of knowledge transmitted to them without the key that would enable them to gain access to it, that is, without the intellectual methods that had made possible its discovery.

Their attitude was somewhat ambiguous. There was a tendency (doubtlessly derived from St. Augustine) to relate all doctrines of the heathen to the same source of truth as that from which Christian truth emanates: "The truths found in the books of the learned men of the century must be attributed solely to Truth and Wisdom, for these truths were not established from the outset by those in whose books they are read; instead, they have emanated from the eternal being and been discovered to the degree that Truth and Wisdom have permitted learned men to discover them; thus everything must be related to a single term, whether it be what is found to be useful in the books of the heathen or what is salutary in Scripture" (chap. ii).

The method of science did not differ essentially from the philological method of the commentator. The object of science was to discover what God had instituted in nature, just as the object of the commentator was to discover what God had instituted in Scripture. This entailed the separation of the bad sciences and the good sciences: the bad sciences had to do with "the institutions of men" (chap. xvi), that is, with the worship of idols and the magical arts; and the good sciences were in turn divided into two classes: those relating to the corporal senses—history, through which we know the past, knowledge of the present through the senses, and conjectures concerning the future (for example, astronomy), based on experience (*experimentum*)—and the seven liberal arts.

But the notion of a unique source of truth tending to bring about fusion and unity was counteracted by a wholly different principle. According to this principle, commentary of Scripture dominated all else, and inventories of the profane sciences should serve only to provide materials for illuminating the spiritual meaning of Scripture. Grammar, for example, contains in Hrabanus Maurus' view one element indispensable to the understanding of the Psalter; dialectic will teach the rules and interrelations of truths that will show what can be deduced correctly from the truths taught by Scripture; arithmetic and the science of numbers will reveal the hidden meaning of Scripture, inaccessible to the ignorant; geometrical porportions utilized in the construction of tabernacles and temples help us to penetrate the spiritual meaning of Scripture; and astronomy is indispensable in reckoning time.[10]

Knowledge of the universe serves the same end as the liberal arts. A comprehensive image is the prime requisite. Bede in the *De natura rerum* described the world according to the order of the elements: the sky with its planets and stars; the air with its meteors, comets, wind, thunder, lightning, rainbow; the waters, the ocean with its tides, the Red Sea, and the rising of the Nile; the earth with its inner life, its volcanoes. *De temporibus* gives a complete catalogue of the six ages of history, the last of which began with the establishment of the Roman Empire. The information contained in these vast, all-inclusive catalogues, in which, with but few exceptions, we find no trace of direct, personal experience, and in which everything is based on tradition (and on Pliny the Elder in particular), appears in encyclopedias like the *De universo* by Hrabanus Maurus, who derived his knowledge mainly from Isidore

[10] Migne, CVII, 395–98; cf. Augustine *De ordine* ii. 13.

of Seville. The work owes its unity (to the extent that it possesses unity) to its vast allegorical interpretation of the whole universe in which every detail has a spiritual meaning. The inspiration of the Holy Scripture permeates every page.

We see, then, what Christianity absorbed from the Hellenic culture: materials for the great religious work of effecting the salvation of man. We find not the slightest trace of the spirit that animated the Hellenic age. The emphasis is placed not on understanding it from within but on cataloguing it and putting it to use. In enlightened circles, after St. Augustine, the ancient philosophers were accorded a warm reception. "If those who are called philosophers, especially the Platonists," says Hrabanus Maurus, following his discussion of the liberal arts, "are found to have said things that are true and in harmony with our faith in their treatises and essays, we must not be afraid but must wrest from them these things, as from wrongful possessors, and make use of them" (chap. xxvi).

If we try to picture to ourselves the means that a man of the eighth century had of picturing to himself his philosophical heritage, we find that he had three sources of information. The first was a series of works which, though authentic, were decadent, detached from their origin, disparate, and linked together by a common Neo-Platonic spirituality. Such were Chalcidius' *Commentary on the Timaeus,* the translation of the beginning of the same dialogue by Cicero, and Macrobius' *Commentary on the Dream of Scipio,* which passed from Plotinus and Porphyry to St. Augustine. The second source was the great number of doxographies that provided many historical details, which were increasingly distorted and falsified with time, about schools that had disappeared. These doxographies, a good example of which is offered by Hrabanus Maurus,[11] were used by the Fathers as background to their identification of the pagan philosophical sects and Christian heresies. Finally come Boethius' technical treatises on logic, based on Aristotle.

[11] *De universo* xv. 1 (Migne, CXI).

The catalogue of their philosophical heritage, incomplete and distorted, explains the confidence as well as the distrust of Hrabanus Maurus and others like him. Philosophy, indispensable as a logical tool and illuminated by rays of truth in the hands of men like Plato, is dangerous when it brings us to the brink of heresy.

Pedagogical concern dominates the work of Alcuin (735–804), who was called from England by Charlemagne in 781 and whose name symbolizes the intellectual renaissance projected by the king of the Franks. Alcuin reformed the clergy of the Frankish Empire which had sunk to its intellectual nadir,[12] and he established the Palatine school for the purpose of promoting secular education. His handbooks on education, grammar, rhetoric, and dialectic, and his treatise on orthography added nothing to earlier compilations. Alcuin's correspondence shows that he wielded great authority in his time and that he upheld the utility of profane studies with respect to theology. In his treatise *De fide sanctae et individuae trinitatis* he cited St. Augustine to prove that "rules of dialectic are necessary and that the most profound questions concerning the Holy Trinity can be elucidated only by virtue of the subtlety of the categories."

IV *John Scotus Erigena*

The work of John Scotus Erigena is the best introduction to the philosophical preoccupations of the theologians of the period. Erigena was the product of the Church of Ireland, which on several occasions had manifested its independence of Rome. Bede in his *Ecclesiastical History* quotes the letter in which Pope John criticizes him for being remiss not only in matters of discipline but also in matters of doctrine; he was falling back into the Pelagian heresy. The classic poets were still read in Ireland, and Greek was still studied.[13] Erigena, who was born in Ireland at the beginning of the ninth century, was one of the "Scots" brought to the continent

[12] Cf. the precept in *De spiritu: Disce ut doceas.*
[13] Migne, XCV, 113.

to teach. He was welcomed to the court of Charles the Bald around 840. He translated into Latin the works of Dionysius the Areopagite and those of his commentator, Maximus the Confessor. These works, previously sent to France by the pope during the reign of Pippin, were then handed over once again in 827 to Louis the Pious by the ambassadors of Emperor Michael II. Erigena's translation is not really a translation in the strict sense of the word. Like most of the translations made during the Middle Ages, its word-for-word fidelity is exasperating and suggests that the author, like a mediocre school-boy, tried to decipher the meaning of the sentence only after he had translated each word separately. Dionysius was not translated again until the end of the twelfth century.

The works of Dionysius were one of the important sources of the Neo-Platonic conception of things found in Erigena. That they were not the sole source is shown by the fact that in his treatise *On Predestination,* which was written in 851 and which contains no references to the works of Dionysius, his Neo-Platonism shows up clearly. He refers in sufficient detail to his authorities to enable us to identify his sources: in the *De divisione naturae,* in addition to Dionysius and Maximus, he relied mainly on St. Augustine, then on Gregory of Nyssa, less frequently on Basil of Caesarea, Gregory of Nazianzen, and Epiphanius, and very rarely on St. Ambrose, Origen, and St. Jerome. He often turned for support not only to the Fathers but also to philosophers or the learned men of the world: the treatises on logic by Boethius, which acquainted him with Cicero and Aristotle, Plato's *Timaeus,* sometimes Pythagoras, more often Pliny the Elder, and also the poets Ovid and Vergil.

Erigena, unlike his predecessors, was not simply a compiler. He had a mind sufficiently strong and independent to enable him to use his sources without being enslaved by them. His system was not a mixture, in different proportions, of Dionysius and Augustine; it was a carefully considered reply to the awesome question that was to dominate thinking all during the Middle Ages. The Christian image of the universe and the Neo-Platonic image share a common rhythm: both are theocentric images that describe the dual motion of things, the way in which things move outward from their first principle and then return to the principle. In the Christian image the succession of these moments is a series of events, each of which has as its starting point a free initiative: creation and fall, redemption and a future life of bliss. In the Neo-Platonic image, successive moments are derived from a natural, eternal necessity: outward motion or movement away from the first principle represents a change in that the same reality that was initially in a state of absolute unity (the first principle) is divided more and more as it proceeds through the lower levels of being, and the return represents a reversal of the process of division, which now gives way to unity.

But the opposition between the two images of the universe is by no means as clear-cut as suggested here. Hellenic Christianity was indisputably hypnotized by Neo-Platonism and tended (without ever succeeding completely) to interpret the sequence of events recounted by the Christian myth as a sequence of moments necessitated by the nature of things. After the Stoics, the Greek mind was dominated by the image of a life of the universe alternating between the emergence of God and absorption in God, a pattern that had of necessity profoundly influenced the Christian image of creation, the fall, and redemption.

This is precisely the pattern rediscovered by Erigena, and his great work *De divisione naturae* is a comprehensive interpretation of Christian theocentrism on the basis of Platonic theocentrism.

His Neo-Platonism appears clearly in his earlier work *On Predestination*. The monk Gottschalk posited the existence of dual predestination, that of the elect and that of the damned; just as divine predestination caused the elect to achieve justification and eternal life, so the other type of predestination forced the condemned to fall into a state of godlessness and to suffer eternal punishment.[14] From his argument were deduced the conclusions that orthodoxy and good works were useless and that God forced certain men to sin. Hrabanus Maurus, and later Hincmar, Arch-

---

[14] *Ibid.*, CXXII, 359c–360d.

bishop of Rheims, saw that the Church was in danger. Not content with having Gottschalk condemned by the Synod of Quierzy (849), Hincmar invited Erigena to write against him.

Erigena begins by stating, with St. Augustine, that the true philosophy is the true religion[15] and actually refutes Gottschalk by speculating on the divine essence: in the first place, dual predestination is contrary to the unity of the divine essence, for the same cause cannot produce two opposite effects; and if God—according to Gottschalk—produces justification in man, he cannot produce in him sin. Furthermore God, being the supreme essence, is the cause solely of good, which is a reality; he cannot be the cause of sin, which is nothingness. It is obvious that Erigena has found in St. Augustine two basic principles of Neo-Platonism: God is identical to the Good, and evil is not a positive reality.

The *De divisione naturae* follows the rhythm of Neo-Platonic philosophy: procession from God to his creature, then the return from the creature to God; or moving through nature from God as principle to God as end.[16] It is obvious that his idea of rhythm is drawn mainly from Maximus the Confessor. Erigina quotes Dionysius' interpreter to show that man's state after the fall will be characterized by extreme division and digression from the first principle (God), while redemption will be followed by the final union of beings with each other and with God. Furthermore, he states explicitly that the interpretation of redemption as the beginning of total reabsorption in God "has received scant attention" and that only scattered references appear in the writings of the Fathers.

This rhythm simply denotes the division of nature according to all logical differences, as if reality were nothing but the logical division of a genus into its species. First comes nature that creates and is not created, or God as the principle of things; then comes nature that is created and creates, or the Word that is engendered by the principle and that produces the sensible world; then comes nature that is created and does not create, or the sensible world;

---

[15] *Ibid.*, 358, according to Augustine *De vera religione*, CXXII, v.

[16] Cf. the general plan, Migne, CXXII, 528c–d.

last comes nature that is neither created nor creative, or God as the supreme end in whom the motion of things in search of perfection is terminated. But beneath these differences we detect an essential unity. According to the old Orphic formula, which Erigena quotes (in the eleventh chapter of the first book) although unaware of its origin, God is at the same time the principle, the middle term, and the end. The first division, with God as the principle, is identical to the fourth, with God as the end; the second with the Word as the creator,[17] is identical to the third, the created world; and finally the second and third, which together constitute the totality of created beings, are shown through redemption to be identical to the fourth.

It is the simultaneous presence in his thinking of these differences and of this identity that permeates the work of Erigena. By seeking always to identify the whole in the parts and the parts in the whole, he imbues his work with the same sort of tension that we find in thinkers of his sort from Plotinus to Hegel and Bradley. What he is actually describing is the God of Plotinus, the God who seemingly moves from principle to end through the whole cycle of beings, but in whom there is in reality no opposition between motion and immutability, the God who does not move to find repose. He is said to move only because he is the principle of the motion of created beings (Book I). The Plotinian triad of hypostases is identified with the Trinity, in which the Father has no positive determination, while the Son contains the primary causes in all their simplicity and unity, and the Spirit distributes them according to genera and species. The images of the Trinity which Erigena, with the help of St. Augustine and Dionysius, finds in beings—the triad *essentia virtus operatio,* the triad *intellectus ratio sensus interior*—in turn symbolize the movement of procession or evolution from the simple to the multiple, from hidden essence to its manifestations, on the one hand, and from the idea to its expression, on the other, suggesting the fundamental identity of the multiple and the simple. Among primary causes, as Plotinus states in dis-

[17] On the place of the word, cf. *De divisione naturae* ii. 2 (Migne, CXXII, 526).

cussing his intelligibles, there is no inequality, no true diversity: they are separated and isolated by intelligence. That is why the sensible world created and unfolded in time can no longer be separated from the Son and the Spirit that contain its cause; it represents but a further step in the division. What was simultaneous in the eternal becomes a succession or progression, just as from their eternal unity is gradually evolved an arithmetic that progressively reveals all the numbers and their properties.

After this extreme division the return of things to God begins (Book IV). And it is here and only here that man, whose creation marks the beginning of the return, intervenes. The enigma of man is that he is a dual being: he is an animal with respect to his senses, his passions, and his nutritive life, but he is above animals with respect to his reason and intellect. According to an old interpretation of Genesis by Philo, he is at the same time the being shaped from earth and the being created in the image of God. The solution of the enigma is that God sought to create a microcosm in which all his creatures might be reunited; they are all in him, at least as ideas and through his notions of them; primitive man, before his transgression, had perfect knowledge of himself and of his creator, of the angels and of things inferior to himself. He is therefore the vehicle for the return of all things to God, and because the return is effected through him, every creature is in him. But man transgressed, and his fall resulted in his expulsion from Paradise; in other words, it tied him to his animality and made him dependent on it but did not detract in any way from the integrity of his essence. Hence the necessity of redemption: it will not only re-establish the primitive state of man but will also be marked by the annihilation of the material world and the spiritualization of all things.

This discussion indicates the restrictions that must be imposed on any attempt to compare the system of Erigena and Neo-Platonism. To begin with, in the second part of his doctrine—the part that concerns the nature of man and the return to God—Erigena followed the Fathers with scrupulous fidelity: the dual nature of man, his state before and after his transgression, man as a microcosm, the interpretation of Paradise—all of these notions came from Ambrose's *De paradiso,* borrowed largely in turn from Philo's *De opificio mundi,* Gregory of Nyssa's *De imagine,* and other works. And through these writers he managed to reconstruct the tradition of the old myth of Anthropos, the intermediary between God and things, a myth fully developed in the writings of Philo and completely absent from the works of Plotinus. Through them he also assimilated the anti-Hellenic idea (which he recognized as such) of the end of the world and substituted it for the eternal order of Plotinus. There is nothing in the salvation or return of nature to God through man to recall the Plotinian retroversion in which the emanative being returns eternally to its principle to receive the overflow and thus be constituted as being.

If we now return to the first part of the work, we shall see that it is not, in a strict sense, a true system of emanation in which the principle radiates its influences through natural necessity. Of course God, being and willing, nature and will, are identical terms; but the act of creation is primarily a *theophany.* The Father, invisible and unknown, is manifested through the divine Word; and the divine Word is born in the same sense that intelligence, at first invisible and unknown, is manifested in us when we come into contact with sensible things; and the creation of the other things is simply an opportunity or a means for the Word to be made manifest. Theophany and reabsorption in the first principle are different from procession and retroversion in that the latter imply that reality has a history and involves initiatives, while the former designate an eternal, unchangeable order.

BIBLIOGRAPHY

Texts

Beiträge zur Geschichte der Philosophie (und Theologie) des Mittelalters.
   39 vols. Münster in Westfalen, 1891——.
Corpus scriptorum ecclesiasticorum Latinorum. 77 vols. Vienna, 1855——.
Les philosophes Belges. Louvain, 1901–42. Continued as Philosophes médié-
   vaux. Louvain, 1948.
Migne, J. P. Patrologiae cursus completus. "Series Latina." 221 vols. Paris,
   1844–64.

Useful Translations and Anthologies

Fairweather, E. R. A Scholastic Miscellany: Anselm to Ockham. (The Library
   of Christian Classics, Vol. X). Philadelphia, 1956.
Fathers of the Church: A New Translation. Edited by R. J. Deferrari. New
   York, 1947——.
McKeon, R. Selections from Medieval Philosophers. 2 vols. New York, 1929.
   (Paperback reprint).
Pegis, A. C. The Wisdom of Catholicism. New York, 1949.

Histories and Studies of Medieval Philosophy

Burch, C. B. Early Medieval Philosophy. New York, 1951.
Chevalier, J. Histoire de la pensée. Vol. II: La pensée chrétienne, des origines
   à la fin du XVIᵉ siècle. Paris, 1956.
Copleston, F. A History of Philosophy. Vol. II: Augustine to Scotus. Vol.
   III: Ockham to Suarez. Westminster, Md., 1950, 1953.
——. Medieval Philosophy. London, 1952.
Curtis, S. J. A Short History of Western Philosophy in the Middle Ages.
   Westminster, Md., 1950.
De Wulf, M. History of Medieval Philosophy. Translated by E. C. Messenger.
   2 vols. New York, 1935.
Gilson, E. History of Christian Philosophy in the Middle Ages. New York,
   1955.

23

Gilson, E. *La philosophie au moyen âge*. 2 vols. Paris, 1944.

———. *The Spirit of Medieval Philosophy*. Translated by A. H. Downes. New York, 1936.

———, and Böhner, P. *Die Geschichte der christlichen Philosophie von ihren Anfängen bis Nikolaus von Cues*. Paderborn, 1937.

Grabmann, M. *Die Geschichte der scholastischen Methode*. 2 vols. Freiburg im Breisgau, 1909, 1911.

———. *Die Philosophie des Mittelalters*. Berlin, 1921.

———. *Mittelalterliches Geistesleben. Abhandlungen zur Geschichte de Scholastik und Mystik*. 3 vols. Munich, 1926, 1936, 1956.

Hauréau, B. *Histoire de la philosophie scolastique*. 3 vols. Paris, 1872 and 1880.

Leff, G. *Mediaeval Thought: St. Augustine to Ockham*. London, 1958.

Maurer, A. A. *Medieval Philosophy*. New York, 1962.

Pieper, J. *Scholasticism, Personalities and Problems of Medieval Philosophy*. Translated by R. and C. Winston. New York, 1960.

Ueberweg, F. *Grundiss der Geschichte der Philosophie*. 11th ed. Revised by B. Geyer. Vol. II: *Die patristische und scholastische Philosophie*. Berlin, 1928. Vol. III: *Philosophie des Mittelalters*. Edited by P. Wilpert. 1965.

Vignaux, P. *Philosophy in the Middle Ages: An Introduction*. Translated by E. C. Hall. New York, 1959.

Weinberg, J. R. *A Short History of Medieval Philosophy*. Princeton, N.J., 1964.

Bibliographies

The histories of philosophy by De Wulf, Gilson, and Ueberweg have good general critical bibliographies.

Bibliography of Philosophy. Paris, 1937———. N. S. 1954———.

Bochenski, I. M. (ed.). *Bibliographische Einführungun in das Studium der Philosophie*. Bern, 1948–53.

Bulletin Thomiste. Le Saulchoir, France, 1924———.

Farrar, C., and Evans, A. *Bibliography of English Translations from Medieval Sources*. New York, 1946.

Glorieux, P. *Répertoire des maîtres en théologie de Paris au XIII⁰ siècle*. 2 vols. Paris, 1933, 1934.

McGuire, M. *Introduction to Medieval Latin: A Syllabus and Bibliographical Guide*. Washington, D.C., 1964.

Progress of Medieval and Renaissance Studies in the United States and Canada. Edited by S. Harrison Thomson. Bulletin 22. Boulder, Colo., 1952.

Recherche de théologie ancienne et médiévale. Separate fascicle, *Bulletin de théologie ancienne et médiévale*. Louvain, 1929———.

Journals

Franziskanische Studien. Paderborn, 1914——.
Gregorianum. Rome.
Revue des sciences philosophiques et théologiques. Paris, 1907——.
Revista di filosofia Neo-Scolastica. Milan, 1909——.
Scholastik. Freiburg im Breisgau, 1926——.
The Modern Schoolman. St. Louis, Mo.
The New Scholasticism. Washington, D.C.
The Thomist. Washington, D.C., 1937——.

I

Studies

Harnack, A. *Lehrbuch der Dogmengeschichte.* 3 vols. Freiburg, 1894–97.
Tixeront, J. *Précis de l'histoire des dogmes.* 6th ed. Vol. II. Paris, 1921. 4th ed. Vol. III. Paris, 1919.

II

Texts

Boethius. *Opera.* Migne, LXIII, LXIV.
———. *The Consolation of Philosophy.* Translated by H. Stewart and E. Rand. New York, 1918.
Claudianus Mamertus. *Opera.* Migne, LIII.
Cassiodorus. *Opera.* Migne, LXIX, LXX.
Martianus Capella. *Opera.* Edited by A. Dick. Leipzig, 1925.

Studies

Barrett, H. *Boethius: Some Aspects of His Times and Work.* Cambridge, 1940.
Courcelle, P. *Les lettres grecques en occident de Macrobe à Cassiodore.* Paris, 1948.
Dürr, K. *The Propositional Logic of Boethius.* Amsterdam, 1951.
Grabmann, M. *Die Geschichte der scholastischen Methode.* 2 vols. Freiburg, 1900, 1910. See I, 148 ff.
Patch, H. *The Tradition of Boethius.* New York, 1935.
Stewart, H. *Boethius.* London, 1891.
Vann, G. *The Wisdom of Boethius.* Aquinas Paper No. 20. Oxford, 1952.

III

Texts

Alcuin. *Opera*. Migne, C, CI.
———. *Rhetorica*, in W. Hornell, *The Rhetoric of Alcuin and Charlemagne*. Latin and English translation. Princeton, N.J., 1941.
Bede the Venerable. *De natura rerum*. Migne, XC.
———. *Historia ecclesiastica*. Migne, XCV.
———. *De temporibus*. Migne, XC.
Hrabanus Maurus. *De institutione clericorum*. Migne, CVII.
———. *De universo*. Migne, CXI.
Isidore of Seville. *Etymologiarum libri XX*. Migne, LXXXII.
Vincent of Lérins. *Commonitorium*. Migne, L.

Studies

Duckett, E. *Alcuin: Friend of Charlemagne*. New York, 1951.
Gillett, H. *Saint Bede the Venerable*. London, 1935.
Gilson, E. *Les idées et les lettres*. Paris, 1932. Pp. 171–96 on Alcuin.
Turnau, D. *Rabanus Maurus, praeceptor Germaniae*. Munich, 1900.
West, A. *Alcuin and the Rise of the Christian Schools*. New York, 1892.

IV

Texts

John Scotus Erigena. *De praedestinatione*. Migne, CXXII, pp. 355–439.
———. *De divisione naturae*. Migne, CXXII, 442–1022. Book IV, chaps. 7–9, translated in McKeon, *Selections*, I, 106–41.

Studies

Bett, H. *Johannes Scotus Eriugena*. Cambridge, 1925.
Webb, C. "Scotus Erigena: De divisione naturae," *Proceedings of the Aristotelian Society*, II (1892–94), 121–37.

THE TENTH AND
ELEVENTH CENTURIES

NOT UNTIL the end of the eleventh century was there a real revival of intellectual activity in the Western world. This does not mean, however, that the intermediate period was void or unimportant. Everywhere in monasteries and cathedral cloisters schools were being founded. These centers were widely separated but united by a common culture. From the ninth century on, there were cathedral schools in Auxerre, Rheims, and Paris, and studies were pursued in Aurillac, Saint-Gallen, and Chartres. Material difficulties were always present: after the Arabs conquered the East, papyrus and parchment became so rare that libraries necessarily remained impoverished; in 860 one of the richest, the library of Saint-Gallen, contained four hundred volumes. The intellectual revival at the end of the eleventh century coincided with the creation of religious orders actively engaged in copying manuscripts, and during the twelfth century the library of St. Vincent of Laon contained eleven thousand volumes.[1]

We know the approximate holdings of the late Middle Ages with respect to philosophical works: in the ninth century Saint-Gallen, for example, possessed Apuleius' works on logic, works by Cassiodorus, Isidore, Bede, and Alcuin, and Aratus' *Phenomena*; to these holdings were added Boethius' *Consolation,* Lucan's

[1] L. Maitre, *Les écoles épiscopales et monastiques de l'Occident depuis Charlemagne jusqu'à Philippe Auguste* (Paris, 1866), especially pp. 278 ff.

Pharsalia, and *The Dream of Scipio* (perhaps with Macrobius' commentary) in the tenth century, and Boethius' treatises on logic in the eleventh. The listing reveals the narrow limits of the intellectual horizon at a time when culture was based solely on books, which were very rare.

We have practically nothing from the period other than marginal glosses and commentaries (most of them unpublished) of the writings of Boethius or Martianus Capella. Education, apart from the Christian doctrine, was given over almost exclusively to dialectic. Eric of Auxerre (died in 876), Rémi of Auxerre (or Remigus), who taught in Chartres around 862, Bovo of Saxony, living at the beginning of the tenth century, Gerbert of Aurillac, who became pope under the name of Silvester II (999–1003), and his pupil Fulbert, who opened a school in Chartres in 990, are the principal authors of commentaries. A document from the eleventh century had preserved a listing, in the order in which they were presented, of the subjects taught in dialectic at Chartres.[2] Students took up in succession: Porphyry's *Isagoge,* Aristotle's *Categories,* St. Augustine's *Categories* (with a preface by Alcuin), Boethius' *Definitions,* Cicero's *Topics,* Aristotle's and Apuleius' *Peri Hermeneias,* Boethius' *Topical Differences,* anonymous compositions on rhetoric, Boethius' *Divisions,* Gerbert's treatise *De ratione uti et rationali,* and finally Boethius' *Categorical Syllogisms* and *Hypothetical Syllogisms.*

The art of discussion was obviously perfected by such a system of education, which endured for years. Every art other than dialectic would seem to have been neglected. The only exception is Gerbert's *Geometry* (*ca.* 983), which seems because of the methods of measurement employed in it to betray the influence of the Arab mathematicians.[3] But dialectic reigned supreme and inculcated in the minds of men a predilection for discussion, for the endless distinctions and divisions that dominated the whole of medieval philosophy.

[2] Quoted by A. Clerval, *Les écoles de Chartres au Moyen âge* (Paris, 1895), p. 117.
[3] Würschmidt, "Geodätische Messinstrumente und Messmethoden bei Gerbert und bei den Arabern," *Archiv der Mathematik und Physik* (1912), p. 315.

1 *The Controversy of Berengar of Tours*

What matters in the history of philosophy is not so much dialectic as the art of discussion as the use to which it is put in an attempt to arrive at a conception of reality. To be specific, we recall that Boethius' collection posed several metaphysical problems, the first of which is the problem of the reality of universals in Porphyry's celebrated text; next (just as in the case of St. Augustine) comes the problem, no less celebrated during the Middle Ages, of the limit of the application of categories. The ten categories or genera of being apply only to the sensible world, and dialectic, since it works only with the categories that embrace genera and species, is incapable in its turn of attaining to a superior reality. But then the problem is to determine how it is possible to refer to a superior reality. Finally, we note that in his commentaries Boethius brought to light some of Aristotle's technical notions of philosophy, for example, the notions of form and matter and of act and potency.

Much more is involved here than the simple art of discussion. We notice this in Fredegisus' *Epistola de nihilo et tenebris,* which according to Prantl, the historian of logic, is rather "stupid and artless." The author, a pupil of Alcuin, maintains that nothingness (*nihil*) exists, for to say that it *is* nothing is to imply that it is.

Gerbert's little treatise *De rationali et rationalibus uti* is more instructive than such artless realism. Porphyry says in the *Isagoge* (vii) : "Since *reasonable* is the specific difference, *using reason* is said of this difference; and it is also said of all species of beings subsumed by this difference." One might confront Porphyry with the rule of logic which holds that the predicate must have an extension superior or at least equal to that of the subject. Here the rule is violated since the term *reasonable* is a potency whose act is *using reason,* with the result that the subject has an extension superior to its predicate. Gerbert replies by making a distinction between predicates that are a part of the essence of the subject, as *reasonable* is a part of the essence of *man,* and accidental predicates, such as *using reason* when it is said of *reasonable*. The rule of logic applies only to predicates of the first type.

The sharp distinction between essential and accidental attributes makes possible a clear statement of the problem of universals. For universals, whose reality was the subject of speculation, are nothing but the genera and species—for example, "animal" and "man"— which are essential attributes of an individual like Socrates. On this point Boethius' commentators, such as Pseudo-Hrabanus Maurus (whose *Super Porphyrium* is generally assigned to the first half of the eleventh century), followed the hints that appeared in the writings of their master and that had their source in Aristotle. They repeated what had been said by Boethius and also by Simplicius: that the *Categories,* the study of attributes, cannot refer to things (since *res non praedicatur*) but only to words as signifiers of things. Hence the solution, imbued with the spirit of Aristotle, of the problem of universals: genus and species exist only by virtue of predicates essential to the individual. "Individuals, species, and genus are one and the same reality (*eadem res*), and universals are not, as is sometimes stated, something different from individuals." We hear an echo of Aristotelian thought, through the intermediary of Boethius, in the statement that genus is to species and species is to the individual as matter is to form.

The controversy over the Eucharist, which took place in the middle of the eleventh century, also involved dialectic. Paschasius Radbertus (died *ca.* 860) had taught that in the consecration "through the power of the Spirit, the substance of the bread and wine is changed into the flesh and blood of Christ." His theory of transubstantiation implied, first, an omnipotent God whose will is restricted by no law of nature and, second, radical independence of what the eyes perceive through the senses and the mind through faith, since "in the visible species the mind apprehends something more than that which sight and taste can perceive." Berengar of Tours had no intention of denying that the Eucharist was a sacrament in the sense in which the word is used by St. Augustine: a sacred sign that takes us beyond the sensible appearance to an intelligible reality. We must guard against making of him a rationalist or an apostate. Imbued with the dialectical teaching of Fulbert of Chartres, however, he could not conceive of transubstantiation, which requires us simultaneously to affirm and deny that bread and wine are on the altar after the consecration, since "an affirmation cannot be allowed to stand in its entirety if one of its parts is struck down." [4] The question implied is this: Do we have the right to contradict ourselves in formulating dogmas?

Many different refutations appealed to Berengar, but they were all marked by the same ambiguity. On the one hand he was told that neither dialectic nor philosophy had anything to do with the establishment of a dogma. On the other hand he was assured that no real contradiction was entailed by the affirmation of transubstantiation. The letter written by his schoolfellow from Chartres, Adelmann of Liège, is a good example of the first line of argument. It might well be quoted in its entirety because of its biting criticism of philosophy: "Certain pagans and noble philosophers have rightly been scorned for their false opinions, not only about God the creator, but also about the world and what is in it. What is more absurd than stating that the sky and the stars are motionless, that the earth turns on itself with a rapid rotary motion, and that those who believe in the motion of the sky are deceived in the same manner as sailors who see shores with their towers and trees recede from them?" [5] He dismisses Heraclitus' old notion, which the eleventh century knew through Chalcidius' commentary on the *Timaeus*, in the same way that he dismisses the opinion of those who believe that "the sun is not warm and that snow is black." All the more reason why, in matters of dogma, neither our senses nor our intelligence can enable us to apprehend that which is apprehended only by a virtue that issues from grace—faith.

Alger of Liège, who wrote toward the end of the controversy, also took the authoritarian viewpoint: the question must be resolved "not by human reason, which is completely inadequate,

[4] Exposition by Lanfranc (Migne, CL, 416d).
[5] In Heurtevent, *Durand de Troarn,* p. 290.

but by the testimony of Christ himself with regard to his saints."
He explained the relation between reason and faith by the following comparison: our intellect with regard to God is like our senses
in comparison with intelligence or one sense in comparison with
another, that, is unable to understand but forced to believe what it
does not understand. It would hardly be possible to state in a more
radical manner the fundamental discontinuity of the mind. And
yet the same Alger, at the end of his treatise, tried to show that
there was no contradiction in transubstantiation. He explained that
the reference is not the same when we state thaat bread is present
on the altar and when we state that the body of Christ is on the
altar: "With respect to their appearance and their form, the elements are bread and wine; with respect to the substance into which
they have been changed, the bread and wine are truly and distinctly
the body of Christ." [6]

Finally, in the same way Lanfranc, Abbot of Le Bec, while
criticizing Berengar "for abandoning the sacred authorities and resorting solely to dialectic," and while asserting that he would prefer to settle the debate solely on the basis of authority and "that in
treating of divine things, he desires neither to propose dialectical
questions nor to answer such questions," nevertheless pointed up his
shortcomings with respect to "the rules of discussion." And although Lanfranc censured him for "putting nature before divine
power, as if God could not change the nature of anything and
everything," [7] he still was unable to grant that there was anything
in dogma that contradicted dialectic. Thus, while the question was
settled by convoking synods that upheld faith (the synods of Rome
and Verceil in 1050, which condemned Berangar, the synods of
Rome in 1050 and 1079, which forced him to recant), every attempt was made to make dogma conform to the rules of common
reason.

[6] Migne, CLXXX, 740c–d and 753d.
[7] *Ibid.,* CL, 419c.

II *Criticism of Philosophy Until the End of the Eleventh Century*

With the reform of the monastic orders and the movement toward asceticism that characterized the last part of the eleventh century (intense faith culminated in the crusade of 1095), people felt the need for placing stricter limitations on the role of the profane disciplines. Peter Damian (1007–1072), named Cardinal of Ostia in 1057, who sought to shun honor and fame by withdrawing to the solitude of a hermitage, is one of the reformers who proclaimed the complete inadequacy of dialectic in matters of faith. He stated "that dialectic must not arrogantly usurp the role of a master but be like the servant of a mistress (*ancilla dominae*)." What lies behind his condemnation? The famous dialectical argument (first framed by the Megarians) that demonstrated fate and the impossibility of contingent futures by means of the principle of contradiction. Thus a rule of logic eliminated the omnipotence and complete freedom of God, the very foundation of faith. Peter Damian judiciously observed that rules were invented for use in syllogisms, "they do not have reference to the essence and matter of reality but to the method of discussion."[8] This meant a return, brought about by a sure instinct, to the doctrine of Aristotle, who had declared premises and definitions to be indemonstrable. So long as there was no other method of thinking than the syllogistic one, it was fitting to reduce it to the status of a simple organon and not to try to make it the instrument for investigating reality.

But in addition to dialectic, which could be relegated with relative ease to its role of organon, profane books, particularly Macrobius' *Commentary on the Dream of Scipio,* spread doctrines about God and the world that were diametrically opposed to the Christian doctrine. Through them access was given to Pythagoras' speculations on the transmigration of souls and Plato's concept of the

---

[8] *De divina omnipotentia* v (Migne, CXLV, 604); cf. E. Bréhier, *The Hellenistic and Roman Age* (Chicago, 1965), pp. 3–8.

fabrication of the world soul, to say nothing of the discussion between Platonists and Aristotelians which suggested that the immortality of the soul implied its divinity. In them it was stated
that there were on the earth inhabited but inaccessible regions,
necessitating the conclusion that Jesus had not saved all men. In
them was something more than dialectic: a conception of the
world in which salvation through Christ had no place. Manegold
of Lautenbach (who died in 1103 in an Alsatian monastery) turned
on his adversaries, declaring that readers too attentive to such
dangerous philosophers were under diabolical inspiration.[9]

Nothing is easier in theory than to separate theology and philosophy, but in practice nothing is more difficult. Theology used
words such as *substantia* and was forced to consult Aristotle's *Categories* for definitions. Manegold himself, conceding the kinship
between certain philosophical doctrines and faith, accepted the
Plotinian division that he found in Macrobius of political, purify-
ing, and purified virtues. On the whole, then, the eleventh century
was characterized by the inability of thinkers to dispense with
profane philosophy or to determine the limitations of its applicabil-
ity.

III *St. Anselm*

That is why the reasoning of St. Anselm of Aosta (1033–1109)
is of great interest. Taking up the Augustinian tradition he made
every effort in his teaching at the monastery of Le Bec, where he
succeeded Lanfranc, to establish a more stable equilibrium between
reason and faith. The reasoning of St. Anselm, who in 1093 became Archbishop of Canterbury, is easy to follow: Scripture and
the Church impose dogmas on our faith, such as those of the existence of God and the Incarnation; man accepts them solely on the
basis of authority, and reason contributes nothing to his understanding. But when faith exists, man has in addition a tendency to
reflect on dogmas and to seek to understand them. As Isaiah puts it

[9] *Contra Wolfelmum* (Migne, CLV, 147–76).

(7:9), "If you will not believe, you will not understand." Furthermore, faith seeks to understand (*fides quaerens intellectum*) and the illumination of dogmas that one can acquire by reasoning in this way is like an intermediary between pure faith and the direct vision the elect will have of the divine reality. St. Anselm's attitude is in turn an intermediary between fideism that rules out any normal exercise of reason and mysticism that introduces the beatific vision into this life.

It is clear that St. Anselm, through the strength of his genius and through his meditation on the works of St. Augustine, rediscovered elements of Plato's dialectic. The path from faith to understanding and from understanding to the beatific vision is closely related to dialectic, which leads from belief to discursive reflection and from the latter to intellectual intuition; but belief has become faith, that is, a theogonic virtue that reaches man only by the grace of God and a set of dogmas on which depends man's salvation, and intellectual intuition has become the beatific vision accorded to the elect by the grace of God. Man is incapable of taking the initiative and of attaining the end: the *intellectus* receives from the outside, from faith, that which it is to understand. Except for this datum, it requires nothing more than the dialectical subtlety that Anselm took pains to have his pupils acquire through exercises such as those in the *De grammatico*; separated from faith, however, the most subtle line of reasoning cannot attain to certainty, but merely states "that which seems to me."

We should note that St. Anselm's work is dominated by a practical consideration which befitted a prince of the Church. By using logical arguments to prove the necessity of the Incarnation, for example, he was trying to refute the objections of the infidels who said that the Christian faith contradicted reason. That explains the peculiar character of his works, which he himself pointed out clearly at the beginning of the *Monologium*: nothing that he said must be grounded on the authority of Scripture; he must write clearly, using only common arguments and restricting himself to simple discussion in which everything was based on "the necessity of reason and the clarity of truth." This meant freeing himself completely from the literary conventions of his age and from slavish dependence on scriptural commentary. And here we see that even though we must approach his "rationalism" with some degree of caution, St. Anselm nevertheless took pains to determine what reason could accomplish independently.

His effort was of course restricted to purely theological matters. The *Monologium* and the *Proslogium,* written in that order between 1070 and 1078, dealt successively with the nature of God and the existence of God. The *De veritate,* a later work, had as its subject the radical unity of all truths in God. The *Cur deus homo,* completed in 1098, explained the Incarnation. He attempted to show that reason was helpful, that it had a place in the salvation and conversion of infidels; he did not show the slightest concern for the independent development of reason for its own sake.

Yet his very method (and completely apart from the end he sought to attain) implied conclusions on the nature of reason which were of universal import and which were independent of his subject. To begin with, he rediscovered in the *Monologium* the Platonic method that posits for each category of similar things perceived by the senses and reason the existence of a model in which they participate as equals. The whole work might bear as its epigraph the fundamental theorem of Proclus' *Elements of Theology*: "A term equally present to all terms in a series can explain them all only if it is not in one of them or in all of them but prior to all of them." In the same way St. Anselm saw that good things are as they are by virtue of a common essence, the good, which is independently good and then supremely good. Thus for each category of qualities shown by experience to be of higher or lesser degree, he established a supreme greatness through which things are great, an absolute being through which they are, a supreme justice through which there are just things. He demonstrated that these terms all designate the same reality since there can be but one supreme nature.

Thus dialectic leads from imperfect multiplicity to a unique, perfect reality, from the *per aliud* to the *per se*. Moreover, the unique being, if it exists, exists of itself (*ex se*); for if it had a cause it would be inferior to its cause. Finally, the universe comes from it and was created or produced by it from nothing, but in a rational manner which would have been impossible had there not been in the mind of the creator "something resembling a model of the thing to be done or, putting it a better way, a form, a resemblance, or a standard." It is the Word of God, identical to him: all created things are in the Word, just as design exists in art not only when it is produced but before its existence and after its disappearance.

It is easy to untangle in the arguments of the *Monologium* two elements that never quite interpenetrate: on the one hand, the Platonic dialectic, which is a general method consisting in proceeding from the sensible to the intelligible, from diversity to unity, from *per aliud* to *per se,* and on the other hand, a transformation of this method into a religious metaphysics, as a result of which being *per se* is defined as God the Creator *ex nihilo* of Genesis and the intelligible world as the Word. Alselm's confusion is surely explained by the *Timaeus,* with its demiurge and its model, and by all those who from Philo to St. Augustine perpetuated it, but there is no justification for it.

The *Monologium* had determined what reason knows of God, if he exists. The *Proslogium* (chaps. ii, iii) demonstrated his existence by means of a unique argument that has immortalized the name of St. Anselm: "We believe that you are something greater than which no other being can be conceived to exist (*quo nihil majus cogitari possit*). Is it possible that such a nature does not exist because a fool has said in his heart: 'There is no God'? But at the very least this fool, on hearing me say 'something greater than which no other being can be conceived to exist,' understands what he hears; and that which he understands is in his mind, even if he does not understand that this thing exists. The very idea of such a being implies its existence. . . . And surely the Being that is something greater than which no other being can be conceived to exist cannot be solely in the mind; indeed, even if he is only in the mind, one can imagine a being like him who exists also in reality and who is therefore greater than he. It follows that if he were only in the mind, the being who is something greater than which no other being can be conceived to exist would be such that something greater could be conceived to exist."

His proof starts not from the contemplation of Providence as revealed through nature, but from meditation on God, for which St. Augustine had provided the model.[10] "No soul," he had said, "has ever been able or will ever be able to conceive of anything better than you . . . and if you were not incorruptible, I could attain through thought to something better than my God." The trend of thought is the same: one can surely attribute to God that which one cannot deny him without diminishing his perfection. "God and things that are of God are in every way perfect," Plato had said.[11] And that was the starting point of all rational speculation on God. But in no instance had the notion been advanced of making existence an attribute that could not be denied him by virtue of his greatness and the immensity of his perfection. Philosophers implicitly acknowledged the existence of God because this alone could in some way clinch their image of the universe: there would be no eternal motion of the heavens without Aristotle's prime mover, no perfect rationality of things without a Stoic *logos* that permeates the universe. In Christianity the existence of God is implied by the drama that is to end with the salvation of man and is, as in every other instance, a revealed truth. But St. Anselm, who did not conceive of God in his relation to a cosmic order to which he is indispensable, and who did not wish by supposition to make use of revelation, had but one aim: to prove God's existence by the same method of meditation that allowed him to conceive God. His is not, as has been aptly observed,[12] an ontological proof that goes from essence to existence, for God's essence is unknown to us. Therefore his proof has as its starting point, not the essence of God but the notion of God as it exists in our understanding and as it is revealed

[10] According to Draeseke, *Revue de philosophie* (1909), p. 639.
[11] *Republic* 381b.
[12] Koyré, ed. and trans., *Proslogium* (Paris, 1930), p. 201, n. 1.

only through sedulous meditation. It is this notion which, no matter how remote it is from real essence, allows us to infer the existence of its object.

All these proceedings imply the affirmation of the possibility of a type of meditation that consists in sharpening our awareness of the notion of God that is in our understanding, and this was indeed a daring affirmation to make at the end of the eleventh century. It meant that one could meditate on God without benefit of the instruction given by the Church. The line of argument by which Gaunilon, Prior of Marmoutiers, countered St. Anselm's proof in the name of the fool is based wholly on apprehension. Gaunilon was in truth attacking St. Anselm's whole theological method: "The reality that is God—that I do not know. Nor is there anything similar that will enable me even to guess what it is like. Besides, you yourself state that it is that which can be likened to nothing else." Gaunilon challenged Anselm's premise, the *esse in intellectu* of God: having no notion of God, we are unable legitimately to affirm or deny anything about him. The implied conclusion is that there is in theology no method other than authority and revelation, and this negates the role assigned by Anselm to *intellectus* as the intermediary between faith and the vision of the elect.

St. Anselm offered a new application of his method in the *De veritate.* Here, as in the *Monologium,* he depicts in a particular instance the movement that takes us from multiplicity to unity. He starts from the multiplicity of truths: the truths of enunciations, of opinions, of the will (that is, right intention), of actions (right actions), of the senses, and of essences. The mere enumeration of these truths shows how the problem of truth is not restricted to judgment but relates also to will, to the senses, and to the essences. The common character of all these truths is their conformity to a certain standard or rectitude. A verbal statement is intended to signify that which is, and the statement is true when it actually signifies what it is intended to signify; the same is true of an opinion; an act of will is true when its aim is what it should be; and in the same way actions and the senses, taken in themselves, are always true because a sense always does what it should do; finally, the essences are true in the sense that things always have the essence which God has willed that they should have and are what they should be. The notion of truth refers in every instance, then, to a supreme standard that exists eternally, to a truth that is rectitude, not because it must be something, but because it is, and to which all other truths are reduced. It would be impossible to provide a clearer statement of theocentric rationalism, which originated with Stoicism and Neo-Platonism and in which reason, transcending particular truths, is not the immanent method that discovers them but the eminent and unique reality that they represent. It is obvious in this treatise, as in the whole of St. Anselm's work, that the contrast between faith and intellect is mainly the contrast between two ways of presenting theocentrism: on the one hand is the Christian God of salvation and on the other the intelligible and transcendent world of Neo-Platonism. Both views bend human reason toward a region where it cannot be exercised normally and where it must be transformed into a vision.

But there is a deep-rooted divergence between the two theocentrisms: on the one hand the divine drama of Christianity with its discontinuous universe, whose events—creation, sin, and redemption—are due to unforseeable initiatives on the part of a free being; on the other hand a continuous universe without a history, and one whose order is eternal and invariable. Their divergence shows up plainly in the Incarnation, which binds together two natures that are separated in Platonism—the divine and the human—and introduces into the universe a radically new law. In the *Cur Deus homo,* St. Anselm applies his method of *fides quaerens intellectum* to the dogma of the Incarnation and tries to show the necessary and rational character of the death of Christ. If nothing were known concerning the death of Jesus, reason would show that men cannot be happy unless a God-man appears and dies for them, for only God can atone for a sin that has offended the divine majesty. To be sure, Anselm does not reduce Christian truth to a necessary phase of an eternal order; but once sin has been posited, he introduces a rational necessity that directs him toward the Platonic vision of things.

IV *Roscelin (Roscellinus Compendiensis)*

Despite its difference from Christianity, Platonism must have seemed to Anselm, when he saw the consequences of the doctrine of Roscelin of Compiègne, to be linked by necessity to the dogma of the Trinity. Roscelin's views, which are summed up under the label of nominalism, seem to be grounded on the logic of Boethius. Roscelin's views are known only through a few extracts from those who contradicted him (Anselm and Abelard). Boethius, it will be recalled, held with Simplicius that Aristotle's *Categories* and the whole of the dialectic it engendered referred not to things but to words as signifiers of things, and that the *Isagoge* was but the classification of the five terms through which they are expressed. Roscelin said the same thing: all the distinctions made by dialectic between genus and species, substance and quality, are merely verbal distinctions and relate to human discourse. But he added that the only distinction grounded on reality was that of individual substances. That is exactly what Anselm says in the passage in which he summarizes in three articles the doctrine of the dialectician: "The universal substances are but verbal expressions (*flatus vocis*); color is nothing other than a colored body; man's wisdom is nothing but his soul." [13] Roscelin meant that it is only through speech that we are able to separate man from Socrates, whiteness from a white body, and wisdom from the soul, but that the man of whom we are speaking is in reality Socrates, the whiteness a white body, and wisdom a wise soul. That which, according to Abelard, seems to Roscelin completely arbitrary and conventional is not simply the division of things according to terms and categories but the very division of a body into corporeal parts. Any body, such as a house, is indivisible. To say that it is in reality made up of foundations, walls, and a roof is to consider one of its parts, such as the roof, as

[13] Migne, CLVIII, 265a.

being at the same time a part of a whole and a distinct thing in a list of three things.[14]

Roscelin seems then to have had the feeling (and this is the meaning of nominalism) that all distinctions made by the dialectician existed only in speech and not in things. Yet we know that he was ordered at the Council of Soissons (1092) to retract his opinion concerning the Trinity. It seems that he had drawn his inference from the opinion of Boethius, who used the word "person" to designate a rational substance; it follows that there are in God as many substances as persons (tritheism); the Father and the Son, the begetter and the begotten, are two distinct realities; the three persons are separated just as three angels would be, and if there is unity between them it is merely a unity of will and of power. What relation is there between this opinion and nominalism? St. Anselm explains it clearly when he speaks of dialecticians "whose minds are so obsessed by corporeal images that they cannot extricate themselves. If we cannot understand how several persons are specifically one single man, how can we understand how several persons are one single God? If we are unable to distinguish between a horse and its color, how can we make a distinction between God and his multiple relations? If we are unable to distinguish the individual man from the person, how can we understand that the man assumed by Christ is not a person?" According to this decisive text, tritheism was but one of Roscelin's errors. His nominalism was a principle subversive of all theology, for he made distinctions where none should be made and failed to make necessary distinctions. He saw in the Trinity three individual and distinct substances; in return (this is the second point raised by Anselm), he did not try to make a distinction between the attributes of God (goodness, power, and so forth) and his substance, nor was he able to make a distinction (this is the third point) between the divine person incarnate in Jesus, and his humanity. There was in this cleric from Compiègne a need to see clearly, a need not satisfied by the residue of thought from Aristotelianism

[14] Cousin, *Ouvrages inédites d'Abélard*, p. 471.

and Platonism. It has been aptly observed that we have here something "other than an academic question; if universals are realities,
the theologian is dealing not just with formulas but with things
themselves." [15]

[15] Seeberg, quoted by Grabmann, *Geschichte der scholastischen Methode,* p. 311.

I

Texts

Berengar of Tours. *De sacra coena adversus Lanfrancum.* Edited by A. and F. Vischer. *Berengarii Turonensis opera.* Berlin, 1834. P. 100. On the dispute, cf. the writings of Hugh of Langres (Migne, CXLII, 1325); Adelmann of Liège (Migne, CXLIII, 1289); Heurtevent, *Durand de Troarn,* pp. 287–303; Lanfranc (Migne, CL, 410–12); and Durand of Troarn (Migne, CXLIX, 1375).

Fredegisus. *Epistola de nihilo et tenebris.* Migne, CV.

Gerbert. *Opera.* Edited by A. Olleris. Clermont-Ferrand, 1867.

———. *De rationali et ratione uti.* Migne, CXXXIX, 159–68.

———. *Opera mathematica.* Edited by N. Bubnov. Berlin, 1899.

Paschasius Radbertus. *De corpore et sanguine domini.* Migne, CXX, 1263–1350.

Pseudo-Hrabanus Maurus. *Super Porphyrium.* In V. Cousin, *Ouvrages inédites d'Abélard.* Paris, 1836. Pp. xvi, lxxvi.

Studies

Ebersolt. *Essai sur Bérengar de Tours et la controverse sacramentaire au XIe siècle.* Paris, 1903.

Endres, J. "Fredegisus und Candidus, ein Beitrag zur Geschichte der Philosophie des Mittelalters," *Philosophisches Jahrbuch* (1906), pp. 439-46.

Heurtevent, R. *Durand de Troarn et les origines de l'hérésie bérangarienne.* Paris, 1912.

McDonald, A. J. *Berengar and the Reform of Sacramental Doctrine.* London, 1930.

Picavet, F. *Gerbert: Un pape philosophe d'après l'histoire et d'après la légende.* Paris, 1897.

Thomas Aquinas. *Summa theologiae,* III, 75, 1. A reply to Berengar.

II to IV

Texts

Anselm. *Opera.* Migne, CLVIII, CLIX.
———. *The Proslogium, Monologium, Cur Deus homo.* Translated by A. N. Deane. Chicago, 1910.
———. *Dialogue on Truth.* Translated by R. McKeon in *Selections,* I, 150–84.
Peter Damian. *Opera.* Migne, CXLIV, CXLV.
Roscelin. *Letter to Abélard.* Migne, CLXVIII. Translated into French in Picavet (see below).

Studies

Barth, K. *Fides querens intellectum. Anselms Beweis der Existenz Gottes in Zusammenhang seines theologischen Programms.* Munich, 1931.
Blum, O. *St. Peter Damian: His Teaching on the Spiritual Life.* Washington, D.C., 1947.
Clayton, J. *St. Anselm: A Critical Biography.* Milwaukee, 1933.
Endres, J. "Die Dialektiker und ihre Gegner in XI Jahrhunderte," *Philosophisches Jahrbuch* (1906).
———. *Petrus Damiani und die weltliche Wissenschaft. Beiträge zur Geschichte der Philosophie des Mittelalters.* Vol. VIII. Münster in Westfalen, 1910.
Gilson, E. "Sens et nature de l'argument de saint Anselme," *Archives d'histoire doctrinale et littéraire du moyen âge,* IX (1934), 5-51.
Gonsette, J. *Pierre Damien et la culture profane.* Louvain, 1956.
McIntyre. *St. Anselm and His Critics.* 1954.
Phelan, G. *The Wisdom of Saint Anselm.* Latrobe, Pa., 1960.
Picavet, F. *Roscelin, philosophe et théologien d'après la légende et d'après l'histoire.* 2d ed. Paris, 1911.
Spedalieri, F. "Anselmus an Gaunilo? sen de recta argumenti sancti doctoris interpretatione," *Gregorianum,* XXVIII (1947), 55-77.

THE TWELFTH CENTURY

THE TWELFTH CENTURY was a century of fiery and varied intellectual activity, a century of tumult and confusion: on one hand there was a need for systematization and unity that gave birth to the encyclopedic works of theology called books of Sentences; on the other hand, a great intellectual curiosity, translated in certain circles into a return to ancient humanism and a new interest in the sciences of the quadrivium. Furthermore, antiquity was gradually unveiled by translations of hitherto unknown authors and the resources of libraries were gradually expanded.

Four main intellectual tendencies are discernible, each against a different background: theologians in their Sentences brought together and unified the elements of the Christian tradition; Platonists—true humanists—were linked to the school of Chartres; mystics were associated with the cloister of St. Victor; finally, pantheists and naturalists constituted a group whose activities were certain to disturb the spiritual power. But there were, in addition, independent thinkers who cannot be placed in any category, among them Abelard, whose complex and perceptive mind reflected all the passions of his epoch.

1 *The Sententiaries*

The twelfth century was the period of the great theological encyclopedias that were intended "to unite in a single body," as Yves

46

of Chartres expressed it, everything relating to the Christian life, discipline, faith, and morals. Philosophical preoccupation had no part in all this. But there was a practical necessity in bringing together a vast array of scattered data. All of these data, often seemingly contradictory, had to be unified if the spiritual unity of Christianity was to be preserved. The works of the sententiaries were prompted by a need not unlike that met by our codes: they were by nature juridical rather than philosophical. Consequently they were based on philology and on textual criticism. Bernold of Constance indicated each point on which the authorities seemed to contradict each other and, as Vincent of Lérins had done before him, gave rules for reconciling their views or for choosing between them. The seventeen-volume *Decretum* of Yves of Chartres (died in 1116) is a survey (*speculum*) of doctrines of faith and ethical precepts. From the same period comes Radulphus Ardens' *Speculum universale,* something resembling a history of Christianity, in which we find, alongside specifically Christian teachings, all that remained of ancient humanistic ethics. Before discussing salvation through Christ (1.2), he explains the basic moral concepts of good and of virtue (1.1); before explaining faith and the sacraments (1.7 and 1.8), he develops human thinking concerning virtue and vice (1.6); and before dealing with theological virtues, he speaks of cardinal virtues. In each instance he juxtaposes Christian truths and a humanistic ethic that he tries naïvely to integrate with faith. For example, if he finds that—according to the ancient system of classification—the sciences (transmitted by Isidore or Bede) comprise theoretics, ethics, and logic, to which is added mechanics, he hastens to note piously that the four sciences are four remedies to be used against the defects that issue from original sin: ignorance, injustice, error, and weakness of the flesh.

This codification of Christianity occasioned a series of works that continued throughout the twelfth century: the *Questions* or the *Sentences* of Anselm of Laon (died in 1117), the *Sentences* of William of Champeaux (1070–1121), Robert Pulleyn (died in 1150), Robert of Melun (died in 1167), and especially those of

Peter Lombard, the Master of Sentences (died in 1164), which soon after his death were being used for instruction by Peter Comestor (died in 1176) and Peter of Poitiers (died in 1205). These collections were to serve as the basis for all theological instruction during the following century.

The *Sic et non* of Abelard, who was one of Lombard's teachers, belongs to the same literary genre, since on each point of the Christian faith he cites the opinions of the Fathers, classifying them according to whether they say "yes" or "no." Abelard surely did not intend to draw any skeptical conclusion, but simply "to provoke readers to further pursuit of truth and to sharpen their perception in the process." [1] He begins, moreover, by giving rules for reconciling the opinions of the Fathers.

These works naturally presuppose a rational basis without which any codification is impossible. The subject matter is determined solely by authority, but logical discussion must establish the significance and value of an authority. In each of the paragraphs that make up the divisions or chapters in his book, Peter Lombard compares one text with another, the pro and the contra, and chooses on the basis of discussion rather than of citations. This is the origin of the so-called scholastic method, a dialectical method designed not for discovery but for examination and evaluation: the subtle mind is not one that discovers a new truth but one that grasps correspondences or contradictions between opinions. The scholastic method is the only intellectual method possible in a domain in which truth is considered as already given.

Another important point is the distribution of materials in the work of Abelard and Lombard. The substructure of their work is the recital of the Christian drama, and its elements are studied in this order: God and the Trinity, Creation, the Angels, man and original sin, the Incarnation and Redemption, the sacraments, and eschatology. Here we have a concept of the universe that gradually gained ascendancy, became dominant, and continued to appeal to many philosophers long after the Middle Ages had drawn to a

[1] Migne, CLXXVIII, 1349a.

close. First, the hierarchy of realities—God, the angels, and man; then the drama itself—original sin, redemption, and the return to God of the elect. The dual theme includes many variations, but they are bounded on the one side by a Platonism of which Erigena is representative and which makes the descent of man and his return to God an eternal necessity, and on the other by the orthodoxy of men like Lombard and St. Thomas, who posit a completely free and contingent initiative at the beginning of each act in the divine drama.

II *The School of Chartres
in the Twelfth Century:
Bernard of Chartres*

Offsetting the work of the sententiaries was the development of a philosophical theology in the school of Chartres. Nothing is more moving than the efforts made by the adherents of the school to extend the intellectual horizon of their era beyond Boethius, Isidore, and the Fathers. Among the initiators were Constantine the African and Adelard of Bath, who provide valuable testimony concerning the beginnings of the establishment of relations between East and West. At the end of the eleventh century, Constantine, born in Carthage, traveled throughout the East. He translated, besides the medieval books of the Arabs and the Jews, Hippocrate's *Aphorisms* with Galen's commentary, and two of Galen's treatises. His translations gave access to Democritus' theory of corpuscular physics.

Adelard of Bath traveled through Greece and through the Arab lands at the beginning of the twelfth century and brought back many translations of mathematical works. He translated Euclid's *Elements* from Arabic and introduced to the West, in addition to astronomical works, Alchwarismi's arithmetic. This represented an extraordinary addition to the quadrivium. Adelard was a mathematician who also exhibited a predilection for Platonism, and his Platonism came not from St. Augustine but directly from the *Timaeus,* Chalcidius, and Macrobius. He wrote his short treatise *De eodem et diverso* to justify philosophy; in it, Philosophy and the seven arts engage in a debate, following the pattern set by Boethius and Martianus Capella, with Philocalia. The theory of knowledge outlined in the treatise presupposes the whole Platonic myth of the psyche: intelligence in its state of purity knows things and their causes; "in the prison of the body" such knowledge is partially lost; "then it searches for what it has lost and, betrayed by its memory, has recourse to opinion"; "the tumult of the senses" (cf. the *Timaeus,* 44a), which allows us to ignore "very small and very big things," prevents rational knowledge (the minima are probably atoms, whose existence Adelard granted). It follows that Aristotle is right in saying that we cannot actually know without the help of the imagination; but Plato is also right in stating that perfect knowledge is knowledge of the archetypal forms of things, as they exist in the divine intellect before they enter the body. They are simply taking opposite courses: Plato starts from principles, Aristotle from sensible, composite things.

Such is the basis of his solution to the problem of universals: the distinction between genus, species, and individual—for instance, the distinction between animal, man, and Socrates—has no meaning other than in sensible things; the words designate the same essence viewed from a different angle. "When we consider species, we do not eliminate individual forms but simply ignore them because they are not implied by the name of the species." The same is true of genus with respect to species. But one must guard against confusing these universals, which are designated by speech, with archetypal forms as they exist in the divine intelligence; universals, according to Aristotle, are still only sensible things themselves, although considered with more penetration. Archetypal forms are neither genera nor species, which are conceivable only in relation to individuals, but "they are conceivable and exist apart from sensible things, in the divine mind." And here we are not dealing with knowledge comparable to the beatific vision but with ordinary human knowledge, for the aim of dialectic is the contemplation of ideas.

Bernard of Chartres, who taught in Chartres from 1114 to 1124, seems to have had the conviction, wholly characteristic of his group, that the aim of scholarship was not to consolidate the knowledge of the past but to expand it. "We are as dwarfs on the shoulders of giants; we can see farther and farther into the distance than could the ancients, not by virtue of the keenness of our sight or the size of our bodies but because we are supported and elevated by them as by giants." [2] John of Salisbury called him "the most perfect Platonist of our time" [3] and said that according to Bernard, universals are identical to Platonic ideas. Was Bernard also the author of the short outline of Platonism that follows in the *Metalogicus?* In it John stresses the contrast between the immutability of ideas and the mutability of sensible things, drawing his inspiration from Seneca (Eps. 58, 19, and 22), whom he quotes, and the *Timaeus* (Ep. 49d-e). One thing seems certain in any case, and that is that Bernard's brother, Thierry, wrote a commentary on Genesis in which he explained the world through the concurrence of four causes: God the Father as the efficient cause, the four elements as the material cause, the Son as the formal cause, and the Holy Spirit as the final cause. There is obviously in this passage an attempt to apply the Aristotelian theory of the four causes to the cosmogony of the *Timaeus,* and the Christian formulas scarcely hide the four Platonic notions of the demiurge, matter, the order of the world, and the good (besides, later on Thierry explicitly identifies the Holy Spirit with the world soul of the *Timaeus*). This interpretation of the *Timaeus* is found in the letters of Seneca (65. 8–10), who compares each of Plato's principles of the world with one of Aristotle's four causes. The same interpretation is also found in the preface to the *Theology,* a ninth-century Arabic work falsely attributed to Aristotle (see below chap. iv, sec. ii).

The *Timaeus* also served as the source of inspiration for Bernardus Silvestris in his *De mundi universitate sive megacosmus et microcosmus* about the middle of the century. A pupil of Bernard

[2] John of Salisbury *Metalogicus* iii. 4.
[3] *Ibid.* iv. 35.

of Chartres, William of Conches (died in 1145) wrote a *Commentary on the Timaeus* and a *Philosophia* imbued with Platonism. It is worth noting that, contrary to Abelard who also followed Plato but assigned him a subordinate role and tried to use him to support the Christian apologetic, the Platonists of Chartres explained Platonism as an independent philosophy, without trying to reconcile it with dogma but not without introducing an element of humanistic imagination and a concern for style that gives all the productions of the school a very special savor. Bernardus Silvestris' work on cosmogony is a good example. In his work—a "mystery play" written before the term was invented—Nature tearfully complains to Nous (that is, to Providence) about the confusion that reigns in matter; Nous gives in and separates the elements (as in the first book of Ovid's *Metamorphoses*); then Nous turns to Nature and promises to create man in order to bring the work to perfection; Nature will in turn shape the body of man from the four elements (an adaptation of the account in the *Timaeus*). This seems to be the Christian Trinity dressed in Platonic garments: the Father is identical to the Good (Tagathon), the Son to Nous, the Spirit to the world soul or Entelechia, which emanates from Nous. But the comparison is illusory for we are dealing not with co-equals but with a hierarchy of terms, since the world soul connotes an inferior hypostasis, nature, and since Nous bears no resemblance to the incarnate Word, but is an intelligible world that contains species, genera, and individuals, "everything engendered by matter, the elements and the world . . . the whole series of fates (*fatalis series* is the Stoic term), the order of the centuries, the tears of the poor, and the fortunes of kings." [4]

III *Alan of Lille (Alanus de Insulis)*

Nature, the unity of nature, and natural laws probably constitute the essentials of the Platonism of Chartres. One of the best thinkers of the last part of the century was Alan of Lille (1115–1203), the "Universal Doctor," who taught in Paris and in Montpellier.

[4] Cousin, *Ouvrages inédites d'Abélard*, p. 628.

Though he did not depend directly on the school of Chartres, he retained much of its spirit. He represented nature as a young virgin wearing a crown embellished by stones that symbolized the planets and dressed in a mantle on which were embroidered living beings of every type. Thus the twelfth-century cleric rediscovered the ancient image that Pherecydes of Syros probably borrowed from the Babylonians in the sixth century B.C. And to his representation of nature was linked that of man as a microcosm, shaped from the same elements as nature. He was in all probability acquainted also with Nemesius' treatise *On the Nature of Man,* translated by Alfanus in 1058, but he gave first place to the images of the *Timaeus*: reason in man is like the motion of the sphere of fixed stars, and sensibility with its variations is like the motion of the oblique spheres of the planets; the soul is like a divine city where reason, in the head, corresponds to God and heaven, ardor in the heart to angels and the air, and the kidneys in the lower part of the body to man and the earth. Thus the dominant image is that of a universal life, all of whose parts are bound together by secret affinities.[5]

An orthodox cleric like Alan could not deify nature, of course, and he subordinated nature to God. But the manner in which he interpreted the relation of God to nature was borrowed from Proclus' *Theology,* which he knew through the *Book of Causes,* translated from Arabic around the middle of the century and quoted elsewhere by him under the title of *Aphorisms on the Essence of Supreme Goodness.*[6] When he has nature say, "The operation of God is simple and mine is multiple," we must recall the Platonic theories that posit between the diverse levels of reality only the difference between an enveloped unity and a developed unity.

IV *William of Conches*

It was the very concept of philosophy that tended to change in the atmosphere of Chartres. Abundant proof of this is provided in

[5] *De planctu naturae* (Migne, CCX, 431–82).
[6] *Contra haereses* i. 25.

the work of William of Conches (1080–1145), a pupil of Bernard of Chartres. What set him apart was the radical distinction that he made between the trivium and the quadrivium: the former (grammar, dialectic, rhetoric) was merely a study preliminary to philosophy, whereas the latter (mathematics and astronomy) was the first part of philosophy, of which the second part was theology. The contrast between the seven arts and theology tended to be replaced by a contrast between belles-lettres (*eloquentia* or the trivium) and the scientific and philosophical study of nature.[7] And this was indeed the situation depicted by William, who stated in his preface that many teachers would like to restrict instruction to eloquence.

A new image of nature was taking shape. William tried to introduce the corpuscular physics of Constantine the African. "Constantine, discussing as a physicist the natures of bodies, applies the word elements, in the sense of first principles, to the simplest and smallest parts of these bodies; philosophers, discussing the creation of the world and not the natures of particular bodies, refer to the four visible elements." But the common image of the four elements was good for "those who, like peasants, ignore the existence of everything that cannot be apprehended by the senses."[8] Here, then, intelligence was timidly reclaiming its role not only in the acquisition of knowledge of divine things but also in the determination of the substance of sensible reality: invisible atoms were contrasted with visible elements, a simple alloy with transmutation. William encountered considerable resistance, particularly within the circle at Chartres.

The history of the controversy is easily reconstructed by comparing William's *Philosophia* (pp. 49–55) and the fragment of his commentary on the *Timaeus* with the ideas advocated by Gilbert of Poitiers (Gilbertus Porretanus, 1076–1154), also a pupil of Bernard of Chartres and for a long time Chancellor of Chartres. William referred to those who, to refute him, drew support from a famous passage in the *Timaeus* (43a) which, because of the fluidity

[7] *Philosophia mundi* iv. 40 (Migne, CLXXII).
[8] Migne, CLXXII, 50a and 49c–d.

of the sensible world, denied that the elements were stable substances. Gilbert, we can be sure, thought that he was faithful to the
Timaeus in making a distinction between the four sensible elements,
which in conjunction with a certain matter (called by Plato necessity, illusion, nurse, mother) produce diverse bodies, and the Ideas
of the four elements, pure substances that are formed of intelligible
matter and exist as models (*exemplaria*) in God. He therefore refused to see anything but flux in the intelligible world, and found
stability only in the divine reality.[9] Physics, he observed elsewhere,
is concerned only with forms attached to matter and their arrangement, and must therefore refer always to the intelligible world.
Against this, William seems to have envisioned an independent
physics. For example, after showing that the firmament could not be
made of frozen water, he added: "But I know that others will say,
'We do not know what it is but we know that God is capable of
creating it.' Nonsense! What ill-chosen words! Can God make a
thing without seeing what it is like or having a reason for it to be
as it is or showing its utility?" Thus William did not hesitate to
seek a "natural" explanation of the origin of beings and, with respect to the origin of animals, to return to the speculations of Lucretius: the formation of living beings must be attributed to the operation of nature (*natura operans*).[10] To those who countered that
his conception detracted from the divine power, he answered that
the opposite was true, that he was exalting it since it was this divine
power "which has given such a nature to things and which therefore, through the intermediary of the operation of nature, has created
the human body." Such criticisms, he said, come from men who "are
ignorant of the forces of nature," whereas "I maintain that we
must search for reason in all things, but if it fails us, put our
trust in the Holy Spirit and in faith." Inspired perhaps by
Lucretius and the *Timaeus,* he was quick to acknowledge that in
such matters we can attain only to that which is probable. His
naturalism is a rather vague blend of Platonic and Epicurean

[9] *Ibid.,* LXIV, 1265.
[10] *Ibid.,* CLXXII, 53–56.

themes (and even of Stoic themes, for William defined the world soul as the *vigorem naturalem,* "the natural force which is infused in things by God and through which some things have life, others have life and sensation, and still others have life, sensation, and reason").

v *The Mysticism of the Victorines*

In addition to the sober sententiaries who codified Christianity, and those from Chartres who revived Platonism, the twelfth century gave birth to an important mystical movement linked to a radical reform of the monastic orders. Its most important representatives were St. Bernard (Bernard of Clairvaux, 1091–1153) and Hugh of St. Victor (1096–1141). The monastic ideal, that of the *status religiosus,* is a life of renunciation; the pursuit of perfection is based on adherence to the common code of poverty, chastity, and obedience. The history of the monastic orders shows a continual alternation between neglect of basic rules, leading to contamination by the world outside the cloisters, and reforms that re-establish the standard. The eleventh century was dominated by the reform of the Abbey of Cluny, but the monastic spirit then suffered a relapse until the twelfth century, when it was revived by the Cistercian reform and the founding of the Carthusian order by St. Bruno of Cologne. The Cistercian monk was a "composite of the peasant, the artisan, and the ascetic"; the spiritual life, in his view, consisted only in spiritual meditation on the fundamental truths of Christianity to which he gradually subjected his intelligence and his will.

Such meditation, in which cultivation of the imaginative faculty practically replaced critical reflection, gave birth to the monastic mysticism of the twelfth century. Typical is the treatise *De diligendo Deo* by St. Bernard, the celebrated Cistercian and Abbot of Clairvaux. St. Bernard also preached the second crusade (1146) and was counselor to Pope Eugene III, whom he had once instructed and to whom he addressed a treatise, *De consideratione,* on the evils of the Church and the duties of the sovereign pontiff. In the thinking of this dedicated and enthusiastic man "the sum and substance of philosophy is knowledge of Jesus crucified" or, putting it another way, knowledge of God's love for men, which leads men to love God. This love explains the whole Christian drama. Through love God ordained salvation for all men; but he gave them a free will (defined by the Stoic word for assent, *consensus*) which led to their fall; after the fall, God provided through the Incarnation and sacrifice of Jesus a means of satisfying both his justice and his mercy; the Christian since that time has been able to save himself by following Christ; the Christian life is the description of the way that starts from thought or inquiry (which is meditation on ourselves, the world, and God) and leads through contemplation, which is "a sure and not a dubious conception of truth," to ecstasy: separated from the physical senses and no longer aware of itself, the soul is caught up (*rapitur*) and delivered to God; finally, after it has become quite different from itself and quite similar to God, it is deified.

We should note the traditional elements in his portrait of the inner life. They have reappeared from century to century since the time of Philo, Plotinus, and St. Augustine. But one fact stands out: in this instance mysticism is religious and sensible and is in no way speculative. It is a way of life for the soul and not, as in Plotinus, the basis for a philosophical conception of the universe. It is the tradition of Augustine's inner meditation, not the tradition of Neo-Platonist metaphysics. We find the same tendency in Hugh of St. Victor and in those who succeeded him as head of the cloister of St. Victor in Paris. They were no longer great politicians like Bernard, but masters of theology who devoted all their attention to the instruction of clerics. Quite different also from the school of Chartres, they adhered to a traditional conception of education, and the six books in Hugh's *Didascalicon* (with the *Epitome in philosophiam*) were handbooks in the style of Isidore, comprising the liberal arts and theology. Much importance was attached to complete studies, ranging from grammar to mechanics and embracing ethics and theoretical philosophy (mathematics, physics, and theology), and protests were lodged against those who sought "to mangle and lacerate the collective body and who through perversity of judgment choose arbitrarily that which pleases them." [11] In the twelfth century the tradition of universalism, very important in the history of philosophy, was being threatened. We shall soon see who was responsible for this.

Mystical contemplation, the stages of whose attainment are described in detail in numerous Victorine works, is buttressed by thorough intellectual instruction. The fullness of the inner life of the Christian is described in works such as the *De contemplatione et ejus speciebus,* a handbook of spiritual exercises of increasing difficulty: meditation on morals and the divine orders, the soliloquy in which "the inner man" scrutinizes the secrets of his heart, circumspection (*circumspectio*), which is the defense against the seduction of sensible things, and ascension. There are three degrees in ascension: *ascensio in actu,* which consists in confessing our sins, in distributing alms, and in scorning wealth; ascension in our feelings (*in affectu*), which consists in perfect humility, consummate charity, purity of contemplation; finally, and at the highest level, ascension in intelligence (*in intellectu*), which consists in knowing created beings and eventually the Creator. Knowledge of God, in turn, is attained through five modes, each of them more perfect than its predecessor: through created beings whose contemplation leads to the idea of the Creator; through the nature of the soul which is an image of the divine essence that permeates the body as God permeates the universe; through Scripture that reveals to us the attributes of God; through a flash of insight that enables us to ascend to him; and finally through the vision which is "possessed by very few at present and in which, enraptured by divine sweetness, calmly and peacefully one contemplates only God." The mysticism of the Victorines is meticulously orthodox; contemplation at the highest level is but a sublimation of the fundamental Christian virtues of faith and charity.

Hugh's work was continued by Richard of St. Victor, whose

[11] B. Hauréau, *Les œuvres de Hugues de Saint-Victor,* pp. 169–70.

mysticism was even more thoroughly imbued with rationalism and intellectualism. Like St. Anselm, he sought to find "necessary reasons" for divine dogmas, and his *De gratia contemplationis* played an important role in the intellectual preparation for a state of ecstasy.

VI *Peter Abelard*

Members of the school of Chartres, sententiaries, and Victorines seem to have been quite different and even hostile to one another, but they were nevertheless fired by the same spirit. In all of them we find a feeling of liberation, an exuberance over a dawning civilization, an intellectual drive held in check by the inadequacy of their resources. The twelfth century was the first century truly to free itself from encyclopedias and commentaries. Literary forms became more supple and more personal.

Peter Abelard (1079–1142) is the most typical representative of his epoch. For many years and with growing success he taught dialectic: at Melun, at Corbeil, then in Paris at the cathedral school and on Mont Ste Geneviève. The *Introductions for Novices,* the *Glosses* and the *Short Glosses on Porphyry,* and the *Dialectic* (1121) were the result of this teaching. But about 1112 he began to apply himself to theology under the guidance of Anselm of Laon, and his instruction at the cathedral school in Paris in 1113 is wholly theological. His teaching career ended catastrophically in 1118 as a result of his love for his pupil, Heloïse. Cruelly mutilated by her uncle, Fulbert, a canon of Notre Dame, he sought seclusion in the Abbey of St. Denis. He nevertheless resumed his teaching, first at Nogent-sur-Seine, then from 1136 to 1140 at Le Paraclet. From this period of his life came the inspiration for the *Sic et non* (1121), the *Theologia Christiana,* the *Introductio ad theologiam* (*ca.* 1136), and the *Ethica.* From the same period came also his *History of My Misfortunes* (*Historia calamitatum*), which bears a closer resemblance to Rousseau's *Confessions* than to St. Augustine's, and his celebrated correspondence with Heloïse.

Abelard's teaching was of the type which during the Middle Ages invited censure by theologians. Condemned by two councils, at Soissons in 1121 for the *De unitate et trinitate,* and at Sens in 1141 for the *Introductio ad theologiam,* his theological opinions were viewed as a summary of all the great heresies: Arianism, Pelagianism, Nestorianism. According to a letter written by the Archbishop of Rheims to Cardinal Guido of Castello (1141),[12] he denied the equality of the divine persons, the efficacy of grace, and the divinity of Christ; and all his denials sprang from one source— the vast intellectual pride for which he had been censured by his great adversary, St. Bernard:[13] the pride that makes "the human genius (*humanum ingenium*) arrogate everything to itself, reserving nothing to faith," or from the fact that he refused to attach "any merit to faith, thinking that he can understand the fullness of God through reason."

Thus he was accused of trying to change the whole pattern of Christian life by substituting a dogma that eliminated every element of mystery and made tradition useless, and a moral philosophy that rested on man's confidence in himself and rendered grace and the sacraments useless. The truth is that Abelard did not subscribe to such rationalism. "I do not wish to be so philosophical that I resist Paul," he wrote, "or so Aristotelian that I am separated from Christ." Or again: "See how presumptuous it is to discuss rationally that which transcends man and not to stop until all words have been clarified through the senses or through human reason." [14]

What, then, was Abelard's conception of reason? It was based entirely on dialectic, to which he devoted himself with passion to the almost complete exclusion of the sciences of the quadrivium. He was the founder of a school of dialecticians who restricted philosophy to this art. Moreover, his *Dialectic* (1121) was based exclusively on translations of the works of Boethius and showed no trace of the

---

[12] Ep. 192 (Migne, CLXXXII).
[13] Letter written in 1140 (Migne, p. 331).
[14] Ep. 17 to Heloïse (Migne, CLXXXII, 375c–378a): *Introductio ad théologiam* 1223d.

great logical treatises of Aristotle—the *Prior* and the *Posterior Analytics,* the *Sophistical Refutations,* and the *Topics*—which were not translated into Latin until 1125. Dialectic remained for him what it was for Boethius when he was preparing his commentary of the *Categories*: a science dealing not with things themselves but with words as signifiers of things. It is important to note that dialectic has no bearing on our direct knowledge of things; if we wish to discover the way in which a man like Abelard envisions the universe, we must consult, not his dialectic, but a certain passage in the *Ethica* in which this "rationalist" speaks of the influence of the demons on us by virtue of their knowledge of natural forces: "For there are in herbs, in seeds, in the natures of trees and stones many forces capable of agitating or assuaging our souls." [15] We must not forget the contrast between this vivid, passionate knowledge of nature and the dry dialectical classification whose nets could hardly be expected to catch things.

Yet dialectic cannot be totally disinterested in knowledge of things. Abelard's program of dialectical instruction seems at first to be quite simple: he studied the non-complex terms (the five predicables and the categories), then the complex terms, that is, the categorical proposition and syllogism and the hypothetical proposition and syllogism, and finally definitions and division. Its simplicity is illusory, however, for in connection with hypothetical propositions he introduces everything that he knows through Boethius of Aristotle's *Topics,* as well as questions on physics and metaphysics, such as the question of matter and form and of the theory of causes.

The equivocal character of dialectic, which appeared first in Aristotle's attempt to convert a method of discussion into a universal method, is at the heart of the celebrated quarrel over universals: If words signify things, what things are signified by words that designate the genera and species of individual substances? We re-call that genera and species ("animal" or "man") are attributes of

[15] *Opera,* ed. Cousin, II, 608.

an individual subject ("Socrates"), but that unlike accidents ("white," "wise"), they are contained in the essence of the subject, that is, they are such that without them the subject would cease to be what it is.

We also recall that Porphyry and later Boethius asked whether these genera and species, these universals, existed in the nature of things or were the simple product of a vain imagination. We have already considered Roscelin's opinion on this point. William of Champeaux, Bishop of Châlons (1070–1121), had a different opinion. He thought that the attribute "man," posited by Socrates, Plato, and others, was essentially the same reality, and that it was wholly in each of these individuals at the same time; he added that these individuals did not differ at all through their essence, as men, but through their accidents. Besides, we are told, his was a very ancient opinion. The genus ("animal") retains its identity when to it are added specific differences ("rational," "lacking in reason"), and the species retains its identity when accidents are added to it.

Abelard tells us that he discussed the thesis of William (under whom he studied) and even forced him to change his views. William then conceded that universals, in different individuals, were the same reality "not essentially but through the absence of difference (*non essentialiter sed indifferenter*)." That is the negative side of the same thesis—the impossibility of differentiating between man as such in Plato and in Socrates. William went even further and ended by admitting that between the humanity of Socrates and the humanity of Plato there was neither essential identity nor absence of distinction, but simply similitude.[16]

It should be noted that this dispute was not on the same plane as the conflict which, sixteen centuries earlier, had separated Aristotle from Plato on the subject of the existence of Ideas. It is easy to reconcile theological Platonism, which assumes that Ideas are divine thoughts and models of things, with nominalism, which assumes that universals—as we name them and conceive of them—do not designate any true reality. The origin of nominalism is sometimes

---

[16] Quoted in G. Lefèvre, *Les variations de Guillaume de Champeaux.*

attributed to the Platonist Erigena because he thought that dialectic had to do only with words (*dictio*).[17]

Abelard, who in matters of theology was a Platonic realist and who believed "with Macrobius and Plato that divine intelligence contains the original species of things, called Ideas before they are manifested in bodies," [18] still did not accept William's interpretation of the realism of universals. He raised the old objection of Boethius: *"Res de re non praedicatur."* A universal is an attribute; therefore "no reality can be attributed to several things, but only a name." Thus, whereas William considered genus and species in isolation, as members of a classification beginning with the highest genus and ending with the lowest species, Abelard followed Boethius and refused to overlook the fact that the universal is before all else a predicate that implies several individual subjects of which it is the predicate. This explains the theory of universals attributed to him by his pupil John of Salisbury: "He sees subjects of speech in universals as discourses (*sermones*) and reinterprets accordingly everything that has been written on universals"; in other words, he holds that the universal cannot exist apart from the subjects of which it is the attribute (*sermo praedicabilis*). His theory cannot even be called conceptualism.[19]

There is, it seems, a close link between his theory of universals and the Aristotelian theory of abstraction which Abelard borrowed from the passages in Boethius inspired by the third book of Aristotle's treatise *On the Soul* and of which he seems to have been the first to grasp the significance. He describes the process through which the imagination, after sensation "attains superficially to reality," fixes the reality in the mind, and through which the intellect apprehends no longer the reality itself but the nature or property of the reality. This nature or form, if it is apprehended through abstraction as separated from matter, is never known as a separate reality: "There is no intellect without imagination."

[17] Prantl, *Geschichte der Logik,* II, 28.
[18] *Opera,* ed. Cousin, II, 24.
[19] John of Salisbury *Metalogicus.*

After Abelard, universals were never discussed apart from the conditions of the formation of general ideas. Thus the whole century seems to have been inclined toward a kind of "moderate realism" that granted that general words had a real meaning but not that they designated real things to the same degree as sensible things. Such was the attitude of the author of the anonymous treatise *De intellectibus*.[20] The treatise is preceded by a remarkable analysis of intellectual knowledge: an intellectual perception (*intellectus*) of a composite thing, such as three stones, can be simple when perceived by a single intuition (*uno intuitu*) or composite when known through more than one impression (*pluribus obtutibus*); but intellect, whether simple or composite, is always one, provided that its act "be effected continuously and through a single mental impulse." It is clear that simplicity and unity can exist in the intellect that unites things (*intellectus conjungens*), whereas they are not in things themselves. Similarly in abstraction: intellect, as it separates form from matter, divides and separates things that are in reality neither divided nor separated. In neither case does it follow that intellect is useless and vain. Nor is it so when I use universal terms such as "man." The fact that man is in reality always such and such in no way implies that I conceive of him as such and such. Thus we are dealing not simply with a general term and an individual reality but with the meaning of the term, which is the peculiar object of the intellect. As stated in an anonymous fragment, Socrates, man, and animal are the same thing, but considered from a different viewpoint: genus when life and sensibility are considered, species when reason is added, individual when accidents are considered.[21] There is no longer a trace of nominalism or of realism in any of these doctrines. Platonic realism, though frequently advocated, applies to a problem wholly different from that of universals, and we would search in vain for a doctrine to give rigid support to the reality of genera and species within things. Gauthier

[20] In *Opera,* ed. Cousin, II, 733–55.
[21] Cf. the anonymous fragments in *Beiträge zur Geschichte der Philosophie des Mittelalters,* IV, Heft 1, 105, 108.

of Martagne, the writer whom John of Salisbury presented as a typical realist, argued that universals must be united with individuals.[22] And Peter Lombard, in contrast to St. Anselm, freed the dogma of the Trinity of every supposition of realism by making a radical distinction between the unity of the three persons in God and the unity of species in the genus or the unity of the individuals in the species.[23] The field was therefore open to a doctrine that came from Aristotle and Boethius and that can be summarized in two statements: there are in things universal forms that are like images of divine Ideas; these forms have no independent existence but are apprehended separately through intellectual abstraction.

The theological problem as posed by Abelard derives from the same intellectual setting as the problem of universals. Dialectical teaching eventually created a certain mentality or, to put it another way, imposed a certain method for classifying reality: in each instance one must ask to which of Porphyry's five predicables or to which of Aristotle's ten categories a particular thing belongs. The question must be asked of each thing, even of the divine reality to which the most orthodox theologians applied the words "substance," "essence," "quality," "relation," "identity," and "difference." That is the question which poses itself after Boethius, whose *De Trinitate* deals exclusively with the application of the terms of dialectic to the divine reality. We recall Erigena's solution to the problem.

The question is one that engrossed twelfth-century thinkers, and Abelard's *Christian Theology* contains not only his own teaching on this point but also an outline of the teaching of his contemporaries. We have noted that St. Bernard and his party accused Abelard of exaggerating the role of dialectic in acquiring knowledge of divine things. It would be ridiculous to assume that all of Abelard's work is directed specifically against the dialecticians whom he accuses of the mistake for which others have criticized him. "In this tract we find not an exposition of truth but a defense of truth, especially

[22] *Metalogicus* ii. 18.
[23] Dehove *Temperati realismi antecessores*, p. 122.

against the pseudo-philosophers that attack us with philosophical arguments."[24] Abelard then has a middle position between the radical theologians who considered dialectical distinctions as being true of sensible things alone, refusing to apply them to divine reality, and the rabid dialecticians who sought to apply dialectical distinctions as such to the Trinity.

From the second position were derived the "heresies" described by Abelard: the heresy of Alberic of Rheims who, starting from the idea that the Father and the Son are one God, concluded that God begot himself; the heresy of Gilbert the Universal who sought to identify in God, besides his divinity and the three persons, the three essences—paternity, filiation, and procession—that differentiate the three persons; the heresy of Ulger, a teacher from Angers, who made a distinction between the attributes of God, such as justice and mercy, and between the properties of the persons; the heresy of Joscelin of Vierzy who taught that God can err since certain things happen in a manner other than that which he ordained; and the heresy for which Abelard censured the school of Chartres, the belief that God was not prior to the world.[25]

It is easy to discern the application of dialectical rules in all of these "heresies": Alberic applies the notion of substance; Gilbert applies the principle that each being has a distinct essence; Ulger sees in the *Categories* no means of separating the persons (Father, Son) from the other attributes of God; Joscelin of Vierzy applies to the sacred texts the notion of the modality of propositions; the school of Chartres applies the principle that cause cannot exist without effect.

Abelard's solution seems at first to be a radical one. He holds that God or what is said of him fits into no category. We cannot even say that he is substance since substance, according to Aristotle, is the subject of accidents and of contraries. No name befits him. "God

[24] *Opera,* ed. Cousin, II, 519. Cf. his attack on Roscelin (*Theologia* 1215c): "His life and his prattle have made the dialectic of impudent professors contemptible to almost all religious men."

[25] *Introductio ad theologiam,* ed. Cousin, pp. 84–85; commentary by Robert, *Les Écoles,* pp. 198 ff.

violates the rules of the philosophers." But running parallel to the brutal application of dialectic is the path indicated by Plato and St. Augustine, the path of similitude. We can say, for instance, that the Father is to the Son as wax is to the image formed from it: it is the same wax with respect to its essence (*essentialiter*), yet the image comes from the wax, and both the image and the wax have an exclusive property.

It is the same kind of image that Abelard seeks and finds in the *Timaeus* and in the writings of Macrobius. He does not take Plato's doctrine literally, and he reserves the right to subject it to allegorical exegesis: "The language of enigma is as familiar to philosophers as it is to prophets" (*Opera,* ed. Cousin, p. 46). And his exegesis of the *Timaeus,* which like the interpretation of the school of Chartres identifies the Christian Trinity with the triad of God, Intelligence, and the world soul, is wholly allegorical, with the result that it eliminates whatever might be heterodox in Plato's work. He takes pains especially to identify the world soul, the first creature of the demiurge and the creature through which the demiurge made the world a living being, with the Holy Spirit. If Plato ascribes to the world soul a beginning in time but makes the Holy Spirit eternal, the reason is that he is referring to the operation of the Spirit in the world, to a temporal and progressive operation. If Plato ascribes to the world soul two essences, the indivisible and the divisible, the reason is that the Holy Spirit, simple in itself, is multiple in its effects and in its gifts to the human soul. If Plato views the world as a rational being animated by the world soul, the reason is that he is using figurative language, for the world is not in any way a living being; but just as our soul confers life on our body, the world soul or Holy Spirit confers spiritual life on our souls.

His intention is clear: to eliminate from Plato all the naturalism that later appealed so strongly to the Renaissance. Abelard was well aware that his procedure was "violent," and he wrote these characteristic lines: "I am accused of being a violent, troublesome interpreter and of resorting to false explanations to make the texts of the philosophers support our faith and to attribute to them ideas that they never had. Let my accusers recall the prophecy that the Holy Ghost proffered through the mouth of Caiphas, attributing to it a meaning other than that of the one who pronounced it" (*Opera,* ed. Cousin, p. 53).

Now we understand Abelard's theology: it is neither Anselm's dialectical method, which seeks to establish through reason what is believed through faith, nor the philosophy of the school at Chartres, which is to a certain degree independent of dogma; it is rather an effort to find in philosophical notions an image of divine reality so that he can at least conceive of it through analogy.

VII *Polemics Against Philosophy*

The tendencies exhibited by Abelard and by William of Conches were disturbing in circles preoccupied with monastic reform based on a very simple faith. St. Bernard and those around him were violently opposed to such tendencies. Their viewpoint is represented in the *Aenigma fidei* by William of St. Thierry (died in 1153). William was concerned mainly with the common faith that "must be that of everyone in the Church of God, from the youngest to the oldest." [26] He recalls the simplicity of the Gospel and the peculiar style of the Holy Spirit; here we find no allusions to the complex questions concerning the Trinity that theologians were obliged to ask to defend themselves against heresies. "The predicaments of substance, accident, relation, genus, species, and the like, are alien to the nature of faith; common, vulgar instruments of reason, they are unworthy of divine things" (pp. 409a and 418b).

This is the crux of all the criticisms that William of St. Thierry directed against William of Conches. [27] To understand them we must recall that the *Timaeus* was a cosmogony describing, in the divine realities, that which related to the creation of the world. Against this, revealed Trinitary theology aimed to attain to God through other means than his relation to the world. William of

[26] Migne, CLXXX, 407c.
[27] *Ibid.,* CLXXX, 333–40.

Conches, drawing his inspiration from Plato (and also from St. Augustine), identified the Father with the power through which God created the world, the Son with wisdom according to which he created it, the Spirit with the will through which he administered it. Hence "the Father is what he is, not with respect to the Son (as in orthodox theology) but with respect to his creature, not through his nature but through his mode of being" (p. 338d). The Trinity no longer describes the intimacy of the divine life, but rather relations between God and his creature—for instance, charity or mercy.

The criticism directed at Abelard is essentially the same: by identifying the Trinity with the triad of power, wisdom, and goodness, he is attributing to God considered in himself that which is true only of God considered in his relation to his creature. His analogy is nevertheless a classic one; it is found in St. Augustine and subsequently in Bede and Peter Lombard; but it is dangerous because it destroys the meaning of the mystery. William of St. Thierry censures him also for attributing creation to "God's benevolence to his creatures," as the *Timaeus* does, and for saying that the Holy Spirit is a soul that permeates everything. "Here is a theologian who knows the flesh better than the spirit and man better than God," he says. "It is plainer than day that these terms—being moved by affection and reaching out to something—are not applicable to the immutable God."

VIII *Gilbert of Poitiers* (*Gilbert de la Porrée*)

But even William of St. Thierry is forced to admit that "the doctrine of faith cannot repress and reject completely the names supplied by men, but must simply adapt them one by one to its principles." Here he is referring to the program followed by Boethius in his *De Trinitate* and later by Gilbert of Poitiers in his commentary on *De Trinitate*. According to Gilbert, all heresies have their source in the application to "theological things" of certain principles that pertain only to "natural things." Despite all his precautions on this point he is well aware of the impossibility of speaking of God "unless we transfer to him categories borrowed from natural things." But it is necessary to guard against distortion: a perilous task which Gilbert himself was not able to perform to the satisfaction of St. Bernard, who had him condemned by the councils of Paris (1147) and of Tours (1148).

Gilbert, a student of the school of Chartres, adhered to its Platonism. Moreover, he ranked with the best students of Aristotelian logic in his era: he knew the *Analytics,* translated in 1125; under the title *De sex principiis* he wrote an essay that will remain a classic on the last six categories—action, passion, where, when, habitus, and posture. He stressed particularly the notion of form or of essence, basing his discussion on a passage from Seneca which, as we have already seen, was utilized at Chartres.[28] Seneca makes a distinction between the Platonic Idea and the Aristotelian form (εἶδος), between the model that exists apart from a work and the form that is inherent in the work. This is precisely the distinction that Gilbert makes.[29] And what is referred to as his realism consists in his stating, not that the forms subsist in themselves, but that the individual substances that do subsist independently possess being or essence by virtue only of the forms inherent in them. A man has being or essence only because he has within himself the form *humanity,* which in turn is composed of the forms *rationality* and *corporeality*. In contrast, the forms that make substances subsist (the *subsistentiae* of *subsistentes*) cannot subsist by themselves, that is, they cannot be subjects.

But Gilbert found in his examination of form a principle common to *naturalia* and to *theologica*. Common to both orders, he said, is the principle that "being always comes from form." [30] It is therefore necessary to posit in God himself, prior to the three persons, a form, the divinity or deity through whom the persons are given form. It was this very distinction that Bernard attacked. Here

---

[28] *Epistulae morales* 58, 21.
[29] Cf. John of Salisbury *Metalogicus* ii. 17 (Migne, CLXXXIX, 875d).
[30] Migne, LXIV, 1268 ff.

we have a good indication of all the difficulties raised by the critical problem that wore away the intellectual strength of the twelfth century: "To what degree is the divine reality subject to the rules of knowledge that apply to natural things?"

IX *Abelard's Ethic*

The criticism that was directed against Abelard's doctrine of the Trinity and which culminated in his condemnation at Soissons (1121) probably hides the more serious criticism that led to his second condemnation at Sens in 1141. In the twelfth century, as in the previous centuries, it was impossible to separate speculative debate relating to dogma from a whole set of ideas, more practical than theoretical, concerning the Christian life. Just as St. Bernard the theologian took issue with Abelard the theologian, and for the same reasons, the monastic reformers, seeking to return to a strict code, were confronted by opponents who proclaimed that marriage between monks and nuns was licit, or even that salvation was possible prior to the Incarnation and in the absence of belief in the Incarnation. What might be called theological naturalism was offset by a liberating movement that finally resulted in a declaration of the futility of the monastic life, the sacraments, and faith. Such were the circumstances under which Abelard wrote his *Ethica* or *Scito te ipsum*. Here indeed, as St. Bernard said, "human intelligence reserves everything for itself and nothing for faith." [31] To be sure, the *Ethica* is a dialogue between a philosopher and a Christian. The philosopher himself adheres to Christianity, and Abelard, represented by the Christian, criticizes him for his inconsistency in viewing as unsound the doctrine of the Apostles which he has yet found convincing. Still, Abelard—who denounced as scandalous the priests' remission of penitence for money and contested the bishops' power to forgive sin—nevertheless defends an individualistic ethic totally independent of Christian discipline: an upright will guided solely by man's conscience and his concept of

[31] *Ibid.,* CLXXXII, 331.

the good. His ethic leads to the concept of purely personal sin and the impossibility of original sin or of the reversibility of transgressions; to the radical separation of moral transgression, which is wholly internal and which is assent to that which is thought to be bad, and legal transgression; to the impossibility on the part of any other man of knowing an intention, which alone constitutes a transgression; and finally to the idea of a personal salvation not contingent on the reversibility upon us of the merits of Christ.[32] All in all, his was a penetrating intuition that brought to the foreground once again the Greek and human morality. Such was "the new Gospel and the new faith"[33] that was judged dangerous to the tradition of the Church and condemned at Sens. Pope Innocent II, in the rescript that he prepared on the subject, recalled the letter (in reality a forgery) of Marcian the emperor, who told Pope John: "Let no cleric, no military man, no person in any position try to discuss publicly the Christian faith." But we must remember that the *Ethica* is a dialogue between a philosopher and a Christian, that the philosopher clings tenaciously to Christianity, and finally that Abelard is represented by the Christian who criticizes the philosopher for being inconsistent in viewing the doctrine of the Apostles as unsound and in declaring at the same time that he finds it convincing.

x *The Theology of Alan of Lille*

Such condemnations did not stop the irresistible movement that impelled theologians to try to find in the Christian faith a rational structure that would constitute a coherent whole. Underlying their search was a practical necessity which must not be overlooked and which Abelard used to advantage several times: the method of logical argumentation was the only possible method against heretics who would not acknowledge the truth. That is also what Alan of Lille says in his *De arte seu articulis catholicae fidei,* written to-

---

[32] *Opera,* ed. Cousin, II, 637–38.
[33] Letter (1140) from St. Bernard to Innocent II (Migne, CLXXXII, 354).

ward the end of the century. In his book he used (as Proclus had once done in his *Elements of Theology,* with which Alan was acquainted) the form of Euclid, his axioms, his postulates (*petitiones*), and his theorems.

Yet Alan did not pretend, any more than Abelard, to go beyond probability through logical argumentation; instead, he held that faith was "based on certain reasons that are not sufficient for science." Thus there was in his thinking a contrast between the contingent character of Christian truths, most of which announce events that depend on a mysterious decision made by an incomprehensible God, and the rational character of the method that is supposed to prove these facts. The fathomless power of God always limits the reason that could be given for the truths of faith; for example, "God could have ransomed mankind in wholly different manner" (iii. 15); there was no necessity for the Son, rather than some other person, to become incarnate.

Like Gilbert of Poitiers, he tried in his *Theologicae regulae* to show the extent to which the rules of *naturalia* can be transferred to *theologica.* He had a dual principle. First, the common rules of attribution do not apply to God, for God cannot be considered as a logical subject whose attributes can be classed according to the categories of substance, quantity, quality, and the like. It is impossible to fit God, who is a singular term, into a genus and a species, and the diversity of his attributes never designates anything other than a unique essence. Second, rules relating to causes apply both to natural things and to the divine reality. If a predicate is true of a subject, whether the subject is God or a created being, we always have the right to say that there is a cause through which the predicate pertains to it and that the cause of the attribution is different from the attribute itself. If it is true that God is just, there is a cause that makes him just, and this cause is different from the attribute "just" which designates our interpretation of its effects.

In the second principle we see a new application of the ideas in St. Anselm's *Monologium*: revealing the nature of God by referring to the variety of his attributes or, as Dionysius the Areopagite phrased it, of his names.

XI *Twelfth-Century Heresies*

The last part of the twelfth century and the beginning of the thirteenth, marked by the pontificate of Innocent III (1198–1216) and his struggle against the Empire and by the conflict of the English barons against the kings of the Angevine dynasty, is one of the most troubled and tumultuous of all eras. It came to an end with the Lateran Council (1215), which confirmed the doctrines of papal authority and at the same time instituted courts of inquisition and authorized the creation of the mendicant orders. The Magna Charta, which laid the foundation for the security of English political and personal liberty, was signed during the same year. One year earlier (1214) the power of the Capetians had been established at Bouvines.

To understand the importance of these events, which were to have a momentous impact on the history of ideas, we must picture to ourselves the conflicting trends of the closing years of the twelfth century: on the one hand, a vast social upheaval against the Church, manifested in popular heresies and heterodox doctrines, and on the other, a humanistic and doctrinaire trend, of which the best representative is John of Salisbury, who studied under Abelard and the dialecticians of France and who was the counselor of Thomas à Becket, Archbishop of Canterbury.

In the numerous heresies of the era, and in the associations of the Beguines, the Capuciati, the Humiliati, and the Catholic Poor, as well as among Cathari and Albigenses or Waldenses, it is difficult to determine where questions of discipline end and questions of doctrine begin. Toward the middle of the century, Arnold of Brescia, a pupil of Abelard, preached that clerics could not be saved if they possessed land. (He was powerful enough to drive the pope from Rome in 1141.) The substantial basis of these heresies seems always to be the same: the preaching of an ideal of a holy, religious life attainable through a return to evangelical simplicity and total liberation from the Church and the sacraments. Illuminati proclaimed that they were sons of God. Men like Peter of Bruys denied the validity of baptism and the presence of Christ during the Eucharist and sought to destroy churches and to eliminate external forms of worship. About 1170, Peter Waldo of Lyons, the founder of the Waldenses, "usurping the office of Peter," preached evangelical poverty. Alan of Lille tells us that he denied all religious authority and even all human authority, the validity of the sacrament of the Holy Orders, the institution of absolution, and indulgences.

The same Alan of Lille speaks in his *Contra haereticos* of heretics whom he does not name but who are easily identified as the famous Cathari or Albigenses who were dominant in the south of France. Here we see how doctrinal opinions are related to the ideal of the holy, religious life. The yearning for pure, undefiled holiness is always accompanied by the belief that the soul is a fallen heavenly force imprisoned by opposing evil forces. But this belief was transformed among the Albigenses into a precise doctrine in which we recognize, not Manicheism, as has sometimes been said, but rather the doctrine of the Gnostics: the world was created by an evil principle, a demiurge which is at the same time the author of the Mosaic law; the soul is of heavenly origin; a fallen angel, it is being punished here on earth; this soul is not to be confused with the soul conceived as a simple vital principle which, like the soul of an animal, perishes with the body. Christ, who came to save souls, was in no way human; his body was but an illusion. Christ did not institute any of the sacraments and yet the Church owes its power to the fact that they are presumed to be necessary for salvation. The sole aim of the Christian life is to attain to a state of purity in which the soul, wholly delivered from sin and incapable of doing evil, is no longer the prisoner of evil. The pure, or the Cathari, are those who have reached such a state.

The religious independence demanded by the Albigenses was matched by the political independence which the rulers of southern

France, the counts of Toulouse, wished to acquire for themselves. The crusade ordered by Innocent III and characterized by unspeakable cruelties (1207–1214) brought an end to both the heresy and the power of the counts.

Among the doctrines condemned at the Lateran Council was that of Joachim of Fiore, Abbot of the monastery of St. Giovanni at Fiore in Calabria (1145–1202). Jesus said in the Gospel of St. John (14:16): "And I will pray the Father, and he shall give you another Comforter (Paraclete), that he may abide with you for ever." To Joachim, the Paraclete was the Holy Spirit, and this verse indicated the three periods in the history of salvation: Mosaic law, the period of the Father, was the past, and prefigured the Christian Church; the Church was the present, and prefigured the reign of the Spirit; the Spirit was the future announced by Joachim in apocalyptic visions in which he represented the Church as transformed and spiritualized in a new era that was supposed to begin in 1260. This was the birth of the idea of an eternal Gospel that would give the definitive spiritual meaning of the Gospel of Christ. The idea was to persist in Franciscan circles until the fourteenth century.[34]

Between the ideas of Joachim and those of the Waldenses or of the Albigenses there was surely a kinship—the desire to bring to birth a new spiritual order, different from the existing order. But the contrast was great: the Joachimites saw in the eternal Gospel the consummation of Christianity, something long anticipated; they had a sense of historical continuity. The Cathari simply denied the role of the Church and held that the new spiritual order was realized then and there by the pure or the perfect who had been initiated to their divine origin. Thus they stood for progress on the one hand, violent revolution on the other.[35]

The doctrine of Amaury of Bène (died 1207), Professor of Theology at Paris, though quite different from that of the Albigenses, leads to the same practical attitude. The Albigenses rediscovered

[34] Cf. Gilson, *Saint Bonaventure*, pp. 22 ff.
[35] Cf. Delacroix, *Le mysticisme spéculatif en Allemagne*, p. 44.

the drama of salvation as it had been described by the Gnostics: the deliverance of the soul, the divine essence imprisoned by evil. No such drama is found in the work of Amaury. He taught that each man is a part of Christ; according to the commentaries of his disciples he meant that the only reality that might exist eternally identical to itself was God, and that salvation consisted in nothing but the knowledge that God is all things. In his teaching there was nothing that resembled faith and hope, which are the expectation of something better: no evidence of fear of Hell or hopes of Paradise; no evidence of the belief that God is present in a special way in Christ or in the Host, since he is everywhere and incarnate in all creatures. But there was complete assurance, based on personal revelation, of the birth of the definitive reign of the Spirit that was to replace the Church.

Here we recognize a pattern of thought that began with the Stoics, continued through Plotinus and Dionysius, and reached Amaury by way of Erigena.

We see also that the theoretical doctrine of the unity of all being in God was strong enough at this time to be translated into overt opposition to the whole spiritual system of the Church. The Church recognized the danger, and the doctrine of the Amauricians was condemned at the Synod of Paris in 1210 and at the Lateran Council in 1215. At the same time Erigena's *De divisione naturae* was condemned, for in it was seen the source of the doctrine. During the same period the doctrine persisted in the writing of David of Dinant, also condemned in 1210. We know only the title of his book, *De tomis hoc est de divisionibus,* which recalls Erigena, but we know his ideas through Albert the Great and St. Thomas. The division to which he refers is that of realities into bodies, souls, and separate substances; each reality has its indivisible principle—matter (*hyle*) for bodies, Intelligence (*Nous vel mentem*) for souls, God for separate substances. But the triad of matter, intelligence, and God designates but one substance. To establish this conclusion David seems to have employed the principle of the *Book of Causes*: if we saw them as distinct terms we would have to posit beyond them a simple and indivisible principle that contains whatever they have in common (Avicebron, whose *Fons vitae* was known to David, followed an analogous line of reasoning); this brings us back, then, to a unique reality. We recognize in his triad, not the Neo-Platonic triad of Macrobius (One, intelligence, and soul), but a triad drawn from the *Timaeus* (demiurge, intelligence or being, and matter).

XII *John of Salisbury*

One of the most striking figures of the period was John of Salisbury (1110–1180), who was taught by Abelard, by Gilbert of Poitiers, and by William of Conches. He was the friend of Thomas à Becket and died while serving as Bishop of Chartres. A distinguished writer, well versed in the classics, he was familiar not only with poets like Ovid and Vergil, but also with Seneca and especially Cicero, from whom he borrowed his knowledge of Stoic moral philosophy as well as academic doubt. His two great works, the *Metalogicus* and the *Policraticus,* vividly reflect all the preoccupations of a great ecclesiastical official of the period.

The *Metalogicus* gives us a catalogue of all the questions raised around 1160 by the diffusion of instruction in dialectic. A belief that had prevailed for a long time was now threatened: the belief that dialectic was but one of the seven liberal arts which, collectively, were destined to serve as an introduction to theology. Many twelfth-century theologians feared that their neat hierarchy was on the verge of collapse. Dialectic resisted subordination and started to invade theology. Such men as St. Bernard viewed it primarily as a sin, "a shameful curiosity that consists in acquiring knowledge for its own sake, a shameful vanity that consists in knowing for the sake of being known." Such criticisms were heard constantly until the end of the twelfth century and they applied even to the authors of Sentences and compendiums, who were censured for not being satisfied with the Fathers. In his *Contra quatuor labyrinthos Fran-*

ciae, Gauthier, Prior of St. Victor, took issue with Peter Lombard and Peter of Poitiers as well as with Abelard and Gilbert of Poitiers. But orthodox theologians were frightened by something more than a mere dialectical invasion that profaned the sacred science and made dogmas the object of public debates. They were also witnessing, not without apprehension, the emergence of extremism in dialectic: the purely formal cultivation of the art of discussion which finally becomes an end in itself. Prohibition of the teaching of theology, enforced upon masters of the arts, resulted in an almost monstrous development of the art of discussion. John of Salisbury described the "pure philosophers" who scorned everything apart from logic and were ignorant of grammar, physics, and ethics. "They devote their lives to it, and in their old age they are puerile doubters; they discuss each syllable and even each letter of words and passages; they are always groping, always searching, and they never attain wisdom. . . . They compile the opinions of everyone, and the mass of conflicting opinions is such that the author of a book can scarcely recognize his own." [36]

This pointed up the danger of cultivating subtlety for its own sake and of reviving along the banks of the Seine—as Adam du Petit-Pont did—the pursuit of sophistry that had ruined certain Greek schools. Adam candidly acknowledged that he would have had very few auditors if he had taught dialectic using simple, easily understood formulas.[37] People preferred collections of sophisms such as this one that typifies the spirit of the Megarian school: "One hundred is less than two, for one hundred in relation to two hundred is less than two in relation to three."

John of Salisbury was no enemy of logic, and he took issue with those who declared it useless, such as the enigmatic man whom he calls Cornificius, who boasted of his method to short-cut education.[38] But John made logic a simple intellectual tool: Adam's dialectic, "wallowing in its own mire and muddling its own secrets, is con-

[36] *Metalogicus* i. 6 and 7.
[37] Cf. Grabmann, *Geschichte der scholastischen Methode,* II, 112.
[38] Cf. Robert, *Les Écoles,* p. 69, note.

cerned with subjects that are useful neither in the family, nor in war, nor in law, nor in the cloister, nor in the Court, nor in the Church—nowhere except in school" (viii). Logic was designed not to hide ignorance but to advance knowledge. On this point John was guided mainly by Aristotle's *Topics,* his favorite among the five treatises of the *Organon,* which was then becoming known in its entirety throughout the West. The *Topics* was of considerable importance; it was then new to readers, and its style was much clearer than that of the *Analytics.* With a sure sense of history, John saw clearly that it constituted a complete and independent treatise. To the foundations of logic, presented in the first book much more clearly than in Porphyry and Boethius, he addded the ethical and physical questions listed in the third book, and he ended with the eighth book, the most useful of all, in which are given the rules for discussion and debate. With respect to the other treatises in the *Organon,* the *Categories* and the *Peri Hermeneias* are designed only to lay the foundation for the *Topics,* and the *Analytics* are merely appendices. The art of demonstration taught in the *Posterior Analytics* is useless, for the nature of things is so mysterious that man can never know the modality of propositions, possibility, impossibility, and necessity. "That is why the method of demonstration almost always vacillates in physics and has its full efficacy only in mathematics" (xiii, end).

Here we see clearly outlined the ideal of an epoch: not to discover the nature of things but to find a general method of devising arguments applicable in the most diverse circumstances. Scholars were well aware that in this way they would reach only that which was probable: "the apprehension of truth itself pertains only to the perfection of God or an angel" (ii. 10). John was no exception. He knew that beyond reason, which he defined in the manner of the Stoics as stability of judgment, there was intelligence (*intellectus*) that attained to the divine causes of natural reasons, and wisdom that was as the savor of divine things. But he sets it distinctly apart from the sphere in which purely human interests struggle with human tools.

The same spirit, humanism subordinated to theology, character-izes the *Policraticus,* in which human, moral, and political wisdom is subordinated to a theocracy. With respect to its ethical content, the work is permeated by Stoicism. The rebirth of the doctrine of Stoicism during this period coincided with the spread of naturalism, whose many manifestations we have noted. The Stoic arguments relating to fate were known and disputed.[39] John speaks of a Neo-Stoic (*novus stoicus*) from Pouille, an Italian named Louis who had written a commentary on Vergil and who, taking up again Dio-dorus' ancient discussion of contingent futures, concluded that it was impossible to know "whether an action that a man will not perform is nevertheless a possible action" (ii. 23). Elsewhere John proves according to the old Stoic doctrine that "the providence of God does not suppress the nature of things and that the order of things (*series rerum,* the Stoic definition of fate) does not alter providence." The whole of the fourth book, which is on politics, is imbued with the Stoic ideas of Cicero's *De legibus.* In it we find that the prince is the servant of the law and of equity, and that law (Chrysippus' formulation) is mistress of all divine and human things. The state, he adds, must be constructed in the image of na-ture; and he cites as a model in this context the description of the republic of the bees given in the *Georgics* (v. 21). He finds precepts for the conduct of the prince in a letter from Plutarch to Trajan, which he cites in his fifth book. The same Stoic tendency is mani-fested in his moral philosophy, particularly in the eighth book, in which he deals with the passions and follows Cicero's *Tusculan Disputations.* His Stoicism, like Cicero's, is restrained by academic doubt.

Naturalism imbued with Stoic rationalism fits remarkably well into a theocracy that subjects temporal power to spiritual power. If "the prince is the minister of priests and inferior to them," this is because "it is an established fact that the prince, by virtue of the authority of divine law, is subject to the law of justice" (iv. 3, 4).

[39] In the fourth chapter (546a) he quotes Epicurus' χυρία δόξα against the fatal necessity of the Stoics.

The priest, then, is the first interpreter of the divine law that "the prince must always have before his eyes" (iv. 6). Rationalism, naturalism, and the predominance of spiritual power go hand in hand with statements like these: "The state is an animate body, by the grace of God, governed by sovereign equity and administered by the rule of reason" (v. 6). "The prince is therefore chosen by God; hence his privileges, which make his subjects consider him as an image of the divinity" (vi. 25). Just as the Stoic law was realized in the spiritual power established by Christ, so after John of Salisbury the Stoic ethic was realized in the monastic orders, particularly among the monks at Chartres (vii. 23).

BIBLIOGRAPHY

I

Texts

Anselm of Laon. *Extraits inédits des Sentences.*
Bernold of Constance. *Opera.* Migne, CXLVIII, p. 1061.
Peter Abelard. *Sic et non.* Migne, CLXXVIII.
Peter Comestor. *Opera.* Migne, CXCVIII, pp. 1049–1844.
Peter Lombard. *Opera.* Migne, CXCI, CXCII.
———. *The Four Books of Sentences.* Book I, Dist. III. Translated by R. McKeon, *Selections,* I, 189–201.
Peter of Poitiers. *Sententiae.* Migne, CCXI, 783.
Robert of Melun. *Extract from the Sentences.* Migne, CLXXXVI, 1015, 1053.
Robert Pulleyn. *Sentences.* Migne, CLXXXVI, 639.
William of Champeaux. *Sentences.* Published by G. Lefèvre in *Les variations de G. de Champeaux et la question des universaux.* Lille, 1898.
Yves of Chartres. *Decretum.* Migne, CLXI.

Studies

Epensberger, J. *Die Philosophie des Petrus Lombardus und ihre Stellung im XII Jahrhunderte. Beiträge,* Vol. III. Münster in Westfalen, 1901.
Haskins, C. *The Renaissance of the Twelfth Century.* Cambridge, 1927.
Moore, P. *The Works of Peter of Poitiers.* South Bend, Ind., 1936.
Nash, P. "The Meaning of *Est* in the Sentences (1152–1160) of Robert of Melun," *Mediaeval Studies,* XIV (1952), 129–42.
Nitze, W. "The So-called Twelfth Century Renaissance," *Speculum,* XXIII (1948), 464–71.
Sanford, E. "The Twelfth Century Renaissance or Proto-Renaissance?" *Speculum,* XXVI (1951), 635–41.
Tremblet, P., *et al. La Renaissance du XIIe siècle.* Paris, 1933.

II to IV

Texts

Adelard of Bath. *De eodem et diverso.* Edited by Hans Willner. *Beiträge,* Vol. IV. Münster in Westfalen, 1903. Pp. 3–34.

Alan of Lille. *Opera.* Migne, CCX.

Bernard of Chartres. No known texts extant. Most of our knowledge of Bernard comes from the works of John of Salisbury. (See section XII, below.)

Bernardus Silvestris. *De mundi universitate libri duo.* Edited by C. S. Barach and J. Wrobel. Innsbruck, 1876.

Gilbert of Poitiers. *Opera.* Migne, LXIV, 1255–1412.

Thierry of Chartres. *De septem diebus.* In W. Jansen, *Der Kommentar des Clarenbaldus von Arras zu Boethius De Trinitate.* Breslau, 1926. Pp. 106–12.

William of Conches. Extracts from the commentary on the Timaeus. In J. M. Parent, *La doctrine de la création dans l'école de Chartres.* Paris, 1938.

———. *Philosophia mundi.* Under the name of Honorius Augustodunensis, Migne, CLXXII.

Studies

De Lage, R. *Alain de Lille: Poète du XIIᵉ siècle.* Paris, 1951.

Flatten, H. *Die Philosophie des Wilhelm von Conches.* Koblenz, 1929.

Gilson, E. "La cosmogonie de Bernardus Silvestris," *Archives d'histoire doctrinale et littéraire du moyen âge,* III (1928), 5–24.

———. "Le platonisme de Bernard de Chartres," *Revue Néo-Scolastique de philosophie,* XXV (1923), 5–19.

Haring, N. "The Case of Gilbert de la Porrée, Bishop of Poitiers (1142–54)," *Mediaeval Studies,* XIII (1951), 1–40.

Haskins, C. "Adelard of Bath," *The English Review* (1911).

Jeauneau, E. "Un représentant du platonisme au XIIᵉ siècle: Maître Thierry de Chartres," *Mémoires de la Société archéologique d'Eure-et-Loir,* XX (1954), 3–12.

Parent, J. *La doctrine de la création dans l'école de Chartres.* Paris, 1938.

———. "Un nouveau témoin de la théologie dionysienne au XIIᵉ siècle," *Aus der Geisteswelt des Mittelalters. Festgabe M. Grabmann.* Münster in Westfalen, 1935.

Poole, R. "The Masters of the Schools at Paris and Chartres in John of Salisbury's Time," *English Historical Review,* XXXV (1920), 321–42.

V

Texts

Bernard of Clairvaux. *Opera*. Migne, CLXXVII.
———. *Works*. Translated by a priest of Mount Melleray. 6 vols. Dublin, 1920–25.
———. *On the Love of God*. Translated by A. Pegis in *The Wisdom of Catholicism*. Pp. 230–68.
Hugh of St. Victor. *Opera*. Migne, CLXXV–CLXXVII.
———. The *Didascalicon* of Hugh of St. Victor. Translated by J. Taylor. New York, 1961.

Studies

Butler, C. *Western Mysticism. The Teaching of SS. Augustine, Gregory and Bernard on Contemplation and the Contemplative Life*. London, 1951.
Castrén, O. *Bernhard von Clairvaux. Zur Typologie des mittelalterlichen Menschen*. Lund, 1938.
Gilson, E. *The Mystical Theology of St. Bernard*. Translated by A. Downes. London, 1940.
Hauréau, B. *Les œuvres de Hugues de Saint-Victor: Essai critique*. Paris, 1886.
Hunt, R. "The Introductions to the 'Artes' in the Twelfth Century," *Studia mediaevalia* ("Miscellanea Martin"). Bruggis (n.d.), pp. 85–112.
Kleinz, J. *The Theory of Knowledge of Hugh of St. Victor*. Washington, D.C., 1944.
Weisweiler, H. "Die Arbeitsmethode Hugos von St. Victor," *Scholastik*, XX and XXIV (1949), 59–87 and 232–67.
Williams, W. *The Mysticism of St. Bernard of Clairvaux*. London, 1931.

VI, VII

Texts

Peter Abelard. Theological works. Migne, CLXXVIII.
———. *Opera*. Edited by V. Cousin. 2 vols. Paris, 1849, 1859.
———. *Ouvrages inédits d'Abélard*. Edited by V. Cousin. Paris, 1836.
———. *Peter Abaelards philosophische Schriften. Beiträge*, XXXI, 1–4. Münster, 1919–33.
———. *Abailard's Ethics*. Translated by J. R. McCallum. Oxford, 1935.
———. *Glosses on Porphyry* (Introduction). Translated by R. McKeon in *Selections*, I, 208–58.

William of Saint Thierry. *Disputatio adversus Abaelardum*. Migne, CLXXXII, 531–32.
———. *Aenigma Fidei*. Migne, CLXXX, 397–440.
———. *De la vie solitaire*. Text, French translation, and notes by M.-M. Davy. 2 vols. Paris, 1914.

Studies

Adam, A. *Guillaume de Saint-Thierry: Sa vie et ses oeuvres*. Bourg-en-Bresse, 1923.
Gilson, E. *Heloise and Abelard*. Translated by L. Shook. Chicago, 1951.
Kaiser, E. *Pierre Abélard critique*. Fribourg, Switzerland, 1901.
Lasserre, P. *Un conflit religieux au XIIe siècle: Abélard contre S. Bernard*. Paris, 1930.
Lefèvre, G. *Les variations de Guillaume de Champeaux et la question des universaux*. Lille, 1898.
Lottin, O. "Le problème de la moralité intrinsèque, d'Abélard à saint Thomas d'Aquin," *Revue thomiste,* XXXIX (1934), 477–515.
McCallum, J. *Abailard's Christian Theology*. Oxford, 1948.
Sikes, J. *Peter Abailard*. Cambridge, 1932.

VIII See II, III, and IV

IX See VI and VII

X See II, III, and IV

XI

Texts

Alan of Lille. *Contra haereticos*. Migne, CCX, 305–430.

Studies

Alphandéry, P. *Les Idées morales chez les hétérodoxes latins au début du XIIIe siècle*. École des Hautes Études, "Sciences religieuses," Vol. XVI. Paris, 1903.
Arnou, R. "Quelques idées néoplatoniciennes de David de Dinant," *Philosophia perennis*, I, 115–27. Regensburg, 1930.
Broekx, E. *Le Catharisme*. Louvain, 1916.
Capelle, C. *Autour du décret de 1210: Amaury de Bène, étude sur son panthéisme formel*. Paris, 1932.

Dondaine, A. *Un traité manichéen du XIIIe siècle: Le "Liber de duobis principiis" suivi d'un fragment de rituel cathare.* Rome, 1939.

Fournier, P. *Étude sur Joachim de Flore.* Paris, 1909.

Runciman, S. *The Mediaeval Manichee.* Cambridge, 1947.

Théry, G. *Autour du décret de 1210: David de Dinant, étude sur son panthéisme matérialiste.* Paris, 1925.

XII

Texts

John of Salisbury. *Opera.* Migne, CXCIX.

——. *Metalogicon.* Translated by D. McGarry. Berkeley, 1962.

——. *Policraticus.* Parts translated by J. Dickinson under the title of *The Statesman's Book of John of Salisbury.* New York, 1927.

——. *Policraticus.* Parts translated by J. Pike under the title of *Frivolities of Courtiers and Footprints of Philosophers.* (He does not translate the same books as Dickinson.) Minneapolis, 1938.

Daniels, H. *Die Wissenschaftslehre des Johannes von Salisbury.* Kalderkirchen, 1932.

Denis, L. "La question des universaux d'après Jean de Salisbury," *Revue des sciences philosophiques et théologiques,* XVI (1927), 425–34.

Haskins, C. *The Renaissance of the Twelfth Century.* Cambridge, 1927.

Webb, C. *John of Salisbury.* London, 1932.

PHILOSOPHY IN THE EAST

THE DESTINY of the western world during the Middle Ages was determined in part by the Arab conquest, which, stretching from India to Spain and as far as southern Italy and the Greek islands, put a screen between Europe and Asia. In 635 the Arabs began to move with lightning speed across the globe; within one century they completed their domination, but were finally stopped at Poitiers in 732 and in Chinese Turkestan in 751. They brought with them a language and a religion that subsequently gained ascendancy over vast territories. They seized control of Syria, Egypt, and Persia, countries where the old Hellenistic culture had been preserved and where, in the sixth century, philosophers were still engaged in writing commentaries on Plato and Aristotle. In this chapter we shall try to assess the impact of such events on the course of the history of ideas.

From the historians we learn that only a handful of Arabs were scattered throughout the vast territories they occupied militarily, and that they preserved the administrative and social organization of the conquered nations. For example, following the dismemberment of the Persian Empire that resulted in its division into independent dominions, the Caliphs of Baghdad enlisted in their service the whole financial and political organization of the ancient Persian rulers.[1] An onologous phenomenon seems to characterize the intellectual sphere: converted to Islam and writing in Arabic,

[1] Cf. Halphen, *Les barbares* (Paris: Alcan, 1926), Vol. I, chaps. x and xi.

the Arab philosophers, most of them of Aryan rather than Semitic origin, found their themes for meditation either in the Greek works which the Nestorian Christians who populated Asia Minor and Persia translated into Syriac and Arabic after the sixth century, or in the Mazdaist tradition which was still alive in Persia and which had assimilated elements of Indian philosophy (the mysticism of the Sufi).

1 *The Moslem Theologians*

The Koran is not the direct source of inspiration for Moslem theologies. For several reasons, though its influence was considerable, the Koran did not engender anything similar to the dogmatic theology that dominated Europe. To begin with, most theological controversies were based on questions tacitly set aside by the doctrine of the Koran. The Trinitarian and the Christological controversies, like the controversy over grace, are meaningless in a doctrine that assumes the radical unity of God and has no place for anything like the sacrament. God and his prophet Mohammed, who consummated the work of the two prophets Abraham and Jesus, are the sum and substance of the religion of Islam: sparse and clear as a desert landscape and shorn of any trace of the Hellenic penchant for complicated speculations on the nature of divine reality. Furthermore, there is in Islam no spiritual authority whose function is to interpret dogma. The Koran is not weighted down by an accretion of binding pronouncements. Islam recognizes the prophets as men inspired by God but holds that not one of them can add to the teaching of the Koran.

The sacred book, much more practical and juridical than theoretical, contains but one dogma, which goes back to an idea that Mohammed borrowed from Jewish monotheism: that of one God, absolutely simple by nature, whose will is omnipotent and inscrutable. The dogma implies a representation of the universe diametrically opposed to the Neo-Platonic representation generally accepted in the countries conquered by the Arabs. The Islamic concept of divine arbitrariness stands in sharp contrast to the concept of a rational order of development which the Greek philosophers introduced into the world. The contrast between the two concepts is the only theme treated in what may properly be called Moslem theology, that is, the theology of the Mutakallimoun and the Mutazilites, who took pains to erect against their adversaries a coherent image of the universe according to the Koran.

All reflection was concentrated around two purely theological questions: negation of multiplicity in God and negation of all power other than that of God. On the first point, Moslems asked how God, if he is one, can be said to be good, wise, just, and so forth. Some of them went so far as to deny that God had any of these properties; others, though they did not deny outright that he had them, considered them as modes or manners of being under which divine essence appeared, but without being in any way enhanced by them; they were not qualities, and "whoever posits an eternal quality along with God is positing two Gods." Still others posited them as eternal qualities that subsist through the essence of God.

On the second point, theologians were wary of both free will and determinism. The first concept limits the power of God, and the second entails natural necessity. The denial of free will had as its counter-effect the emergence of the Mutazilites (seceders) in the eighth century. Under the influence of Wazil, the son of Ata, the Mutazilites conceded that man has freedom to safeguard the goodness of God, who is incapable of decreeing a bad act since he ordains good. It is in the same conciliatory spirit that Wazil, the founder of the sect, posited between the righteous believer and the impious man the intermediate state of the sinner who is at the same time a believer. His idea recalls the moderate solution that the middle Stoics offered to the problem of moral progress.

As for natural determinism, we must bear in mind that it is indissolubly linked by the Greek tradition to the image of an eternal world with a cyclical evolution and to a god who acts in the manner of a natural force. Against this, the thesis of creation entails a radical indeterminism in the production of things not only at the initial moment but also throughout the course of time. Hence the atomistic theory advocated by the school of Askari (876–935): the continuity of substance is impossible, for one would have to assume that God was not free to create one part without the others; bodies, then, are made of discontinuous atoms floating in the void. The same holds true with respect to continuity in time, which is formed by a series of indivisible instants, and in movement, which consists of separate and individual leaps. There is no necessity in the inherence of the atom's properties, for all atoms are identical, and their properties—color and life—are superadded accidents. Finally, there is no necessity for the accidents that exist in substance at a given moment to exist there the following moment; they are at each instant the effect of a direct creation of God, and there is no natural law that requires the existence or non-existence of anything whatsoever. In this atomistic theory, which is for the glory of Allah, we would search in vain for something that recalls the rationalism of Epicurus.

II *The Influence of Aristotle and of Neo-Platonism*

The Greek influence, running counter to Moslem theology, spread initially through translations from Greek to Syriac made by the Nestorian Christians who, first at the school of Edessa (431–489), then in the cloisters of Syria, and finally, in the seventh century, in the convent of Kinnesrin on the Euphrates, translated not only Aristotle's *Organon* but also the pseudo-Aristotelian treatise, *On the World,* and the works of Galen. After the founding of Baghdad in the ninth century, many works were translated into Arabic, either from Syriac or from Greek, and in 832 the Caliph himself founded what amounted to a translation bureau in his capital. Toward the end of the ninth century, an Arab had access to almost the whole of Aristotle's work (except the *Politics*) and to the commentaries of Alexander, Porphyry, Themistius, Ammonius, and John Philoponus; translations were also available of some of Plato's dialogues, such as the *Timaeus,* the *Republic,* and the *Sophist.* The Greek doxography was accessible through translations of Plutarch's *Lives of the Philosophers,* not to mention works attributed to Empedocles and to Pythagoras. Furthermore, medicine was known through Galen and astronomy through Ptolemy's *Almagest.*

How did the Arab philosophers use these materials? Their interpretation of Aristotle was dominated by two treatises falsely attributed to him. Around 840, extracts from seven treatises from Plotinus' last three *Enneads* were translated into Arabic under the title of *Aristotle's Theology.* The translation was preceded by a preface which was a summary of the Neo-Platonic theory of hypostases. To the triad of God, Intelligence, and Soul (in which each term derives from the preceding term), was added a fourth term, Nature, which derives from Soul. And each of the four terms was made to correspond to one of Aristotle's four causes—final, formal, efficient, or material. The extracts included, in its entirety, the second treatise of the fifth *Ennead,* which is an abridgment of the whole doctrine of Plotinus. The second treatise falsely attributed to Aristotle was the *Book of Causes,* which contained extracts from Proclus' *Elements of Theology.*

Under these influences Arab philosophy, to the extent that it followed the Greeks, was essentially a Neo-Platonic interpretation of the whole of Aristotle's work. In the foreground we find, along with the two treatises mentioned above, the fifth book of the *Metaphysics* and the eighth book of the *Physics,* which contain Aristotle's speculations on the moving Intelligence of the heavens, as well as the third book of his *On the Soul,* which deals with the nature of intellectual knowledge. In some ways anything that differs more than the spirit of Aristotle from the spirit of Neo-Platonism is inconceivable. A rational empiricism, a logical technique, and a positive orientation stand in sharp contrast to a mythology of spiritual forces that seems to suffuse the universe and that is apprehended only through intuition.

III *Alkindi*

The prime characteristic of the Arab philosophers was the ease with which they were able to pass back and forth between Aristotelianism and Neo-Platonism. The first of the well-known Arab Peripatetics, Alkindi (died in 872), was a mathematician deeply concerned with positive knowledge: "Anyone who wishes to understand logical demonstrations," he said, "ought to devote much time to the study of geometrical demonstrations and learn their rules, especially the easier ones since they serve as obvious examples." Demonstration was to him an instrument that required "first a correct standard and then correct application." [2] It therefore presupposed prior, indemonstrable knowledge. There are three kinds of such knowledge: the first, knowledge of the existence of the object whose attributes (*an sit*) are to be demonstrated, is given directly by the senses; the second, knowledge of self-evident universal axioms, is common knowledge and requires neither meditation nor reflection; the third, knowledge of the quiddity or definition of an object, enables us to demonstrate attributes by means of axioms.

We recall all the difficulties raised by Aristotle's theory of definition and of quiddity. Alkindi grappled with the same difficulties: the quiddity of a being is known neither through the senses that ascertain only existence, nor through induction that ascertains only properties. To separate the quiddity from sensible data one must have recourse to a special operation which is described in the treatise *De intellectu et intellecto*. In conformity with the fundamental theorem of Aristotle's metaphysics, a being cannot pass from potency to act unless under the influence of an active being; there must exist "an intellect that is forever active" and conceives always of quiddities. This explains why the "potential intellect" that is in the soul (that is, the capacity of conceiving of quiddities) can become "intellect that passes from potency to act," and finally "acquired (*adeptus*) intellect" capable of demonstration. Thus

[2] Trans. Nagy, p. 46.

knowledge of quiddities is acquired only in a soul capable of receiving such knowledge and by virtue of a primary intelligence which is always active and which, being the universal form of things (God) and giving to things their quiddities or forms, also endows these forms with potential intelligence.

IV *Alfarabi*

Alkindi's views on the operation of the intellect implied the rudiments of a vast theology. Such a theology was developed by Alfarabi (born at the end of the ninth century). In it we see the interpenetration of the influence of Aristotle and that of Plato. From Aristotle he borrowed his astral theology, simplified by Arabic astronomy: a supreme God above the worlds; heavens composed of eight concentric and interlinking spheres, each with its characteristic circular motion governed by an intellect—the sphere of the fixed bodies and the seven spheres of the seven planets; and beneath these, the sublunary sphere. From Plotinus (through the work on theology falsely ascribed to Aristotle) he borrowed the general image of the production of living beings: progression as if by a law of evolution from the One to the Multiple, from the Eternal to the Temporal and the Changing. The starting point is the supreme principle, God, who by knowing his essence knows all things: first in their absolute unity, identical to his own essence; then in their infinite multiplicity. The second type of knowledge is essentially the same as the first. How is multiplicity to be derived from absolute unity? We recall how in Plotinus the One gave birth to Intelligence: something indeterminate emanates from the One and, turning back toward the One, becomes intelligence by contemplating the One and becoming conscious of itself. Such is the description given by Alfarabi: from the eternal One can come only a unique and eternal being that is an intellect; since it is derived, it is composite; for by itself it is only possible. It is therefore necessary to separate knowledge that it has of the Principle as the ground of its existence, knowledge of its existence as possible—that is—of its matter (since matter is merely potential being), and knowledge that it has of it-self, which is its form or essence. From the three kinds of knowl-edge are born three beings: from knowledge of the Principle is born a second intellect that will be to the first as the first is to the Principle; from the matter of the intellect is born the matter of the first sphere (this topical matter is the simple possibility of circular motion); from the form of the intellect is born the moving soul of the first sphere. Thus begins the procession of intellects and celestial spheres with their souls; each intellect produces in its turn a sub-ordinate intellect, a sphere, and a moving soul, down to the last of the spheres, the moon, dominated by the last of the intellects, the "active intellect."

Each intellect is as the law of motion of the sphere: "It knows the order of the good that emanates from it, and it produces this order as it acquires its knowledge." It also conceives the motion that car-ries its sphere from one point to the next, and this image is in turn creative: it creates whatever order there is in the transmutation of elements in the sublunary region.

Intellects, and particularly the last or active intellect, contain in-divisibly all the quiddities or forms of sensible things; but these quiddities separate from each other in the sublunary region where each being is merely a being separated from other beings. The state of separation is the starting point of intellectual knowledge in the human soul. Knowledge is a unifying impulse and is the re-verse of a divisive impulse: "The active intellect seeks to reunite as best it can that which has been divided and creates the acquired in-tellect of which human nature is a part." The different intellects identified in the human soul by Alfarabi are merely the principal points in the passage from division to unity. At the lowest point is the potential intellect, which is the capacity to abstract forms from matter and to reunite and classify these forms; above the potential intellect is the active intellect, which is the effective realization of this capacity. The intelligible reality, fused at first with its image and accompanied by individual peculiarities, is gradually purified and disentangled as it passes from sense to the common sense and from the common sense to the imagination, where the potential intellect receives matter for its abstractive activity. Above each active intellect is the acquired intellect which through an intuitive look apprehends the unifying principle underlying separate forms. At the summit is the active intellect of the moon, which is prior to all other intellects and which has unleashed all their activity by causing the potential intellect to become active. His theory of intellects is quite different from the theory of Alkindi who, suffused by the spirit of Proclus, structured the intellects into a hierarchy, with the result that each of them, beginning with the active intellect, is as form to matter with respect to its successor.

But we must not assume that Alfarabi's theory of intellectual knowledge excludes all other modes of linking the human soul to the supreme reality. As in Plotinus, God may be the first term in a series of emanations among which human intelligence finds its precise rank and place; or he may be the absolute being beyond the whole series and the being that can be possessed directly by the soul that eschews the sensible world. "Being beyond everything, he is without a veil of any kind; there is no accident under which he can hide; he is neither near nor far; there is no intermediary between him and us."

v *Avicenna*

Avicenna (980–1036) added nothing essential to the metaphysics of Alfarabi. Like Alfarabi he starts from a God who is pure intelligence; because he knows his essence, he knows all things; he knows the fundamental causes and the pure quiddities of all things, even individual things. In the same way Avicenna describes the emanation of intellects and of efficient souls that cause the spheres to turn uniformly, imitating as closely as possible the immutability of the intellects from which they derive.

Like Alfarabi, he attributes knowledge to the influence that the agent intellect or the intellect of the sublunary sphere exercises on receptive intellects. The agent intellect gives to sensible things their forms or quiddities to the degree that matter is susceptible of receiving them, and it produces knowledge in intellects. But Avicenna identifies several types of knowledge: knowledge of first principles or axioms, knowledge of abstract ideas, and knowledge through revelation, such as knowledge of the future. To the first type corresponds "the intellect that has been prepared or made ready," so called because here potency borders on act; to the second corresponds the active intellect that actually perceives the intelligible forms perceived potentially by the material or possible intellect; and to the third corresponds the emanated or infused intellect that "comes from without."

Avicenna describes in detail the mechanism of the second of the intellects. Slowly one succeeds in separating the abstract notion from the sensible thing. The operation begins with sensation, which receives only the form of an object ("it is not the stone that is in the soul but its form"), before it has been divested of its material appendages—the characteristics that are due to matter and give it its individuality—and the accidents that fall under categories other than that of substance: quantity, position, and so forth. The "imaginative or formative" operation, situated in the left cavity of the brain, still retains the individuality of the image but begins to separate the image from the temporal or spatial conditions of its existence. Then the "cognitive, imaginative, or collective" operation, by associating it with other similar images, produces a kind of rude notion which, though still not divested of individual characteristics, tends toward the universal. For instance, images make possible the "opinion" that allows the lamb, without reflection, to distinguish the wolf from other animals. It is in images prepared in this way that the rational soul, under the influence of the agent intellect, discovers the abstract forms that make possible logical, reflective operations.

But Avicenna is aware of the narrow limits of intellectual knowledge in man: "man cannot know the essence of things but only that which is inseparable from them or the properties of them." For example, he does not know what a body is, but he knows that it has three dimensions. Essences are merely inferred from properties.[3] Yet the soul can reach a more perfect state: in the state of sleep, unencumbered by its body, it becomes more receptive to the influence of the agent intellect which floods the imaginative faculty, producing prophetic dreams; and after death it will attain to even more perfect knowledge.

Alhazen (965–1038), one of Avicenna's contemporaries, exerted a strong influence on twelfth-century Latin writers through his *Perspective* and his study of optics. He prepared an analysis of visual perception which is still a classic and which we shall find again in Witelo.

VI *Algazel (Al Gazzali)*

The work of Algazel (1058–1111), who taught in Damascus and in Jerusalem, betrays the unrest caused by the diffusion of Peripateticism in Islam. His *Tahafut al-Falasifah* ("Destruction of the Philosophers") is devoted to an exposition of Peripateticism and its refutation. He points out that the thesis of the eternity of the world destroys the concept of the indifference of will that one must attribute to God, by imposing upon him eternally the choice of a definite order; the infinity of past time implies an infinite regression of causes, which is impossible since the infinite number is neither even nor odd and is therefore contradictory. Nor have philosophers been able to demonstrate the unity of God or the spirituality of the soul or the necessity of the causal link.

But it is difficult to define Algazel's own views. According to Averroes, "he belongs to no sect; he is an Asharite among the followers of Ashari, a Sufi among the Sufis, a philosopher among the philosophers," and he tried through his *Destruction* "to protect himself against the wrath of theologians, who have always been the enemies of philosophers." [4] Whether or not he was a Skeptic, we

---

[3] *Liber aphorismorum de anima,* trans. André de Bellune, pp. 101–21.

[4] Quoted by Worms, in Bauemker, *Beiträge zur Philosophie des Mittelalters,* III, 51.

find in his works something resembling the Skeptics' critique of knowledge, which corresponds to a current that seems to have been rather general in Islam during the twelfth century: the uncertainty of the senses that contradict each other and are contradicted by reason, the uncertainty of reason whose principles, just as they judge the senses, can be judged according to principles that remain unknown to us. Here we have the old line of argument of the Greek Skeptics, which is also found in the writings of other Arab thinkers.[5]

VII *The Arabs in Spain: Averroes*

The philosophers still to be discussed were products of Spain, where Moslem culture flourished in the twelfth century. Avempace (Ibn Badja, died in 1138) of Saragossa tried in his *Rule of the Solitary* to describe the different degrees through which a solitary man, apart from any social influence, could identify himself with the active intellect and become a member of a perfect state where justice and medicine—appropriate to our imperfect states which have to struggle against evils—are unknown. Beyond the ideas abstracted from matter, described by philosophers, the solitary man must attain to intelligible forms, which are separated from matter of themselves, rather than by intelligence, and which finally reduce themselves to unity.

Abubacer (Ibn Tufail, 1100–1185) of Cadiz imagined in his philosophical novel, *Risalat Hayy ibn Yakzan* ("The History of Hayy ben Yaqdhan"), what Avempace's solitary man would be if he were born on an uninhabited island. Starting from sensible knowledge he would rise to the forms abstracted from bodies, thence to their general causes, the eternal heavens and their movers, and finally to God, completely separated from the senses.

Averroes (Ibn Rochd, 1126–1198) of Cordova devoted himself especially to the task of determining the true meaning of Aristotle in the face of its deformation by his interpreters. Two points deserve

[5] Cf. Carra de Vaux, *Gazali*, pp. 115 and 45.

special attention: his theory of the production of substantial forms and his theory of the possible intellect. The first is directed against Avicenna: we see the substantial form appear spontaneously in nature as something absolutely new and not contained in matter, but Avicenna holds that this would not be true of all generations; that nature produces spontaneously only combinations resulting from the reciprocal action of the four primary or active qualities (cold and heat, wetness and dryness); that the substantial form which through a certain combination produces a certain being comes from a *dator formarum,* which is an intelligence outside and superior to nature. Averroes censures Avicenna for making a natural being not one being but an amalgam of two beings produced by two distinct agents. He holds that a new substantial form is introduced into matter by another form that already exists in it (so-called univocal generation: man engenders man), with the result that we do not have to have recourse to a *dator formarum* outside matter. The body that possesses a substantial form is capable from the outset, by virtue of its active qualities, of transforming matter in such a way as to prepare it to receive form, and then of engendering form in the matter transformed in this way.

His theory of intellect is directed against the interpretation of Alexander of Aphrodisias. In the active intellect, intelligence is identical to the intelligible reality that it contemplates. Since the intelligible reality is eternal, intelligence is also eternal. But if the subject that contemplates intelligibles is eternal, this question arises: How can we, who are corruptible, contemplate intelligibles? Alexander, by making of the material intellect (which is ourselves) a created and corruptible being, is as a result unable to explain how we can conceive of intelligible beings. It follows that the material intellect, if it is capable of reflection, must be uncreated, incorruptible, identical for all men. But then the difficulty is reversed: How can we explain the intellectual activity of each individual, which begins at a certain moment in time? The only possible solution is to suppose that the intellectual act is not a new intellection, an act that joins us at this moment to the agent intellect. What originates in us and disappears with us is the simple disposition called the passive intellect, which consists in the fact that the state of our images allows us to receive the eternal emanation of the agent intellect.

We shall see later the development of Averroes' philosophy among the Latins. Here we need only note that according to him there is no conflict between philosophy and religion, which simply represent two steps in the process of thinking: religion veils the truths, which the philosopher discovers, in order to bring them within reach of the uninitiated. It is by understanding these truths that the philosopher worships God.

VIII *Jewish Philosophy through the Twelfth Century*

Jewish philosophy developed in the Arab world during the ascendancy of Islam. The Cabala designated not so much a particular doctrine as the Jewish form of Neo-Platonic mysticism. In contrast to the Talmud, a juridical and literal commentary on the Law, it represented a state of mind analogous to that of Philo of Alexandria: a mystical interpretation of letters and numbers, which are the signs through which Wisdom is transmitted to men; a mysterious correspondence between letters and the composition of the world, the divisions of the year, the structure of man; the use of the allegorical method that reveals in each word of the Law a higher meaning and a sublime mystery; a mythology of powers and angels that multiplies the intermediaries between God and his creation. No part of all this seems very novel.

Whether he spoke of metaphysics or of the theory of knowledge, Isaac Israeli, an Egyptian Jew (845–940), reasoned in the main as a Neo-Platonist bent on discovering a hierarchy in which the inferior proceeds from the superior and is as its shadow: intelligence, rational soul, animal soul, vegetative soul; in intelligence, active intellect, passive intellect, imagination, and sensation, we recognize classifications. But his compilations were useful and not without historical importance, for thirteenth-century Latins found in his *Book of Definitions* the famous definition of truth: *adaequatio rei et intellectus*.

Saadia ben Joseph or Saadiagaon (882–942), an Egyptian Jew who lived in Babylonia, tried in his *Book of Beliefs and Convictions,* written in 932, to determine how reason and revelation complement each other in law. The command to serve God and the prohibition against blasphemy and doing harm to others are examples of rational commandments. There are others which deal with things that are in themselves indifferent and which become law by the will of God. The second type of commandment, which must be revealed, is indispensable to the execution of the first, which, because it is too general, leaves undefined the circumstances of its application. How is it possible to prohibit theft, for example, in the absence of a definition of property?

Jewish philosophy developed in Spain and in Morocco. Avicebron of Málaga (Solomon ibn-Gabirol, 1020–1070) wrote a work of great historical importance, the *Fons vitae,* which was to become one of the main sources of Neo-Platonism during the thirteenth century. Among other things, it included a hierarchical classification of realities: first, God exalted above everything, then Will, then Form, inseparable from the Matter that it determines. The *Fons vitae* had as its objective the study of form and matter. The thesis of the work is stated in these words: "All things that emanate from a source are concentrated when they are near the source and dispersed when they are far from it." At the highest level is the universal form that contains, united in itself, all forms; at the lowest level are the sensible things that also contain all forms, but separated from each other and dispersed; between the two levels are realities such as intelligence, which contains all forms, united to each other and yet distinct from each other. A second principle stated by Avicebron is that there are no forms without matter and that each level of reality is matched by a matter that corresponds in perfection to the height of the level, for perfection of matter consists in its ability to become one with form in total union. Hence the order in the *Fons vitae*: beginning with the lowest level, that of corporeal substances, Avicebron studies successively the corporeal matter that supports sensible qualities, the spiritual matter that supports the substantial form of the body, the matter of intermediary spiritual substances (souls) and simple substances (intelligences), and finally the universal matter that supports the universal form.

The place of intellectual knowledge in Avicebron's hierarchy is obvious. Forms are mixed together in intelligence and united to it, not through the accidental union that joins them to the body, but through an essentially spiritual union. This is an essential trait of Neo-Platonism, which does not simply add knowledge over and above reality but views it as one of the levels of reality which rise tier upon tier from the Many to the One.

To eleventh-century Spain also belongs a movement characterized by mystical piety and brought to light by a recently translated work of Ibn Pakuda, called *Introduction to Duties of the Heart*.

Moses Maimonides (Moses ben Maimon), a rabbi who was born in Cordova (1135) and died in Cairo (1204), wrote his *Guide of the Perplexed* mainly for the purpose of explaining the Law. He takes up philosophical subjects—the question of separated intelligences, of the motions of the spheres, of form and of matter—only in order to illuminate Scripture. Philosophical speculation is autonomous (as St. Thomas said later), but it confirms the truths of the Law. Such a position makes Maimonides' thought somewhat ambiguous, or at least it makes the different aspects of his thought hard to harmonize. Take the question of demonstrating philosophically the existence of the unity of God (Book II). Maimonides borrows from the Peripatetics a demonstration based on the eternity of the universe, which they grant, for it is through consideration of the motion of the celestial spheres, which has neither beginning nor end, that he infers an infinite moving cause which is God. Yet he does not view the eternity of the world as anything but a hypothesis of possible demonstration. His system of the world, like that of every other

Arab philosopher, is basically Aristotle's system of concentric spheres. But here too he remains quite skeptical about the exactness of his representation, which he does not consider demonstrable.

Maimonides' main concern was apparently the intellectual and social role of the prophet.[6] "Prophecy is an emanation from God which spreads, through the intermediary of the active intellect, first over the rational faculty and then over the imaginative faculty. Spread over the rational faculty only, it makes speculative sages; spread over reason and imagination, it makes true prophets, indispensable for drawing men together into a perfect society and regulating the actions of individuals whose diversity and, consequently, susceptibility to conflicts surpasses anything seen among other species."

IX *Byzantine Philosophy*

In the Middle Ages, the city of Constantinople had all the resources needed for the continuation of the Greek philosophical tradition. But it was a city of jurists, of businessmen and theologians, and it lacked the inclination to do so. The number of chairs of philosophy at the University of Constantinople was minimal in comparison with the chairs of sophistry and of jurisprudence.[7] Thus for the most part we find only scholars and commentators for whom the only vital question is that of the conflict between Plato and Aristotle. Photius (820–897), the scholar in whose *Bibliotheca* are preserved many extracts from and abridgments of the works of the Greek philosophers, showed a predilection for Aristotle. Psellus (1018–1098) took the role of Plato's defender. To him Plato was the true theologian: "Aristotle generally treated theological dogmas in a manner that was too human." Psellus' vast work was the starting point of the stream of Platonic philosophy that traveled through Pletho and Bessarion to Renaissance Italy and to the rest of the

[6] *Guide des égarés,* trans. Munk, p. 281.
[7] *Codex Theodosianus* xiv. 9, 3; five chairs of rhetoric, twenty of grammar, two of juridical sciences, and only one of philosophy.

West. Thus a clear definition of his Platonism is important to the history of ideas. His main source of inspiration was Proclus, "a superior man who penetrated to the heart of everything in philosophy." Elsewhere he states: "I went to Plotinus, to Porphyry, and to Iamblichus before I found my haven in the great Proclus. He has provided me with knowledge and with sound ideas." [8] The doctrine of Proclus was sure to appeal most strongly to a mind trained in law. But restoring the pagan philosophy of Plato was no easy task even for Psellus. Following the example of John of Damascus, who denounced "the satanic errors of the pagan sages," the monks of Mount Olympus treated the Hellenic philosopher praised by Psellus as a "Hellenic Satan." As Psellus said in reply to criticism by his friend Xiphilinus, however, he was merely continuing the tradition of the Cappadocian Fathers and using Plato in the defense of the Christian dogmas: "Are not Plato's doctrines of justice and the immortality of the soul the basis of similar doctrines of our own?" [9] At the University of Byzantium, restored by Constantine IX (Monomachus), Psellus took pains to re-establish the tradition of Neo-Platonic instruction on the basis of the studies enumerated in the sixth book of the *Republic*. For courses in mathematics the textbooks were the works of Nicomachus of Gerasa, Euclid, and Diophantus; for astronomy, Ptolemy and Proclus; and for music, Aristoxenus. Added to these was philosophy, beginning with Aristotle's logic and ending with the commentaries of Proclus. Finally came the allegorical explanation of inspired texts, such as the poems of Orpheus and the Chaldean oracles. Psellus could not lay claim to originality with respect to any part of the program of instruction: "My sole merit," he says, "consists in the fact that I have gathered together certain philosophical doctrines drawn from a fountain that had ceased to flow." [10] The result was a stubborn rationalism that led him to attack (as had Plotinus) the superstitions of his era and particularly the belief in demons, for which he

---

[8] Cf. Zervos, *Michel Psellos*, p. 193, nn. 2 and 3.

[9] *Opera*, ed. N. Sathas, in *Bibliotheca medii aevi* (Paris, 1874–76), pp. 444 ff.

[10] Zervos, *Michel Psellos*, p. 40.

criticized the patriarch Michael Cerularius: Psellus intended to remain a speculative metaphysician and not to deviate toward theurgy.

The tradition revived by him was continued by his pupils Michael of Ephesus and Johannes Italus who tirelessly transcribed the Neo-Platonic commentaries on Aristotle and Plato. Eustratius, the pupil of Johannes and Bishop of Nicaea, was criticized for teaching the same Plotinian doctrine of hypostases that Abelard taught a short time later in Paris. Proclus' Neo-Platonism, though attacked by theologians (we have, for example, a refutation of Proclus' *Elements of Theology* by Nicolas of Modon in the twelfth century),[11] persisted in the twelfth century with Michael Italicos and Nicephorus Blemmydes, in the thirteenth and fourteenth centuries with George Acropolites, Joseph, Theodore Metochites, and Nicephorus Gregoras, and in the fifteenth century with Demetrios Kydonis and Pletho (Georgias Gemistus), who introduced Platonism to Florence at the court of the Medici and who often defended Plato against the Peripatetics.

He seems seriously to have considered Platonism as the foundation for a universal religion. "When we were in Florence," wrote George of Trebizond, "I heard him say that in a few years men from all over the world, by common consent and in the same spirit would embrace one and the same religion. . . . And when I asked whether it would be the religion of Jesus Christ or the religion of Mohammed, he replied: 'Neither of these, but a third religion that will not differ from paganism.' "[12] Such was the outcome of the movement inaugurated by Psellus.

In contrast to Pletho, Theodorus Gaza was the fifteenth-century representative of the old tradition of reconciling Plato and Aristotle.[13] In Byzantium, scholars continued throughout the period to write commentaries on Aristotle. Among Psellus' own disciples,

[11] Ed. Voemel, Frankfurt, 1825.

[12] Trans. Boivin, *Mémoires de l'académie des inscriptions,* II, 1717; cited by Zervos, *Michel Psellos,* p. 239.

[13] Cf. Theodorus Gaza *De fato,* ed. Taylor (Toronto, 1925).

Michael of Ephesus wrote a commentary on part of the *Organon* and on the tenth book in the *Nicomachean Ethics;* Johannes Italus on the *De interpretatione;* Eustratius on the *Nicomachean Ethics* and the *Posterior Analytics.* In the fourteenth century, Nicephorus Blemmydes, George Pachymeres (1242–1301), Sophonias, John Pediasimus, and Leo Magentinus paraphrased or summarized Aristotle's treatises on logic and psychology and copied the commentaries of Simplicius and Ammonius.

Finally, we should at least mention, alongside the official philosophers and professors, the persistence in monasteries of a trend toward mysticism. According to Climacus, Abbot of the monastery of Mount Sinai at the beginning of the seventh century, one of its earliest manifestations was in St. John's *Ladder to Paradise,* a famous work known in the West through Gerson. It shows the influence of a philosophical thought more popular than those of Plato and Aristotle, and in it we find an echo of Stoicism and Cynicism. As a matter of fact, St. John mentions thirty successive steps in his ladder, and the twenty-ninth is impassivity ($\dot{\alpha}\pi\dot{\alpha}\vartheta\epsilon\iota\alpha$). The impassive man is "one who has made his flesh incorruptible, who has raised his thought beyond creation, and who has subordinated to it all his sensations." [14] St. John saw in the Patriarchs of the Egyptian desert (whose lives are recounted in the *Lausiac History*) illustrious examples of such impassivity. His work is therefore a link in the chain that connects Christian mysticism to Pyrrho and to Diogenes.

The trend toward speculative mysticism, going back to Dionysius the Areopagite, also continued in the Greek monasteries. The anonymous author of an eighth-century commentary on the books of Solomon was inspired by the Neo-Platonism of Maximus, a pupil of Dionysius. The trend is also manifested in the writings of Symeon (1025–1092), who held that mystical intuition was incompatible with mundane living and possible only among monks. Gregory Palamas and his pupil Nicholas Cabasilas, successive archbishops of Thessalonica, defended the Hesychasts who held that there existed

[14] Migne, *Patrologia graeca*, LXXXVIII, 1148b, 1149a.

apart from the Trinity an uncreated light that emanated from the Trinity and put the mystic in communication with God. Here we have the supreme manifestation of Neo-Platonic emanationism in Christianity.

I, II

Studies

Abd-el-Djalil. *Le Coran et la pensée musulmane.* En Terre d'Islam, 1939.
Carra de Vaux. *Les Penseurs de l'Islam.* 5 vols. Paris, 1921–26.
De Boer, T. *The History of Philosophy in Islam.* Translated by E. Jones. London, 1933.
Encyclopédie de l'Islam. 4 vols. completed through 1927 (A to K and the first part of S). Paris and Leyden, 1907——.
Gardet, L. "Islam et Démocratie," *Revue thomiste* (May and September, 1946).
——. "Rencontre entre la première théologie musulmane et la pensée patristique," *Revue thomiste* (1947), p. 45.
Kraus, P. "Plotin chez les Arabes," *Bulletin de l'Institut d'Égypte,* XXIII (1940–41), 263–95.
Macdonald, D. *Development of Muslim Theology, Jurisprudence, and Constitutional Theory.* New York, 1903.
Nicholson, R. *The Mystics of Islam.* London, 1914.
O'Leary, D. *Arabic Thought and Its Place in History.* London, 1922.
Quadri, G. *La philosophie arabe dans l'Europe médiévale des origines à Averroès.* Paris, 1947.
Sauter, G. "Die peripatetische Philosophie bei den Syrern und den Arabern," *Archiv für die Geschichte der Philosophie,* XVII (1904).
Sweetman, J. *Islam and Christian Theology.* 2 vols. London, 1945 and 1947.

III, IV

Texts

Alfarabi. Translated into German by F. Dieterici. *Alfarabis philosophische Abhandlungen, aus dem arabischen übersetzt.* Leiden, 1892.
——. Translated by F. Dieterici. *Der Musterstaat.* Leiden, 1900.
Alkindi. *De intellectu, De somno et visione, De quinque essentiis, Liber introductorius in artem logicae demonstrationis.* Edited by A. Nagy in

their medieval translations in *Die philosophischen Abhandlungen des Ja'qub ben Ishaq al-Kindi zum ersten Male herausgegeben*. Münster in Westfalen, 1897.

Studies

De Boer, T. "Zu Kindi und seiner Schule," *Archiv für die Geschichte der Philosophie,* XIII (1900), 153–78.

Fackenheim, E. *The Possibility of the Universe in al-Farabi, Ibn Sina, and Maimonides.* American Academy for Jewish Research. New York, 1947.

Hammond, R. *The Philosophy of Alfarabi and Its Influence on Mediaeval Thought.* New York, 1944.

Ibn Madcour. *La place d'Al Farabi dans l'école philosophique musulmane.* Paris, 1934.

Malter, H. "Al-Kindi, 'The Philosopher of the Arabs,' " *Hebrew College Annual.* 1904. Pp. 55–71.

V to VII

Texts

Algazel. *Algazel's Metaphysics: A Mediaeval Translation.* Edited by J. Muckle. Toronto, 1933.

———. *La destruction des philosophes.* French translation by Carra de Vaux. Louvain, 1903.

Alhazen. *Perspectiva.* Text and German translation by Baarman under the title "Ueber das Licht," *Zeitschrift der deutschen morgenländischen Gesellschaft,* XXXVI (1882).

Averroes. *Averroes Latinus.* Edited by H. Shields, *et al.* A new edition, not yet complete; presently 4 vols. Cambridge, Mass., 1949, 1953, 1956, 1958.

Avicenna. *Opera Philosophica.* Louvain, 1961.

———. *Avicenna on Theology.* Translated by A. Arberry. London, 1951.

———. *Kitab-al-Najat.* Book II, chap. vi. Translated with notes by F. Rahman as *Avicenna's Psychology.* Oxford, 1952.

Studies

Afhan, S. *Avicenna, His Life and Work.* London, 1957.

Bauer, H. *Die Psychologie Alhazens auf Grund von Alhazens Optik dargestellt.* Münster in Westfalen, 1911.

Carra de Vaux. *Avicenna.* Paris, 1900.

———. *Gazali.* Paris, 1903.

Corbin, H. *Avicenna and the Visionary Recital.* Translated by W. Trask. New York, 1960.

Gardet, L. *La Pensée religieuse d'Avicenne (Ibn Sina).* Paris, 1951.

Gauthier, L. *The Philosophy and Theology of Averroes*. Translated by M. Jamil-ur-Rehman. Baroda, 1921.

Gilson, E. "L'étude des philosophies arabe et son rôle dans l'interprétation de la scolastique," *Proceedings of the Sixth International Congress of Philosophy*. New York, 1927. Pp. 592–96.

Goichon, M. *La distinction de l'essence et de l'existence chez Ibn Sina*. Paris, 1937.

Smith, G. "Avicenna and the Possibles," *The New Scholasticism*, XVII (1943), 340–57.

Wensinck, A. *La Pensée de Ghazzali*. Paris, 1940.

Wickens, G.(ed.). *Avicenna, Scientist and Philosopher: A Millenary Symposium*. London, 1952.

Zedler, B. "Averroes on the Possible Intellect," *Proceedings of the American Catholic Philosophical Association*, XXV (1951), 164–78.

VIII

Texts

Avicebron (Gabirol). *Fons vitae*. Latin translation by Jean d'Espagne and Gondissalvi. Edited by C. Bauemeker. *Beiträge*, Vol. I. Münster in Westfalen, 1892–95.

Ibn Pakuda. *Introduction au devoirs des coeurs*. French translation by Churaqui. Paris, 1950.

Isaac Israeli. *Opera omnia Ysaac* . . . Lugduni, 1515.

Moses Maimonides. *Guide of the Perplexed*. Translated by S. Pines. Chicago, 1963.

Studies

Efros, I. "Saadia's Theory of Knowledge," *The Jewish Quarterly Review*, XXXIII (1942–43), 133–70.

Finkelstein, L. (ed.). *Rab Saadia Gaon: Studies in His Honor*. New York, 1944.

Gilson, E. "Maimonide et la philosophie de l'Exode," *Mediaeval Studies*, XIII (1951), 223–25.

Husik, J. *A History of Mediaeval Jewish Philosophy*. New York, 1916.

McKeon, R., *et al*. *Essays on Maimonides*. New York, 1941.

Roth, L. *Spinoza, Descartes, and Maimonides*. Oxford, 1924.

Strauss, L. *Philosophie und Gesetz, Beiträge zub Verständnis Maimunis und seiner Vorläufer*. Berlin, 1935.

Wolfson, H. "Maimonides and Halevi," *The Jewish Quarterly Review*, 3, 2 (1912), 297–337.

———. "Maimonides on Internal Senses," *The Jewish Quarterly Review*, XXV (1935), 441–67.

Vajda, G. *Introduction à la pensée juive du moyen âge.* Paris, 1947.

———. "La philosophie et la théologie de Joseph Ibn Caddiq," *Archives d'histoire doctrinale et littéraire du moyen âge,* XVII (1949), 106–10.

IX

Texts

Works of the following Byzantine philosophers and theologians are included in Migne, *Series Graeca,* in the volumes indicated: Gregory Palamas, CL; Nicephorus Blemmydes, CXLIX; Nicephorus Gregoras, CXLIX; Nicholas Cabasilas, CL; Photius, CL–CLV; Psellos, CXXII; Symeon, CXX.

Demetrios Kydonis. *Sur la crainte de la mort.* Leipzig, 1901.

George Acropolites. *Opera.* Edited by A. Heisenberg. Leipzig, 1903.

John Pediasimus. *In Aristoteles analytica scolia selecta.* Edited by De Falco. Naples, 1926.

Michael Italicos. *Correspondence in Cramer anecdota graeca oxonensia,* III, 158–203. 1836.

Michael of Ephesus, Eustratius, and Sophonias. *Commentaries on Aristotle,* in the Berlin Academy Edition of his works. Vols. XX, XXI, and XXIII.

Pletho. *Traité des Lois.* Translated by A. Pellissier. Paris, 1958.

Theodore Metochites. *Miscellanea philosophica et historica.* Edited by Müller. Leipzig, 1821.

Studies

Anastos, M. "Pletho's Calendar and Liturgy," *Dumbarton Oaks Papers,* IV (1948), 183–305.

Beck, H. *Kirche und theologische Literatur in byzantinischen Reich.* 1959.

Bréhier, L. *La civilisation Byzantine.* Paris, 1950.

Courcelle, P. *Les Lettres grecques en occident de Macrobe à Cassiodore.* 1948.

Karapipéris, M. *Nicéphore Blémmidès comme pédagogue et comme instituteur.* Jerusalem, 1921.

Meyendorff, Jean. *Introduction à l'étude de Grégoire Palamas.* Paris, 1959.

Russack, H. *Un maître de la spiritualité Byzantine: Nicholas Cabasilas.* Paris, 1958.

Salaville, S. "Philosophie et théologie, ou épisodes scolastiques à Byzance de 1059 à 1117," *Echos d'Orient* (Paris), XXIX (1930), 132–56.

Stephanou, E. *Jean Italos: Philosophe et humaniste.* Rome, 1949.

Tatakis, B. *La philosophie byzantine.* Paris, 1949.

Vaccari, A. *Un commentaire byzantin des livres de Salomon.* Congress on Byzantine History. Algeria, 1939. Pp. 105 ff.

Zervos, C. *Un philosophe néoplatonicien du XIe siècle: Michel Psellos.* Paris, 1919. (Editions of Psellos are listed on p. 35.)

THE THIRTEENTH CENTURY

WE RECALL Auguste Comte's encomium to the thirteenth century: the organic age par excellence in which spiritual unity, true catholicity, was realized.[1] It is the century that figures in the dreams of all those who believe that society can never know peace in the absence of a common faith to direct thought and action and to serve as the basis for philosophy, art, and morals.

Surely there is no other epoch during which spiritual life had such a distinct and important role. Circumstances then were especially favorable: the rebirth of powerful commercial cities favored, as it always has, the active exchange of ideas; the University of Paris, which played such an important role in the intellectual life of the thirteenth century, would have been inconceivable without the Paris of Philip Augustus—capital of a realm that was becoming the most powerful in Europe and attracting foreigners from every nation; nor was there any trace of national exclusivism in the instruction, given in the liturgical language of Christianity and given by masters from all countries—Englishmen such as Alexander of Hales, Italians such as St. Bonaventure and St. Thomas Aquinas, Germans such as Albert the Great. It was the university of the whole of western Christianity, and the Pontiff of Christianity, the Vicar of Christ, tried by organizing it and giving it statutes to make it the very center of Christian life. The same pope, Innocent III, created the Inquisition, confirmed the mendicant orders (Franciscans

[1] *Système de politique positive,* ed. Crès (1912), III, 488.

113

and Dominicans), and gave statutes to the University of Paris: three acts inspired by the same spirit, by the desire to strengthen Christian unity. In the Inquisition he found a means of expurging heresies; in the mendicant orders he found men who, freed from any temporal interests or attachment to their native countries, put themselves into the exclusive service of Christian thought; and in the University, which under the names of faculty of arts, faculty of law, and faculty of theology, drew together scattered schools that were already flourishing, he found a means of systematizing all the intellectual life of the epoch through the teaching of theology.

Only the pope had control over instruction at the university; he merely asked Philip Augustus to grant temporal privileges. His aim was to organize instruction in such a way as to protect theology against the danger posed by the excessive development of dialectic. Dialectic must remain an organon, and the "modern doctors of the liberal arts" must be prevented from taking up theological subjects. This is what was said by Innocent III in 1219 and repeated by Gregory IX in 1228: "Theological wisdom . . . must exert its power on each faculty as the mind on the flesh, and direct it into the right path so that it will not err." And theology must be explained solely "according to the traditions tested by the saints," and not through the use of "carnal arms." An order issued in 1231 states that "Masters of Theology must not make an ostentatious display of philosophy." Under such conditions philosophy is, in fact, reduced to the art of discussing and drawing conclusions, starting from premises established by divine authority. Hence the literary form of writings of the period, derived from the method used by Abelard in his *Sic et non,* then by the sententiaries of the twelfth century. Statements of authority or reasons deduced from authority are advanced for each topic; after the pros and cons have been indicated, the solution is given. In this way the theologian ignores or avoids any comprehensive exposition, any synthetic view which, by systematically linking his affirmations, would make the Christian doctrine appear too rational. A certain order is of course inherent in the exposition of the truths of the Christian doctrine: God, the creation, the fall, redemption, and salvation. That is the traditional order, the order that Peter Lombard followed, the order that underlies St. Thomas Aquinas' *Summae*. But we must note that it is an order of revealed truths in which each truth depends logically on the one that precedes: creation, fall, redemption, are free acts that can be known through their effects but not deduced from necessary principles. Each article of faith and each of the affirmations implied by it must therefore be studied separately. Reason is always useful in examining consequences, but not in going back to principles or in making syntheses.

But within its fixed, rigid frame, did thirteenth-century thought have the catholicity that the popes dreamed of imposing on it? Not at all, and notwithstanding the wishes of the popes, the thirteenth century offers the spectacle of sharp conflicts that make it impossible to speak of a single scholastic philosophy even in this period. The conflicts, which did not abate until the Middle Ages had come to an end, stemmed from the attempt to reduce all higher intellectual training to theology and to the disciplines that contribute to theology. A need was felt for a purely human philosophy, but no one knew where it belonged. Should it be a part of theology? How difficult it would be then to maintain the unity of a doctrine that employs simultaneously two methods as divergent as the authoritarian and the rational! Or should philosophy be expelled from theology? Then it would become independent. In either case, the spiritual unity that men were seeking to establish would be broken. It would be broken because they thought, for reasons that were essentially political and religious, that it was not necessary to reckon with the autonomy of human reason. Spiritual unity can be restored only when the attempt to subordinate all studies to theology is abandoned.

The history of philosophy in the thirteenth century is the history of such conflicts. It contains no trace of the anticipated rebirth, the intellectual freedom, the fiery thought that we found in the twelfth century. It is the history of a quest for unity at any price—even at the price of logic and coherence: a unity desired for reasons that were social and political rather than intellectual.

1 *The Diffusion of Aristotle's Works in the West*

Conflicts stemming from attempts to subordinate philosophy to theology were accentuated when the complete works of Aristotle became accessible to scholars through translations into Latin from Arabic or Greek. These translations opened a virgin field to scholars and for the first time provided them with direct knowledge of pagan thought uncontaminated by Christian thought.

After the middle of the twelfth century a college of translators working under the direction of Ramon, Bishop of Toledo (1126–1151), began translating from Arabic the *Posterior Analytics,* with the commentary by Themistius, the *Topics,* and *On Sophistical Refutations.* Gerard of Cremona (died in 1187) translated the *Meteorology,* the *Physics,* and the treatises *On the Heavens* and *On Generation and Corruption,* not to mention the apocryphal works, the *Theology* and the treatises *On Causes* and *On the Causes of the Properties of the Elements.* Then knowledge of Greek spread. We find in the twelfth-century manuscripts a translation of the *Metaphysics* (except for books *M* and *N* which had still not been translated in 1270), and even a commentary on the work. And William the Clerk, in his chronicle of the year 1210, says that the *Metaphysics,* "recently brought back from Constantinople and translated from Greek to Latin," was being read in Paris. Henry of Brabant, William of Moerbeke (1215–1286), a friend of St. Thomas Aquinas, Robert Grosseteste, and Bartholomew of Messina were thirteenth-century Hellenists who translated all or a part of the works of Aristotle, and notably the *Politics,* which had been ignored by the Arab philosophers.

Translations were also made of the works of Arab and even Greek commentators and of the Jewish philosophers. Alkindi, Alfarabi, Avicenna, and Avicebron were known, and by the middle of the thirteenth century all the commentaries of Averroes except the one on the *Organon* could be found in Paris.

The startling impression of such discoveries on minds avid for bookish instruction but unprepared for their task is not hard to imagine. Readers were poorly prepared to understand and evaluate Aristotle because they lacked the historical perspective necessary to assign him his place; because they had access to him only through translations which, in accordance with the common practice of the era, were slavishly literal and often incomprehensible; and finally because they did not have, to combat the magic spell of his philosophy, any opposing doctrine from which they could draw support, or—most important—any method to rival the solid Aristotelian construction. The only works of Plato that had been translated in the thirteenth century were the *Phaedo* and the *Meno*; in the second half of the century Sextus Empiricus' *Outlines of Pyrrhonism* became known; but none of this could counterbalance Peripateticism.

Peripateticism, which drew strength from the weakness of other doctrines, fell far short of meeting the demands of the theologians. Philosophy, always the servant of theology, was supposed to be utilized as a preliminary and auxiliary discipline. It was supposed to provide a method of discussion and not a statement of the nature of things. But what the theologians found in Aristotle was a system of physics and theology that suggested an image of the universe completely incompatible with the one implied by the Christian doctrine and even by the Christian life: an eternal, uncreated world; a god who is simply the prime mover of the heaven of the fixed stars and whose providence and even knowledge do not extend to things in the sublunary world; a soul which is the simple form of an organized body and which must be born and disappear with it, which consequently has no supernatural destiny, and which therefore cancels the importance of the drama of salvation. Creation, fall, redemption, eternal life: Aristotle knew nothing of all this and implicitly denied it. Here was something more than an eclectic Platonism which, though it probably posed a certain danger since it led to the erroneous solutions of Erigena and Abelard, could nevertheless be reconciled with dogma, thanks to St. Augustine and to Dionysius the Areopagite, and which in addition showed concern over the divine reality and the supernatural life of the soul. Aristotelianism refused to take up such problems or to attach any importance to them.

We must also note that the body of doctrine represented by Aristotle's physics, diametrically opposed to Christian theology, contrasted just as sharply with the only experimental science worthy of the name during the Middle Ages—astronomy. The accurate knowledge available of the variation of the distances of planets with respect to the earth during the course of one of their revolutions should have made impossible the formulation of a theory of the heavens that assigned each planet to a sphere that had the earth as its center—a theory that fell back on the doctrine of Ptolemy (the *Almagest* had been translated by Gerard of Cremona in 1175) or the Pythagorean doctrine of the motion of the earth, known since the high Middle Ages. The fact that it did not at this moment did not stop the progress of Aristotelianism, but it *was* one of the most important reasons for its decline later on, once the correct theory had triumphed.

What mattered at this moment was that Aristotelianism, far from serving the academic politics of the popes, threatened to stand as an insurmountable obstacle. Albert the Great himself denounced the influence of Aristotle's physics on the heterodox ideas of David of Dinant. Similarly, in 1211 the Council of Paris prohibited the teaching of Aristotle's physics, and the statutes brought to the University of Paris in 1215 by Robert of Courçon, the papal legate, provided that Aristotle's works on logic and ethics might be taught but prohibited the reading of the *Metaphysics* and the *Natural Philosophy*. The interdiction was probably ineffectual in the face of the public's infatuation, and Gregory IX stipulated that all editions of Aristotle's works should be expurgated of any statement contrary to dogma. It is nevertheless true that the *Physics* and the *Metaphysics* were included in the curriculum of the faculty of arts in 1255, that from this moment on the authorities condemned, not Aristotle, but those who drew from his books doctrines contrary to orthodoxy, and that Aristotle gradually became an indisputable authority. We turn now to the history of the Christianization of Aristotle.

II *Dominicus Gundissalinus*

The philosophy of Aristotle and of the Arab or Jewish Neo-Platonists was first given currency by compilers like Dominicus Gundissalinus (died in 1151), Archdeacon of Segovia, who in addition to his translations wrote works such as the *De divisione philosophiae,* modeled on Alfarabi and on Isaac Israeli's *Definitions.* He tears down the traditional order of the trivium and quadrivium and replaces it with the Aristotelian encyclopedia: physics, which studies mobile and material beings; mathematics, which studies the same beings abstracted from their matter and motion; and theology, which studies immobile beings such as God and the angels. Logic provides a basis for the study of philosophy. He gives Alfarabi's plan for studying Aristotle's writings on physics and metaphysics: *Physics, On the Heavens, On Animals,* and, finally, *On the Soul*; and for metaphysics, the works that study in succession essence and accident, the principles of demonstration, incorporeal essences, their hierarchical arrangement, and divine action. The plan is something completely new in the West, and it is important to note that in it theology as the study of the immovable mover is closely linked to physics, the study of movable bodies, which embraces the study of the soul as the form of the organic body. The new image of the universe is antithetical to the Platonic and Augustinian image that considered the peculiar and wholly supernatural life of God and the soul.

The same inspiration characterizes the *De immortalitate animae,* in which Dominicus criticizes and explicitly rejects the Platonic proof of the immortality of the human soul because it is too general and would also apply to the souls of brutes. He accepts only proof grounded on Aristotelian premises that contain not general principles but characteristics peculiar to the subject under study. But his main proof is, as we know, the independence of the intellect from the body, which entails the concept of an impersonal immortality, something quite different from the continuation of the individual destiny of the soul.

III   *William of Auvergne*

William of Auvergne, who taught theology in Paris in 1228, typifies the uneasiness produced in a traditional Augustinian by the introduction of these new ideas.

One of the aims of the Arab philosophers had been to make a distinction between the first principle and the beings derived from or created by the first principle, without getting outside the framework of Aristotle's philosophy. We see that theirs was indeed a difficult undertaking when we recall the nature of his metaphysics: his speculations on moving bodies and movers led him to posit a multiplicity of unmoved movers, moving intelligences of the heavens, and souls of animals, whose dependence on a unique principle was not clearly seen. It was hard to reconcile his teaching with the monotheism of all the religions that had issued from Judaism. We recall how Alfarabi, then Avicenna, resolved the issue: through an intrinsic characteristic, necessity, the supreme principle is distinguished from the movers derived from it. The necessary being has in itself all that it is; it is simple and unique. Derived movers, however, are potential beings, possible in themselves, that exist only under the influence of the necessary being who makes them pass to act.

Aristotle could become a monotheist only if some such distinction were added to his doctrine. The distinction was introduced by William of Auvergne, who fitted it into the scholastic tradition by linking it to Boethius. It is the celebrated distinction between essence and existence: "God is the being (*ens*) whose essence it is to be (*esse*). In other words, God and the being that we attribute to him when we say 'He is' are one and the same thing." Created being, on the contrary, results from the union of two things: that which is (*quod est*), or its essence, and that through which it is (*quo est*), of necessity distinct from the essence since the latter cannot exist by itself.

But the distinction between essence and existence which was predicated on the method of Avicenna, and which helped to establish monotheism, introduced a new danger. For if the role of the supreme principle is to make potential beings become actual, they must exist as potential beings prior to their becoming actual. Potentiality is then something independent of the supreme being. Only in this way could Avicenna explain multiplicity in created beings. In contrast to Avicenna, William held that potentiality was not something distinct from God but only the power that God has to give being to things.[2]

To this faint difference in interpretation is linked his criticism of the Peripatetics, who advocated the theory of the eternity of the world, basing their argument on the principle we have so often encountered: an immutable essence cannot begin to produce at a certain moment. William answered that there could then be no change in the world that was not reduced to what preceded it— that is, no true change since change is the production of something new. We see that the Peripatetics, basing the eternity of the world on the simplicity of the first principle, could not explain multiplicity and change other than through an independent matter, and the negation of this matter entailed either a denial of the existence of change or the attribution to God of a creative power—something quite different from Aristotle's pure act.

The same spirit is at the heart of his criticism of the Arab theories of knowledge that introduced into the soul itself the opposition of matter and form by showing that the potential intellect becomes actual under the influence of an intellect that is always active. William not only refused to accept the separate agent intellect that Avicenna (and according to him, Aristotle) placed in the sphere of the moon, but also refuted an anonymous theory of the Christian Peripatetics. According to their theory, both the agent intellect and the material

[2] Cf. Roland-Gosselin, in his edition of St. Thomas' *De ente et essentia,* p. 164.

intellect are a faculty of the soul itself; the agent intellect makes the intelligible signs that exist potentially in the material intellect become actual. To the soul the Christian Peripatetics attributed knowledge which is always actual and which, like Platonic reminiscence, would make any instruction useless. William attributed to the soul but one intellect, which he called the material intellect. From it there evolve, as from the seeds of mature beings, and under the influence of sensations and images, the intelligible forms with which it is pregnant. There is an appreciable discrepancy between this theory and the theory that reduces intelligence to an abstractive faculty. According to William, abstraction is not inherent in the knowledge of intelligible forms; it results from our imperfection and from the weakness of our spiritual sight. The exemplar of intellectual knowledge is the knowledge of one's self, that is, of one's opinions, of one's doubts, and therefore of a particular being.

IV *Dominicans and Franciscans*

More positive attitudes than those of William of Auvergne engendered conflicts that disturbed the universities of Paris and Oxford throughout the second half of the thirteenth century. Toward the end of the century (1284), just as these disturbances were abating, the Franciscan John Peckham, Archbishop of Canterbury, wrote the Roman Curia: "Let the Holy Church deign to consider that the doctrines of the two orders (the Franciscan and the Dominican) are almost diametrically opposed to each other on every question open to discussion; the doctrine of one of the orders, neglecting and to a certain degree scorning the teaching of the Fathers, is based almost exclusively on the teachings of the philosophers." [3] And he was more specific in a letter written in 1285 to the Bishop of Lincoln: "You know that we do not condemn philosophical studies in any way so long as they are appropriate to theological dogmas; but we condemn the profane innovations that contradict philosophical truth and the writings of the Fathers—those that struck at the

[3] Quoted by Gilson, *Études de philosophie médiévale*, p. 120.

very roots of theology some twenty years ago and resulted in out-right rejection and derision of the doctrine of the Fathers. Which has a firmer, sounder basis: the doctrine of the sons of St. Francis —that is, of Brother Alexander of Hales, of Brother Bonaventure and their kind whose works . . . are based on both the Fathers and the philosophers—or the new doctrine which is directly opposed to it in almost every way, which devotes its energies to destroying and denying everything that St. Augustine teaches concerning the eternal rules of the immutable light, the powers of the soul, the seminal reasons inherent in matter?"

Here two viewpoints clash: that of the Franciscan, nurtured by St. Augustine and represented by Bonaventure, and that of the Dominican, descended from Aristotle and represented by Albert the Great and St. Thomas Aquinas. The Franciscan embraced a doctrine in which there was no clearcut distinction between philosophy and theology and tried, following the Neo-Platonic model, to attain to the divine reality, or at least to an image of the divine reality. The Dominican, on the other hand, made a sharp distinction between revealed theology and philosophy, which is completely autonomous and independent from theology since it starts from sensible experience and employs a purely rational method.

It is not enough, however, summarily to contrast Franciscan Augustinianism with Dominican Peripateticism. In the first place, St. Bonaventure does not hesitate to follow Aristotle on many points. In the second place, in the very midst of their order, Albert and St. Thomas found many adversaries. It was a Dominican, Robert Kilwardby, who as Archbishop of Canterbury had Thomistic propositions condemned in 1277. In the third place, St. Thomas was no less opposed than St. Bonaventure to a certain manner of interpreting Peripateticism that led to conclusions directly opposed to the Christian faith, namely the interpretation of Siger of Brabant and the movement referred to as Latin Averroism. Finally, the two orders were in agreement on one practical point: the popes were planning to intrust to these orders, rather than to the secular clergy, theological instruction at the University of Paris. Beginning in

1229, a chair was reserved for each of the two mendicant orders, with the result that they became engaged in a violent polemic with the secular clergy. It is reflected in the *De periculis novissimorum temporum* (1255), in which William of St. Amour contests the monks' right to teach, and in St. Thomas' reply, *Contra impugnantes Dei cultum.*

v *St. Bonaventure*

St. Bonaventure was opposed to the spirit of both orders: "The Preachers (the Dominicans) indulge mainly in speculation, which accounts for their name, and then in unctuousness; the Minors (the Franciscans) indulge first in unctuousness and then in speculation." St. Francis of Assisi, the founder of the Minors, had given a new impetus to spiritual life rather than to Church doctrine, and he recommended study to the brothers only on condition that they "act before teaching." [4] There was among the Franciscans one group, the spiritualists, who looked with contempt on any doctrinal instruction; they were partisans of Joachim of Fiore, whose thoughts on the eternal Gospel were related to heresies involving the rule of the Spirit. His views were accepted by the general of the order, John of Parma, who had to resign his position in 1257 and who was condemned by a tribunal presided over by the new general, none other than St. Bonaventure.

Now we have a better understanding of the problem faced by doctrinaire Franciscans and theologians: to reconcile doctrinal and rational instruction with the Franciscan concept of free spirituality, or rather to make the doctrine an inseparable element in the inward illumination that constitutes the spiritual life. There had been doctrinaire Franciscans before the time of Bonaventure: Alexander of Hales (1170–1245), Master of Theology in Paris, who in his *Summa,* modeled on the Lombard's *Sentences,* revealed his knowledge of Aristotle but remained faithful to the Augustinian tradition; and John of La Rochelle (Johannes de Rupello, 1200–1245). Both

---

[4] St. Bonaventure *In hexameron* 22. 21; quoted by Gilson, *Saint Bonaventure,* p. 3.

of them knew and accepted, for the limited sphere of natural knowledge, the Aristotelian doctrine of knowledge: it is through the influence of an agent intellect that the potential intellect can abstract intelligible forms from sensory images; but when we are dealing with objects that transcend man's aptitude, knowledge becomes illuminative and has as its agent God himself.

Giovanni di Fidanza of Tuscany (1221–1274), known as Bonaventure, the "Seraphic Doctor" who taught in Paris from 1248 to 1255 and became general of his order at the age of thirty-six, is the most remarkable representative of this spirit. The teaching of St. Bonaventure is essentially the journey of the soul to God, a title which he ascribed to one of his last works (*Itinerarium mentis in Deum*). He wrote during a period in which the Dominicans were producing many purely philosophical works, but we would search in vain for such a work in the list of his own writings: a vast commentary on Peter Lombard's *Sentences* and a great number of shorter works on purely theological or mystical subjects. But in his journey he finds reason and philosophy, and he assimilates whatever they have to contribute to the higher spiritual life.

Assigned to its place in the search that leads us to God, philosophical reason has significance only to the degree that it is turned toward God. It indicates a transitional step between a lower stage where we have but scant knowledge of God and a higher stage where we have greater knowledge of him. It is one of the moments through which we pass in going from the state of simple belief to contemplation. "We start from stability of faith and progress through the serenity of reason before reaching the sweetness of contemplation." [5] St. Bonaventure adheres closely to the tradition of Neo-Platonic philosophy: reason is an intermediary between belief and an intellectual intuition that apprehends the first principle directly; it is not self-sufficient and provides no rules for the creation of autonomous sciences. Reason no less than faith, on one hand, and contemplation on the other, issue from sanctifying grace, which is manifested first through the virtue of faith (*credere*), then through

---

[5] Quoted by Gilson, p. 115.

the gift of understanding that which is believed (*intelligere credita*), and finally through the beatitude of contemplation (*videre intellecta*). Here we have Plato's scheme of the degrees of knowledge as outlined at the end of the sixth book in the *Republic*. The pious tone superimposed on it changes none of its basic elements.

It follows that philosophy, according to Bonaventure, should not be the fruit of curiosity that seeks to arrive at the essence of reality, but of a religious inclination that leads us toward God. "Creatures can be considered equally well either as things or as signs," [6] and Bonaventure considers them as signs. In everything he searches for expressions, images, vestiges, shadows of the nature of God. The solutions to the most technical questions that he disputes with St. Thomas are provided by the vast symbolism that makes him consider nature, along with the Bible, as a book whose divine meaning must be deciphered. The three unique themes of philosophy are God, the Creation, the return of the soul to God through knowledge and illumination—or God as the exemplary cause, God as the efficient cause, and God as the final cause. The existence of God is an obvious fact: obvious to the soul which through knowledge of itself recognizes itself as the image of God, and which through knowledge of imperfect, composite, mutable things apprehends the perfect, simple, immutable being that causes them to exist. God as the exemplary cause is the object of the study of metaphysics. Bonaventure contradicts Aristotle and asserts the existence of Platonic ideas in which God finds his true, complete expression and his first resemblance. Thus the world of Ideas is not a creature but God himself as the Word or the Son. It is therefore one and indivisible, and it appears multiple only to the degree that it gives birth to a finite multiplicity of sense objects. Bonaventure's intelligible world is not the world of Plotinus, first because it is not inferior to its source, and then because it is not an intermediary between God and the sensible world. Here we find nothing that resembles a first, wholly spiritual creation of the world. Nor is it in this sense related in any way to the world of Plato: here we find nothing to fill the infinite gulf

[6] Quoted by Gilson, p. 209.

that separates creature from creator and, conversely, nothing to impede the return of the soul to God.

That is why God as the efficient or creative cause must be different from God as the exemplary cause. From within the infinite unity of the Word, the model for an infinite number of possible worlds, the will of God chooses one world, and the reasons for his choice are wholly inscrutable. Bonaventure, in effect, refuses to concede that the principle of the best possible world can force God to create the best one: such a notion is senseless, for no matter which world is chosen, one can always conceive of a better one. Through his "voluntarism," which became more prominent in the Franciscan schools, Bonaventure was even more explicitly opposed to any attempt to establish a continuity between God and created beings.

Consequently, all created beings must evidence both God's immediate activity and their separation from him—two contradictory, or at least contrasting, requirements. The first entails the apprehension of the divine irradiation in all created things, the second the proclamation of their deficiency: deficiency, for the multiplicity of created beings is incapable of receiving the communication and effusion of divine perfection other than through multiplication; deficiency, since it is necessary for all created beings to be composed of form and matter, the matter stressing the passive side of their being. Bonaventure did not hesitate to state, along with the other Franciscans and against St. Thomas, that no pure form existed in creation and that angels themselves, which are separate intelligences, and also human souls, which are spiritual beings, result from the union of form and matter. We need only know that a being is mutable, active and passive, individual and capable of belonging to a species or genus, in order to say that it contains matter—that is, potential being or the possibility of being different. This is true of souls and even of angels; contrary to the belief of St. Thomas, they are truly individuals. Bonaventure's awareness of the deficiency of created beings is also responsible for his acceptance, in opposition to St. Thomas, of the thesis of the plurality of forms. In Aristotle's thinking, the form of a being is that which causes it actually to be-come what it is; a man is a man by virtue of the presence in him of the form humanity; each substance, being one, must therefore have a unique substantial form, and this form defines and determines ab-solutely the nature of the substance. Bonaventure does not accept Aristotle's conclusion: to consider form as completing and consum-mating the being in such a way that nothing substantial can be added to it would be to concede that created beings can be perfect and complete; in reality, however, if form gives perfection to a sub-stance, it is not in order to make it something definite but in order to prepare it to receive another degree of perfection which it would be incapable of giving to itself. For example, sunlight added to a body that has already reached a certain state of perfection stimulates activity in it, making it a new substantial form. The same spirit is manifested in his reply to the question of the production of form. We recall one of Aristotle's famous theorems: a potential being can become an actual being only under the influence of a being that is already actual. His theorem implies that the form that is to be cre-ated in potential being is not something already present but some-thing that evolves under the influence of an actual being (eduction of forms). But such a theory would give to actual being an efficacy which it cannot possess and which will be reduced to its proper limits if one admits with St. Augustine that potential being con-tains the seminal reasons that will be manifested and developed un-der the influence of actual being.

The common link between all these theses—on several of which the Franciscan thinker and St. Thomas hold opposing views—is then obvious: multiplicity, hylomorphic composition of all things, plurality of forms, and seminal reasons are all methods of negating an autonomous physical world that has in itself its principle of ex-planation. The theses are in perfect harmony with the second re-quirement, according to which created beings must reveal traces of divine irradiation: through simple analogy, such as the equality of two ratios, and not through true resemblance such as the resemblance of God and Ideas. The exemplar of this simple analogy is the image of the Trinity that St. Augustine identified in the relations between the three faculties of the human soul. But there are different degrees in this analogy, and these range from shadows or vestiges of divine attributes visible in nature to the true image which is found in the human soul and which perceives directly its resemblance to God. Through the influence of supernatural grace, the analogical image will be transformed in the elect into a true likeness, which is the deification of the soul.

It is not so much in itself as in relation to this final state that Bonaventure analyzes intellectual knowledge and evaluates the contributions made in this sphere by Aristotle and the Arab philosophers. He accepts the distinction between the agent intellect and the possible intellect, but like Alexander of Hales and St. Thomas, he first makes each of them a faculty of the soul and refuses to accept the agent intellect as a reality distinct from the last of the celestial intelligences. In his thinking, the negation of the separate agent intellect is another consequence of the principle that rules out the positing of any intermediary between God and the soul. Furthermore, the relation between the agent intellect and the possible intellect is not the same as the relation between pure activity and pure passivity; the agent intellect merely helps the possible intellect to carry out the operation of abstraction through which it extracts intelligible forms from the images of the imagination; but the possible intellect actually performs the operation and provides the agent intellect with the species that it contemplates.[7] Finally, abstraction from sensible things is not the only type of intellectual knowledge. Aristotle's empiricism applies only to knowledge of the sensible world; when we are dealing with principles, with moral virtues, and with God, our method of acquiring knowledge is wholly different. Many sensible species are needed to provide knowledge of principles, such as the principle of contradiction, but the "natural light" within us allows us to acquire them immediately and without recourse to reason. As for moral virtues, knowledge of them is due to no sensible species but to our inwardly felt inclina-

[7] Gilson, p. 354.

tion toward the good and to the immediate knowledge that our inclination is right. Finally, we know God through simple self-reflection, since we are made in his image. In a word, under the name of self-knowledge and knowledge of God, St. Bonaventure assumes direct knowledge that does not pass through the circuit of sensible things.

Any attempt to justify such knowledge and to ascertain its basis results in the reduction of everything to divine illumination. Here Bonaventure starts from the old Platonic principle (revived by Avicenna) according to which there is knowledge only where mind attains to being—that is, to a stable, identical reality. But to attain to being is not precisely to see God or to see the eternal ideas and reasons that are in God. The idea of being is like a framework that we try to apply to realities which do not fit neatly into it and which therefore cannot be known positively and entirely; but it can exist only by virtue of the presence and influence in us of these eternal reasons which we do not possess. Thus the most humble form of knowledge is defined not in itself, but as a blurred image of the full and certain knowledge that God possesses in his own right.

St. Bonaventure's philosophy therefore represents a trend of great historical importance. His thinking is dominated by what he considers the fundamental truth: the soul has a supernatural destiny made known through the revelation of Christ. In searching for other truths, we cannot proceed as though we were ignorant of the fundamental truth and as though we had an independent method for determining truth and falsehood. All truths are subordinate to the first truth. Nature and the soul reach an understanding only when turned toward God: then nature stands as evidence of divine attributes, and the soul unites us to God through its essential function of love.

But it is obvious that his guiding principle, though it was accepted by Christian thinkers, had not the slightest influence on the history of Christian orthodoxy. Here we recognize the old Neo-Platonic principle, evolved in the absence of any Christian influence, that a being is fully what it is only because it turns back toward its own principle and receives its effluviums. One of Bonaventure's successors, Matthew of Aquasparta (1235–1302), Master of Theology in Paris and later general of the order (1287), was to show still more clearly in his work the opposition of this doctrine to the Aristotelianism of St. Thomas. In his *Quaestiones de cognitione* he discusses "certain philosophers" who deny that divine illumination is indispensable to knowledge and who attribute all knowledge to the natural faculty of the agent intellect, repudiating in this way the authority of the "Principal Doctor," St. Augustine. Conversely, he asserts that "all that is known with certainty through intellectual knowledge depends on eternal reasons and the light of the first truth." We find the same fidelity to Platonism in the Franciscan John Peckham (1240–1292), a pupil of Bonaventure in Paris and a Master of Theology at Oxford. The strength of this Platonic–Augustinian movement enables us to understand the conditions under which the Aristotelian counter-movement took shape under the leadership of Albert the Great and St. Thomas.

VI *Albert the Great*

The first of the great Christian Peripatetics was the Dominican Albert the Great (1206–1280), called the "Universal Doctor." Master of Theology, he taught in Paris from 1245 to 1248, and in Cologne from 1258 to 1260 and from 1270 until his death. Between 1240 and 1256 he wrote paraphrases of all the known works of Aristotle and even interpolated his own ideas on questions which were a part of Aristotle's general plan but which he had neglected (such as the *De mineralibus*). He even added a commentary on the apocryphal *De causis* (which he knew to be spurious and which he thought David the Jew had extracted from the writings of Aristotle and Avicenna). He is also the author of treatises on dogmatic theology, such as his commentary on the *Sentences* and his *Summa de creaturis,* and of mystical works, such as his commentary on Pseudo-Dionysius or the *De adhaerendo Deo*. Finally, he played an active role as the defender of the Dominicans against the attacks of William of St. Amour in 1256, as legate of the pope and preacher of the crusade in Germany (1263).

The diversity and scope of his undertaking—the pleasurable task of drawing up an inventory of all the treasures contained in Aristotle's encyclopedia and of contributing to these treasures—concealed from him most of the time the lack of coherence in his own philosophy. Albert seems to have sensed this, and on such occasions to have made statements such as these: "In all of my philosophical books I have refrained from expressing my own opinions, but I have explained as faithfully as I could the opinions of the Peripatetics . . . if I have an opinion of my own, I shall put it, if God so wills, in books on theology rather than in philosophical treatises." [8]

It is not hard, therefore, to show how Albert contradicts himself and how his Augustinianism contradicts his Peripateticism. Sometimes he is content to juxtapose. For instance, in his *Summa of Theology*,[9] he warns that there are two concepts of the soul, the Aristotlelian concept of the soul as the form of an organic body and the theological concept based on the writings of St. Augustine: on the one hand a description of the mechanism of the intellectual and voluntary life, and on the other the description of faculties arranged tier upon tier and showing the progressive elevation of the soul from sensible knowledge to God. There is no similarity between Aristotle's sensation, an act common to the one sensing and to the things sensed, and Augustine's sensuality, which binds the soul to the earth by making it seek after what is helpful and shun what is harmful. Nor is there a parallel, in spite of what Albert thinks, between the Augustinian distinction of higher reason that guides us and lower reason that makes us conscious of moral law, and the Peripatetic distinction of agent intellect and possible intellect. Finally, there is a radical difference, which Albert acknowledges, between Aristotle's will ($\pi\rho o\alpha i\rho\epsilon\sigma\iota\varsigma$ or *electio*) which follows the judgment of the understanding, and the exclusively theological notion of free will, "the faculty of reason and of will through which

[8] Quoted by Schneider, *Die Psychologie des Alberts*, pp. 295 ff.
[9] Tr. 12 qu. 73.

we choose good in the presence of grace and evil in its absence."
Aristotle offers nothing to correspond to *synderesis,* "the spark of
consciousness which, according to St. Jerome, was not extinguished in
Adam's soul even though he was driven from Paradise," the faculty
of knowing the supreme moral rules "not mentioned by the
philosophers because they divide the faculties of the soul according
to their general objects, whereas theologians are able to make a
distinction between divine law and human law." Thus the views of
the "saints," who consider the soul apart from its relation to the
sensible world, complement the views of the philosopher, who knows
the soul only in relation to the body.

Still, in other respects Albert's doctrine evidenced intellectual
propensities that were strikingly new in relation to the dominant
current of Augustinianism. The level to which philosophical reasoning could attain had dropped considerably. The aim was no longer,
as in the case of St. Anselm, to find rational explanations for revealed dogmas, the Incarnation, or the Trinity. These were and remained articles of faith pure and simple. Philosophical reasoning
can proceed only from effects to causes, and that which is first in
the order of knowledge is last in the order of being. In other words,
we can attain to God only through the sensible world, through a
cosmological proof proceeding from effect to cause, and not through
an ontological proof. By contemplating the world we can probably infer the existence of God, but we cannot even know with rational certainty whether the world had a beginning in time. Aristotle's arguments favoring the eternity of the world are for the most
part offset by opposing arguments, and only revelation can decide
the issue.

Albert tended generally to separate the terms that Augustinian
Platonists sought to unify and build into a hierarchy. For instance,
thirteenth-century Augustinians, under the direct or indirect influence of Avicebron, had attributed to all creatures, spiritual as well
as corporeal, a hylomorphic composition: angels and souls as well
as bodies are composed of matter and form. Contrary to this view
and in accordance with Aristotle's theory of the moving intelli-

gence which is a pure act and the soul which is a form, Albert refused to posit matter as a component of spiritual beings. His refusal had the effect of transforming his vision of the universe. Since form (for example, the form of man) is by itself a universal, and since the principle of individuation is in the accidents that have their source in the matter that is added to form, it follows that the nature of an individual man—composed of a soul and a body—no longer has much in common with the nature of an angel. The angels, being pure forms, must for that very reason differ among themselves as species, not as individuals. None of the faculties with the same name is the same in angels and in human souls. Bound to the body, the human soul attains to rationality only through an operation of abstraction on sensible images, whereas the angel, without toil, has impeccable intuitive knowledge. The agent intellect, intuitive in the case of the angel, is in man a faint ray of light that borrows from sensible images all the distinctions of genera and species.[10]

Thus wherever we look, universal continuity seems to be marred by deep cracks. Albert even refused to accept all the elements which, in the Arab Peripatetics' theory of intellectual knowledge, would have brought man and God closer together. The agent intellect, which Averroes posited as the moving intelligence in the tenth sphere, actually containing in itself all the intelligibles and consequently common to all men, is replaced by an agent intellect that is a part of the human soul. There are accordingly as many agent intellects as there are souls. Moreover, the agent intellect is devoid of forms and has no function other than that of abstracting forms from sensible images that come from without. If a separate or angelic intelligence influences us, the result of such an influence is a revelation, which is quite distinct from natural knowledge.[11]

It is understandable that under such conditions the study of nature for its own sake interested Albert and that in his thinking the

---

[10] *Summa de creaturis* tract vi (ed. 1651, XIX, 77–182).
[11] *Summa de homine* qu. 53 art. 3.

sciences, by virtue of the principle that "experiment alone provides certainty in matters relating to zoology, botany, or mineralogy," were beginning to become something more than fantastic bestiaries or traditional systems of symbols.

We know little about Hugh of Strasbourg and Ulrich of Strasbourg, the German Dominicans who popularized Albert's doctrines in Cologne, but it seems that Ulrich was much more critical of the Arab Peripatetics than was his master and that he initiated the mystical movement that was to culminate in Meister Eckart.

VII *St. Thomas Aquinas*

The doctrine formulated by Albert was elaborated and systematized by St. Thomas Aquinas (1225-1274), the "Angelic Doctor." Born at the castle of Roccasecca, of the family of the counts of Aquino, he became a Dominican in 1243. He studied with Albert the Great in Paris from 1245 to 1248, then in Cologne. From 1252 to 1259 he was again in Paris, where he became Master in 1257. From 1259 to 1268 he lived in Italy and became acquainted with William of Moerbeke, the Dominican Hellenist who provided him with translations of Aristotle made directly from the Greek text. From 1268 to 1272 he taught in Paris, where he had to defend himself against the enemies of the regular clergy, against Siger of Brabant and the Averroists in the Faculty of Arts, and against the Augustinians who tried to have him condemned. He left Paris for Naples in 1272 and died two years later while on his way to the Council of Lyons.

During his second stay in Paris (1252-1259) he wrote three treatises in addition to his *Commentary on the Sentences of Peter Lombard*: the *De ente et essentia,* the *De veritate,* and the *Contra impugnantes Dei cultum et religionem* (at the time of William of St. Amour's attacks on the orders). His commentaries date from his stay in Italy and his association with William of Moerbeke (1259-1268): commentaries on Aristotle—the *De interpretatione,* the *Posterior Analytics,* the *Physics,* the *Metaphysics* (twelve books), the *Ethics, On the Soul,* the *Meteorology,* the *De caelo* (i–iii), the *De generatione,* the *Politics* (i–iv); a commentary on the *Book of Causes* (which he recognized as being identical to Proclus' *Elements of Theology,* translated by William of Moerbeke); and commentaries on Boethius' theological works and the Areopagite's *Divine Names.* In the same period he wrote the *Summa contra gentiles* (1259–1260) and began the *Summa theologica,* which he worked on from 1265 to 1273 but never finished. During his last stay in Paris, he wrote polemical works: the *De unitate intellectus contra Averroistas,* against Siger of Brabant; the *De perfectione vitae spiritualis* and the *Contra retrahentes a religiosa ingressu,* against the enemies of the mendicant orders; and the *De aeternitate mundi contra murmurantes,* against the enemies of Peritateticism. During different periods he edited his oral arguments on subjects proposed to him on specific occasions: the *Quaestiones disputatae* and the *Quaestiones quodlibetales.*

In spite of the flawless and perhaps unmatched lucidity of his style, the literary practices of St. Thomas are so remote from our own that it is difficult to determine whether a Thomistic system exists and what it is. In him we find no trace of the emotion and mettle that gave birth in the eleventh and twelfth centuries to the synthetical works in which there is an uninterrupted flow of philosophical thought. For instance, his *Summa theologica* is nothing but a series of questions separated into articles. Each article presents the arguments against the thesis, the arguments for it, and then the rebuttal to the opposing arguments. Only by way of exception (for instance, *Summa theologica* Ia pars, qu. 85, Art. 1–3) do we find a pause or a comprehensive survey in the discussions in which his sole aim is to defeat his adversary. Dialectic, understood as the art of discussion, had become an omnipotent sovereign, and more stress was placed on learning to refute arguments than on their invention.

VIII *St. Thomas: Reason and Faith*

If such conditions were prevalent—if no objection was raised against choppy, piecemeal expositions—the reason was that philosophers and theologians felt that their task was not to make a synthesis, since one had already been made, and not to discover truth, since truth had already been found. St. Thomas' undertaking assumed two great syntheses which he accepted without change as the basis for his own work: the organization of religious truths accomplished by the twelfth-century sententiaries, and the philosophical synthesis of Aristotle. In part of his works, in his *Summae*, we find the rhythm of the *Sentences*, which has its source in the rhythm of Neo-Platonic philosophy: for instance, the *Summa contra gentiles* first discusses God, then the hierarchy of created beings that proceed from him, then the destiny of man and his return to God in the eternal life. In another part of his works, he analyzes and annotates the works of Aristotle.

Furthermore, the relation that he sees between the two syntheses, the theological synthesis of revealed truths and the philosophical synthesis of truths accessible to reason, brings him a sense of tranquility and contentment and makes him much less zealous and passionate for inquiry than men like St. Anselm and Abelard. Whereas they defined the relation between reason and faith in a manner that might be termed dynamic, subjecting the truths of faith to reason, as truths to be progressively and endlessly illuminated, St. Thomas defines it statically: there are truths which belong to faith and which definitely transcend human intelligence, and there are philosophical truths which are accessible to human intelligence, but there is no way of progressing from one order to the other. If reason plays a part in matters of faith, it is merely by drawing consequences from truths belonging to faith when the latter are posited as premises, never by demonstrating such truths. For example, we can demonstrate the necessity of divine grace by showing that without it the supernatural destiny of man would be impossible, but the existence of supernatural destiny must first be re-vealed to us by faith.

It is important to note that St. Thomas does not borrow his purely static concept from the theological tradition but evolves it from his doctrine of knowledge in general, based on Aristotle: "The human intellect is incapable of apprehending the substance of God himself through its natural virtue, for our knowledge in our pres-ent mode of life has its source in the sense organs; that is why any-thing that does not fall under the senses cannot be apprehended by human intelligence unless it is inferred from the senses. Sen-sible things cannot enable our intelligence to see what divine sub-stance is, for they are effects and do not equal the power of the cause." [12] Thus Aristotle's empiricism is hoisted as a bulwark against the indiscretion of reason that would probe mysteries. Sen-sible things are no longer, as in the case of Bonaventure, signs to be interpreted in order to reveal the divine presence, but simple effects through which we are able laboriously to deduce a cause which we do not apprehend in itself but only in its relations to its effects.

Finally, the very nature of his conception of the relations between reason and faith eliminated one of the most powerful forces acting upon philosophical thought during the preceding centuries: the contradictions between reason and faith, which gave rise to an at-tempt to reconcile the two, and which therefore generated philo-sophical discussion. St. Thomas starts from the principle that one truth cannot contradict another; it follows that no truth of faith could weaken a truth of reason, or vice versa. But since human reason is weak, since the intelligence of the greatest philosopher is just as inferior to the intelligence of an angel as the simplest peas-ant's intelligence is inferior to his own, it follows that when an in-tellectual truth seems to us to contradict a truth of faith, we can be sure that the presumed intellectual truth is but a fallacy and that a more penetrating discussion will reveal its falsity. Philosophy there-fore remains the servant of faith, not because faith appeals to reason for clarification, not because the affirmations of faith are interwoven

[12] *Summa contra gentiles* i. 3.

in the fabric of rational arguments (for philosophy as a mode of knowledge is completely autonomous), but because theology dominates it by declaring it incapable of proving all that would be contrary to faith. Such a hierarchy rules out a priori any attempt to establish a reciprocal arrangement. No interpenetration or even friction is possible in the purely external relation between faith and reason, and the same will hold true for temporal power and spiritual power. From above and from without, the spiritual power will determine the conditions of the temporal power and the scope of its functions.

IX *St. Thomas: The Theory of Knowledge*

We must nevertheless understand that between the Thomistic theory of the relation between reason and faith and the Thomistic theory of reality there is, perhaps not an opposition, but at least a contrast that explains the development of the philosophy. Between the mode of knowing through reason and the mode of knowing through revelation there is total discontinuity, and the first will never cause us to rise or even aspire to rise to the second. Inversely, in being itself in reality there is complete continuity, as the Neo-Platonists taught and as St. Thomas believed, with the result that there is no cleavage or gap between the aspects of reality provided through reason and the reality known through revelation, or that attained through the knowledge of the angels or of the beatific vision. From the moment when knowledge, no matter how humble, attains directly to being itself, to simple being, there must be an element common to both intellectual truths and truths of faith; in other words, some truths (such as the existence of God) must be rationally demonstrable as well as revealed.

These abstract considerations have a historical basis. We recall the contrast between Aristotelian and Neo-Platonic theology. Aristotle conceives of God solely as the prime mover of the sensible world; he therefore relies on rational demonstration and the use of the common principles of his physics and metaphysics in formulating his

concept of God. He demonstrates the existence of God by applying the guiding principle of his general concept of the world: the
priority of act over potency. Knowledge of God as the prime mover
or pure act is therefore just as rational as any physical knowledge
whatsoever. Neo-Platonic theology does not start from the sensible.
It assumes a position in an intelligible reality which it pretends to
apprehend through special intuition, and it uses different names to
designate intuition, depending on the height attained in the divine
reality. Thus Aristotle conceived of God as the capstone in his rational explanation of the universe, and that is the most that can be
accomplished by a mind that is forced to start from sensible data. It
can go no farther.

But the mind can go that far because knowledge, as we have already said, attains to being. The Thomistic theory of knowledge can
be studied from two points of view: from one it is universal, embracing all possible modes of knowledge and indicating the conditions
of any type of knowledge; from the other it is critical, defining the
limits and conditions peculiar to human knowledge. The first viewpoint is inspired by an Aristotelian formula which Plotinus and
Proclus (in the *Elements of Theology,* identical to the *De causis*)
had fully elaborated: "The soul is in some way all things." It is in
some way sensible things, which it perceives through the senses in-
asmuch as perception, an act common to the perceiver and to that
which is perceived, leaves in the soul the forms of things, without
their matter, but with all the accidents that account for their individuality. Furthermore, the intelligence in act is identical to the
very thing that it apprehends: there is no difference between knowledge and the thing known. And whether we are dealing with sensible knowledge or the beatific vision, knowledge is a certain presence, impossible to analyze, of the known object in the knowing
subject. It therefore is not, as is often erroneously stated, an assimilation. One must say only (and here we are adopting the second
viewpoint) that by virtue of the principle that "the known object is
in the knowing subject according to the mode of the knowing sub-

ject," there can be instances when assimilation, that is, the operation through which the known object is made similar to the knowing subject, is a preliminary condition of knowledge. For example, when the subject and the object are as different as the soul and a sensible thing, intellectual knowledge can come about only through a "species" that is both a distinctive form in the intellect and an image or likeness of the thing apprehended. It is through the "impressed species" that the intellect, in apprehending a thing, begins the operation that ends with the definition or "expressed species." But no such operation applies to the beatific vision or to the knowledge that God has of his own essence, and therefore it does not define all knowledge. Knowledge in a general sense is a direct presence of being.[13]

x *St. Thomas: Proofs for the Existence of God*

It follows from the limitations of human knowledge that the regions of being to which the soul can attain do not extend beyond the bounds set by Aristotle—that is, the physical world bounded by a theology in which God is envisioned as the prime mover. The notion that one can have direct, positive evidence of the existence of God without passing through the sensible world is as false as the notion that one can attain to God only through faith. The two contrasting notions are based on the same principle: the false principle that one cannot speak of the existence of God without first having learned what he is. Those who support the first view hold (like St. Anselm) that since the name of God means the being greater than which no other being can be conceived to exist, it follows that God exists. They also say that since the being of God is identical to his essence, to posit the essence of God is to posit him as existing. Those who support the second view, distrusting the strength of reason and seeing that neither the quiddity of God nor even the meaning of

---

[13] On this special point, cf. Tonquédec, "Notes d'Exégèse thomiste," *Archives de philosophie,* I, 1.

the name of God is attainable, conclude that any demonstration of his existence is impossible.

Those who support the second view are right with respect to what they deny: our reason is too weak to apprehend in the perfection and greatness of God the reason for his existence. But when they conclude that his existence cannot be demonstrated, they are ignoring the fact that there are two kinds of demonstrations: the demonstration *quid* that takes quiddity as a means and goes from essence to its properties, or from cause to effect; and the demonstration *quia* that proceeds from effect to cause and can define cause with respect to its effect.[14] St. Thomas considers the demonstration *quid* as being inaccessible to man not only in matters relating to the existence of God but in any instance. We recall that one of the difficulties in Aristotle's theory was the impossibility of discovering a rational procedure for attaining to the quiddity of beings. Nobody is more conscious than St. Thomas of this flaw in Peripateticism, and he makes it a flaw in human reason: "Even in sensible things, essential differences are unknown to us; that is why they are designated by accidental differences that have their source in essential differences, in the same way that the cause is signified by its effect; for example, "biped" is posited as the difference of "man."

The type of demonstration that goes from effect to cause or from accident to essence and allows us to posit the existence of a thing without having previous knowledge of the thing and without knowing anything about it other than that it produces the effect that has brought us to it—such is the normal domain of the human mind in all its investigations. And the five "ways" that lead us to posit the existence of God imply no special mode of knowledge but merely apply to the question the most commonplace processes of reasoning.

The first is borrowed from the eighth book in Aristotle's *Physics*: "Everything that is moved is moved by something else; this mover in turn is either moved or unmoved; if it is unmoved we have what

[14] *Summa contra gentiles* i. 12.

we were seeking, an unmoved prime mover, and that is what we call God; if it is moved it is moved by something else, and we must then proceed to infinity (which is impossible) or come to an unmoved mover."

The second is borrowed from the *Metaphysics*: "In all ordered series of efficient causes the first term is the cause of the middle term and the middle term is the cause of the last term, whether there are several middle terms or only one; if the cause is eliminated, that of which it is the cause is also eliminated; therefore if the first term is eliminated, the middle term cannot be a cause. But if there is a regression to infinity in efficient causes, no cause will be the first cause, with the result that all other causes, which are the middle terms, will be eliminated. Since this is patently false, we must posit a primary efficient cause which is God."

The third starts from the experience that we have of the generation and corruption of beings. From the fact that they become corrupted we conclude that they are merely possible beings, that is, that there was a time when they were brought to existence by a being already existing. But if all beings were merely possible beings, it follows that nothing would actually be, and this is patently false. We must therefore posit a being necessary in itself, which we call God.

The fourth is borrowed from the second book of the *Metaphysics*. We can compare two statements with respect to their truth and see that one of them is more false and the other less false. The comparison is possible only because we can refer to an absolute truth or to an absolute being which is God.

The fifth is borrowed from John of Damascus and Averroes and is based on the second book of the *Physics*: "It is impossible for contrasting and incongruous things to be joined harmoniously in a single order other than through the agency of a being that attributes to every and to each thing its tendency toward a determined end. Alternately, in the world we see diverse things form a single order, and this is not the exception but the rule. Consequently there must be a being through whose providence the world is governed, and this being is called God." [15]

In all of his proofs there is an obvious attempt not to introduce any religious sentiment, any flight of the soul to God, anything having to do with the peculiar relations between man with his supernatural destiny and God. St. Thomas introduces only the technical notions of Aristotelian physics. As a result critics soon suggested that the value of his proofs was linked closely to the value of Aristotle's physics. St. Thomas is probably referring to such criticism in his *Summa contra gentiles*: "Two reasons seem to invalidate these proofs. The first is that they proceed from the supposition of the eternity of the world, which is presumed by Catholics to be false . . . ; the second is that in the demonstrations the first thing moved, namely, the celestial body, moves itself and is therefore animate—a belief denied by many people." [16] The eternity of the world and everything implied by it (a world that has no history and consequently no redemption or consummation), and animation of the heavens with all the dangers inherent in astrology—is it only at the price of these errors that reason could succeed in establishing the existence of God?

XI *St. Thomas: A Christian Interpretation of Aristotle*

The above criticism, whether justified or not, may help us understand the peculiar situation of St. Thomas in the eyes of his contemporaries, and the problems that confronted him. His task was to show that there was in Peripateticism a philosophy that was truly autonomous and independent of dogma and that could nevertheless be reconciled with dogma.

But the Aristotelian universe presented features that do not seem to be easily reconciled with Christian beliefs: on the one hand, a God who is only the prime mover of the heavens, who produces motion in matter that exists apart from him; and on the other, an

---

[15] *Summa contra gentiles* i. 13 and *Summa theologica* i qu. 2 art. 3.

[16] Concerning the first and the second, see i. 13.

omnipotent God, the creator of a world that began in time and must come to an end.

The same contrast is found in the notion of spiritual creatures, separate intelligences, or souls. According to the Arab commentators, Aristotle's separate intelligences are the efficient causes of the celestial spheres and have the same nature and even the same function as the supreme God, with the result that their dependence on him is incomprehensible; against this, in the Christian universe the angels are creatures capable of falling.

Souls, too, offer striking differences. Aristotle holds that the soul is the form of an organic body and the principle that determines its biological functions; it has individuality only through its relation to the body, which is its matter. In the Christian drama, the soul is an individual being complete in itself; its connection with the body is transitory, and it has a supernatural destiny.

From the Aristotelian conception of the soul as the form of a body, it seems to follow that the soul perishes with the body. Furthermore, it seems that if the soul has independent knowledge of sensible objects and corporeal organs (such that there is produced intellectual knowledge in it), it is through an intelligence that no longer has any connection with the body, which is beneath the impassible soul and belongs jointly to all men. The eternity of this impersonal intelligence is something quite different from personal immortality and nullifies the image of its supernatural destiny.

The same contrast is also found in the sphere of moral philosophy. Merit, according to Aristotle, depends on virtues that are voluntary acquisitions, that utilize natural endowments, and that are increased by man's civic activities and by political or social relations with other citizens. Against this, the ideal of the Christian mystic is to strip man bare and to isolate him that his soul may be exposed to the influx of divine grace.

Emboldened by these obvious contrasts, St. Thomas' adversaries called attention to these divergent doctrines. St. Thomas' strategy consists wholly in converting all these divergences of doctrine into one basic, definitive pattern of divergence acceptable to all the faithful: a divergence of method. "Human philosophy considers creatures as being such and such, with the result that the divisions of philosophy correspond to different types of things. The Christian faith, however, does not consider them as being such and such; for example, it considers fire, not as fire, but as something that represents divine elevation and directs itself, in some manner, toward God himself. The philosopher considers what is suitable to creatures according to their proper natures: for example, by its nature fire tends to move upward; Christians consider what is suitable to them in so far as they are related to God: for instance, that they are created by him, that they are amenable to him, and so forth." [17]

Now let us see how St. Thomas applies his strategy to the five problems mentioned earlier. First, God the prime mover and God the creator. Aristotelian physics as such generally posits only determinate causes that produce determinate effects. That is why it recognizes only agents capable by their action of drawing from matter outside and prior to this action the being contained there in potency; such agents simply produce a change or motion, that is, passage from ill-defined potential being to clearly defined actual being; and their action is not instantaneous but must be unfolded in time. But all demonstrations, according to St. Thomas, must point to the conclusion that there is a universal cause—that is, an agent of whom all things, no matter what they may be, are in the same manner the effects—and consequently a cause of being, a cause that produces *ex nihilo* and acts instantaneously. This is a point of capital importance, but one that supposes a new interpretation of Aristotle's philosophy: the first "way," as one finds it in the *Physics,* is actually a solution to the problem of the circular motion of the celestial spheres; the unmoved mover is therefore a determinate cause as defined above, that is, a cause that makes the circular motion contained in the matter of the heavens pass from potency to act. But there is no longer any reference to celestial spheres in the Thomistic demonstration, and St. Thomas presents

[17] *Summa contra gentiles* ii. 4.

his proof in such a way that the prime mover appears as the *causa essendi,* or creative cause. The heavens moved by the prime mover, he points out (*Summa contra gentiles* ii. 6), are the cause of generation for things in the sublunary region, which proves that the prime mover is the cause of being. St. Thomas can therefore respond to the objections of his adversaries with consummate calm. They say that his proof implies the eternity of the world, since the prime mover is forever in act and must therefore produce eternally the motion of the heavens, but he sweeps away their objection by observing that the eternity of the world does not imply the independence of the world or the negation of its creation. We need only assume, as Avicenna has already done, that God created the world from eternity; then, whether it is eternal or began in time, the world remains an effect and a creature of God. Furthermore, according to St. Thomas the reasons given by Aristotle for the eternity of the world are not convincing; that God is the prime mover of the world pertains to his relation to his creation and, consequently, not necessarily to his being. Here reason is incapable of reaching a valid conclusion and we must have recourse to faith, which reveals to us with certainty that the world was created in time. In discussing the second way, he understands the efficient cause, not in the simple sense of a prime mover as is generally true in the case of Aristotle, but in the sense of a cause that "transmits its effects to being." That is how the second way leads to a creative cause.

The third way involves speculation on necessity and possibility, on essence and the being introduced by essence—something completely alien to the spirit of Aristotle—and allows St. Thomas to conclude, as we shall see, that there is a universal cause. The fact is that the origin of the problem of the distinction between being and essence is not to be found in Aristotle. To be sure, Aristotle recommends that we determine whether a being exists before determining its quiddity, but this is because the quiddity of a being that does not exist is nothing: the quiddity of the goat-stag is nothing if such a fanciful animal does not exist. Thus the manner in which the Arabs, and subsequently St. Thomas, posed the question of the relation between essence and being, far from being a continuation or an extension of hints provided by Aristotle, was just the reverse. Here the object is not to determine whether a thing exists before determining its quiddity, but on the contrary, to find out whether quiddity can have a determinate meaning before any question concerning existence is raised, to find out (to use St. Thomas' terminology) whether essence is really different from being. But underlying this question, quite abstract and technical to all appearances, is a theological preoccupation: to say that the being of a thing is identical to its essence is to say that it exists of itself, that it is necessary; it is to accord to it a privilege that belongs only to God. All other natures have the property of being merely possible; their being comes to them from something else; essence itself is merely possible and is conceivable in the absence of its being only in the case of the unique being whose essence is to exist. But being is not superadded to essence as an accident; it is rather the realization of the power of which essence consists. At the crux of the matter, then, is the affirmation of a gaping chasm between essence and existence, the negation of which would render God useless. Here St. Thomas contradicts the spirit of Aristotle. Averroes was more faithful to him when he said that there was only a distinction of reason between essence and existence: one can always conceive of essence without conceiving of it as existing, but an essence that could not actually exist is something wholly imaginary. But by positing as the sole necessity the being whose essence is to be, St. Thomas is placing at the base of things the most universal form there is, the form of which all the things that possess being are only participations and effects.

The fourth way leads to the same result. Normally each thing acts and produces its effect according to what it is in act, but the fourth way leads us to a being which, since it is being in act, must be the universal cause of the being of all other things. Finally, the fifth way induces us to posit a cause that is different from particular natural causes.

St. Thomas followed a circuitous road in substituting for Aristotle's prime mover a transcendent being, God the creator, but he satisfied the demands of a faith that required reason to find proof.

Though the issue seems trifling to a modern reader, the theory of angels was one of the most serious stumbling-blocks for Thomistic Aristotelianism. To grasp the significance of the issue we must recall that the proof of the prime mover given by Aristotle at the end of the *Physics* led naturally to a multiplicity of unmoved movers, to as many moving intelligences as there were spheres in his astronomical system, since each of the spheres was presumed to be animated by a distinct and characteristic motion. Furthermore, the relation that might exist among the various intellects was not explored by Aristotle, and his system is equally viable whether interpreted as a monotheistic system in which all intelligences depend on one, or as a polytheistic system in which they all act together but independently of each other. In any event, in Aristotle's system the separate intelligences—which Dionysius the Areopagite, following an already ancient tradition, compared to the angels of the celestial hierarchy—were the equals of God himself.

We recall how the Franciscan school, following not only Avicebron but also Hugh of St. Victor, had resolved the question: these separate substances are not pure forms, but are composed of matter and form. Wherever there is indetermination, wherever there is plurality or finity, there is matter. Thus matter is a common property of every substance, and whether particular substances become spirits or bodies depends on their determining forms; the multiplicity of intelligences proves that they have a common base which is determined by diverse forms.

But St. Thomas denies outright the hylomorphic composition of spiritual substances. One of his arguments strikes at the heart of Avicebron's concept of matter and its relation to form. According to Avicebron, generation consists in the addition of form to matter, as an accident to a substance. Hence there is no true generation and no true unity in the composite being produced in such a way; there is but a simple increment or addition. But Aristotle's concept of matter as being in potency (marble) that becomes actual being (statue) as a result of diverse motions or alterations enables us to understand that hylomorphic composition pertains only to bodies, and his description of the characteristics of intellectual knowledge proves that, unlike bodies, intellects are pure, immaterial forms; furthermore, in the act of understanding, the intellect is identical to the intelligible that it comprehends, with the result that the intelligible is not received in the intelligence as form in matter.[18] When received in matter a form divides; it is individualized as it becomes related to accidents; it excludes the presence of a contrary form; it is introduced into matter as a result of a motion. As an object of the intellect, however, form is simple and indivisible, universal, and free of accidents; it is better known by virtue of the presence of its contrary, better comprehended in proportion as the intelligence is less mobile.

But if separate intelligences are pure forms, how are the difficulties of his thesis to be avoided? The answer is that a being can be a pure form and still not equal the simplicity of God. We have already seen that there is in every creature a mode of composition quite different from that of form and matter: that of essence and being, two terms which are identical only in God. But in every created thing we must make a distinction between essence or substance, that is, what the thing is (*quod est*), and its very being, or that through which it merits the name of being (*quo est*); or to put it another way, we must make a distinction between its potency and its art. It is this distinction which, introduced into Aristotelianism, serves here, as in the case of Albert the Great, to separate the angels from God. This distinction is but the abstract statement of what is to be proven, for to say that an angel is a creature, or that its essence does not have independently the power to be, or that that which it is is distinct from that through which it is, is simply to repeat the same thing. Still, what we have described is not truly an individual being since individuality pertains only to a form engaged in matter; the angels, pure forms, differ among themselves

18 *Summa contra gentiles* ii. 50.

as species and not as individuals, which was the conclusion reached by Aristotle.[19]

The third difficulty is in the peculiar relation that Aristotelianism posits between soul and body. "The individuality of the soul," says a recent interpreter, "must be explained in such a way as to safeguard both its personal immortality and its function as a substantial form."[20]

Here, indeed, is the problem. For St. Thomas, who follows Aristotle, the soul is the form of the organic body; soul and body are not two independent substances, but from their union a unique being, man, is formed. It is a natural union without which the soul cannot apprehend itself, for in effect the soul cannot know itself through itself. St. Augustine's statement to the effect that "the soul has independently notions of incorporeal things" means that the soul perceives that it *is* because it perceives its own actions (*Contra gentiles* iii. 46).

Thus the problem of the individuality of man is resolved in accordance with the general rule that applies to the individuation of beings composed of form and of matter. We know that form in itself is specific and that, for a given species of beings, a specifically identical form is in each individual of the species. What separates individuals from each other is therefore the matter to which form is joined. To understand how matter is the principle of individuation we must nevertheless bear in mind that the fact of being joined to matter in general does not account for individuality. Man, as a species, already includes matter since he is defined as a being composed of soul and body, but he is not for that reason an individual being. What accounts for individuality is signed matter (*materia signata*), that is, matter considered with respect to its determinate dimensions. Signed matter individualizes form and produces numerical diversity within a given species, not only because it gives to form an exclusive position with respect to any other form in time

---

[19] *Metaphysics* A. 8. 1074a, 36.
[20] Roland-Gosselin, in his edition of *De ente*, p. 117.

and space, but also because, by reason of its debility, it can receive form only in a deficient and imperfect manner.

It follows that for a form engaged in matter to become an individual being is in every sense a limitation, a debilitation, a diminution. The human soul, as the form of the body, is subjected to just such conditions and acquires individuality only by virtue of the body whose form it is and with which it has a perfect correspondence. It would seem that we must conclude from this that individuality ought to follow the destiny of the body and disappear with it. But such is not the teaching of St. Thomas: "The human soul," he says, "is a form which by virtue of its being does not depend on matter. Consequently, souls are multiplied as bodies are multiplied, but the multiplication of bodies is not the cause of the multiplication of souls; and that is why it is not necessary, once bodies are destroyed, for the plurality of souls to come to an end" (*Contra gentiles* ii. 81).

Here we see the extent to which the Christian faith is introduced, as if from the outside, to limit Aristotelian biologism. But we need to examine more closely the procedure through which St. Thomas manages to insert into Peripateticism the doctrine of the permanent individuality of the soul. He has but one philosophical reason for accepting the permanence of the individuality of the human soul outside its body, and that is the existence in the human soul, in addition to the operations required by the corporeal organs, of an intelligence that knows its objects without the intermediacy or assistance of matter: "The intelligent soul is therefore not totally attached to matter or immersed in it, like other material forms" (*Contra gentiles* ii. 68).

But the solution raises another serious difficulty: the relation of intelligence to the rest of the human soul. We are already familiar with the series of interpretations that the Greek and Arab commentators had formulated on the basis of Aristotle's handling of this point. They were almost unanimous in seeing in the independence of the intellectual operation, with respect to the organs of the body, proof that the intellect was not included in the definition of the soul as the form of the body; in contrast, the intellect when actively engaged in thinking is identical to its object—to universal or specific forms. It follows that the intellect can be nothing other than a universal form, independent of matter and therefore not susceptible of individuation. Identical in all men, it is not a part of the soul.

On this problem hinges the destiny of Thomistic Aristotelianism in its rivalry with Arabic Peripateticism. Albert the Great had already seen its full significance, and the fact is that under technically different forms it continued to preoccupy Western man.

All of the Peripatetics, whether Christian or Arab, have a common starting point—their manner of interpreting the intellectual operation. It is an abstractive operation through which specific forms, apprehended potentially in sensible data and in the images more or less elaborated from these data, are extracted from the images or phantasms. St. Thomas reduces to two the number of intellects necessary for the operation: the agent intellect and the possible intellect. The agent intellect extracts the specific forms of phantasms; the intellect which is like a blank tablet and susceptible of becoming anything receives the extracted forms. The two intellects never function, therefore, except in connection with other operations that in turn require corporeal organs; by themselves they yield no knowledge.

Once the intellectual operations have been described, the difficulty is in knowing their subject. Are the two intellects "separate"? Or is only one of them, the agent intellect, separate while the possible intellect is part of the soul? Or do both intellects belong to the soul? The first view is that of Averroes, the second that of Avicenna, and the third that of St. Thomas. But Avicenna's thesis is patently illogical, for the relation and proportion between the act of the agent intellect and the potency of the possible intellect is such that the first must belong to the same subject as the second. St. Thomas' real adversary then was Averroes, whose view was championed by many of the professors at the University of Paris (*Contra gentiles* ii. 76).

St. Thomas had only to demonstrate that an intellectual substance could be the form of a body. Finding no support in Aristotle for his demonstration, he could do no more than cite as an example the souls of the celestial spheres, which move their spheres because of the desire that they have for the good.[21] He therefore stated rather than demonstrated that "an intellectual substance can be a formal principle of being for matter" (*Contra gentiles* ii. 58).

But even if his point is demonstrated, it is still necessary to prove that the inclusion of intelligence with the other powers of the soul does not in turn compromise the unity and indivisibility of the soul. Is the intellectual power not different in this respect from nutritive and sensitive power, each of which seems to constitute a separate soul? Here the technical problem of the plurality of forms comes into the picture. The Augustinians, in agreement with Avicebron on this point, held that in material composites, matter is determined by several forms. As we rise from less perfect beings to more perfect beings we find successive additions of higher forms: the body is determined by the simple form of corporeality; to an element is added the form of the element; to a mixture of elements, the form of the mixture; to a plant, the nutritive soul; to an animal, the sensitive soul, and so forth. The higher form is simply added to the lower form: "The lower forms are contained in the higher forms until all are reduced to the primary universal form, which combines all forms."[22] Their thesis, which had already been criticized by Avicenna, seemed unacceptable to St. Thomas. The plurality of forms in a being is incompatible with its unity. A plurality of forms cannot create a true substance; for a composite being endowed with a single form, such as a body, is already a substance, and a new form can be added to an already existing substance only as an accidental attribute.

It is easy to see in this discussion a conflict between the image of a universe consisting of a hierarchy of forms, each of them eager to receive its complement (for unity is never in the individual but only in the whole) and the Peripatetic image of a universe consisting of

---

[21] *Summa contra gentiles* ii. 76.
[22] Avicebron *Fons vitae* 143. 13 (ed. Bauemker).

individual beings each having in itself the principle of its operations. To the second view is linked the thesis of unity of form in each individual being. But it is also by virtue of this thesis that St. Thomas avoids the danger that threatened the unity of the individual human being. For intelligence is not only the form of the organized body; it is also the single and unique form of the body, and from it emanate all the sensitive or vegetative faculties whose operations are executed by the organs of the body. Hence the form of the human body is wholly an intelligent soul that draws its individuality from its relation to the body and its independence from the immaterial character of the operations through which knowledge is acquired.

But there is still one strong argument against this individualization of intelligence: since intelligence is in act identical to its object, and since its object is a universal form, intelligence cannot be multiplied in diverse individuals. St. Thomas' answer is truly a theological master stroke: "Clumsy arguments are adduced to show that God cannot create several intellects of the same species because this implies a contradiction. But even if we grant that it is not of the nature of intellect to be multiplied, it would not necessarily follow that such multiplication would imply contradiction. Nothing prevents a thing from not having in its nature the cause of a characteristic that it nevertheless possesses by virtue of another cause. For instance, a low tone does not have the characteristic of being loud, and yet it can be loud and not imply a contradiction. Similarly, if everyone's intellect were unique because it does not contain a natural cause of multiplication, it could nevertheless accommodate multiplication without contradiction, by virtue of a supernatural cause. Let this be said not so much for our present purposes as to prevent such a line of reasoning from being extended to other subjects, for it could be used to prove that God cannot cause the dead to rise or the blind to recover their sight." [23] In this revealing text we see that St. Thomas does not hesitate to enjoin reason to bend—that is, to support faith or to remain silent.

[23] *De unitate intellectus contra Averroistas*, chap. vii.

There is a rational physics of the sensible world that allows us to ascend through reasoning to God as the cause of the world, and there is a revealed theology that transcends reason; similarly, to direct human conduct there is a natural ethic based on the spontaneous orientation of the will toward happiness and the good, and there is a supernatural destiny with respect to which our only guide is sanctifying grace, something that goes beyond will illuminated by reason.

St. Thomas' fundamental ideas on natural morality are borrowed from Aristotle. From the *Nicomachean Ethics* comes the notion that our will is directed naturally and spontaneously toward the good that is its end, that our free will consists not in choosing our end, which is not free, but in choosing through rational deliberation the means that lead us to our end. There must accordingly be a natural light to provide us with the premises of our practical deliberations. This natural light is manifested in synderesis, which St. Thomas interprets as a natural and immutable *habitus* (stable state) that is divided into particular precepts. From synderesis comes rectitude of will. Virtues are acquired practices deriving from the fact that we are capable through free will of choosing the best means. His view assumes that morality and legality are based on divine reason, to which the divine will is subject: "Eternal law is but the reason of divine wisdom; the divine will, since it is rational, is subject to this reason and consequently to the eternal law." The immutability of law based on reason, contested later by the Ockhamists, nevertheless remains the foundation of one whole group of modern theories of law. And it is from St. Thomas that Grotius received the concept in the seventeenth century, through the intermediacy of the Scholastic, Vasquez (died in 1506).[24]

But natural light provides no means of access to the higher virtues, to the charity and beatitude of the elect. The elect owe their bliss to knowledge of God, which is impossible in this life, and which alone is capable of satisfying all human desires.

[24] Gurvitch, "La Philosophie du droit de H. Grotius," *Revue de Métaphysique* (1927), p. 369.

The great political treatise *De regimine principum,* once attributed to St. Thomas, has been identified as spurious. Ptolemy of Lucca wrote the treatise (or at least the first part of it) around 1301. It illustrates in an exemplary manner the application to political matters of the Thomistic spirit as it is revealed in the philosophy of St. Thomas: civil power pursuing the civic good with the same freedom that reason exhibits in pursuing truth in speculative matters; but at the same time absolute certainty that, if civil power runs counter in any way to the aims of spiritual power that has received from God the mission of guiding man to salvation, civil power is in error and must be corrected. This accounts for the wholly rational, almost realistic character of Thomistic policies in temporal matters: "The kingdom is not made for the king, but the king for the kingdom." The king's power exists only for the pursuit of the good of all; and if he sacrifices the good of his subjects for his own good, the latter are freed from any obligation to him and have the right to declare his power nonexistent. On the other hand, however, it is understood that the rational state must be a Christian state. "For divine law identifies the true good, and its teaching belongs to the ministry of the Church." [25] That is why the Church has the right to excommunicate and depose kings. This type of modified theocracy, which leaves to the temporal power freedom corresponding to the freedom that theology leaves to rational philosophy, contrasts with the *De regimine Christiano,* written during the same period (1301–1302) by John of Viterbo, an Augustinian hermit who advocated a more rigid theocracy in the face of the growing pretensions of national kingdoms.

XII *Latin Averroism: Siger of Brabant*

There is no doubt but that the introduction of Peripateticism into the University of Paris resulted in the destruction of the unity of medieval culture as it had been envisioned up until the twelfth century. The study of the seven liberal arts was supposed to provide

[25] *De regimine principum* i. 13.

the basic knowledge needed by commentators, and theology was grounded in the commentaries on Scripture written by the Fathers. Moreover, encroachment was prohibited, and the faculty of arts had to exclude all theological matters from the curriculum. But where could the philosophy of Aristotle find a place in the system? In the faculty of arts, since there was no possibility of his being considered an authority on theology. As a matter of fact, toward the middle of the century the curriculum included the study of all the Aristotelian encyclopedia, beginning with the *Organon* and continuing through the *Ethics,* the *Physics,* the *Metaphysics,* and so on.[26] This resulted in the introduction of many questions external to the seven arts and relating to theology.

The situation was perilous, for in the faculty of arts scholars were to comment solely on the philosophy of Aristotle and were not to concern themselves in any way with possible disagreement between his doctrines and faith. "Here," said Siger of Brabant, explaining his interpretation of Aristotle's writings on the intellect (in contrast to the interpretation of Albert and St. Thomas), "we are trying to identify the intention of the philosophers, mainly Aristotle. It may well be that the philosopher held an opinion that does not conform to truth and that revelation provides us with information about the soul which cannot be inferred by natural reason; but here we are in no way concerned with divine miracles for we are discussing natural things from the viewpoint of the physician."[27] The Thomistic synthesis did, of course, provide a principle of agreement: what reason teaches us cannot be contrary to what faith reveals to us, and if there is an apparent contradiction, it results from the fact that reason has been misguided.

The Masters of Arts submitted the principle to an experimental proof. Reason was interrogated independently of faith, and determining whether its conclusions were in agreement with faith was a simple matter of collecting the facts. There was no doubt about

[26] Chartulary of the University, quoted by Gilson, *Études,* p. 56.
[27] Ed. Mandonnet, II, 153–54.

the answer in the mind of Siger of Brabant, the celebrated Master of Arts who taught the Averroist interpretation of Aristotle at the University of Paris from 1266 to 1277 and who was the initiator of the movement known as Latin Averroism: Aristotle's theses contradict revealed doctrines. It would seem that his conclusion is to him a simple statement of fact, and nowhere does he infer that there is a "double truth," one truth for philosophers and one truth for theologians. Others may have reached such a conclusion, but he does not hesitate to state that "faith speaks the truth, even though some philosophers have held a different opinion."

The identity of intellect in all men, the necessity of events, the eternity of the world, the destruction of the soul with the body, the negation of knowledge of separate substances in God, the negation of divine providence in the sublunary region—such are the main items on which Siger's Averroism and the Christian faith differ, and which Giles of Lessines collected from the teaching of Siger in 1270 for submission to Albert the Great.[28]

Here we find almost all of the theses which Averroes attributed to Aristotle and which St. Thomas denied. A treatise such as Siger's *De anima intellectiva* also contains a discussion of Aristotle's writings on the intellect and the interpretations of Albert the Great and St. Thomas (who are identified by name). It is not true, according to Aristotle, that the vegetative and sensitive faculties belong to the same subject as the intellectual faculty. Intelligence must be joined to the body during its operation since it can apprehend only whatever is in the images that involve the corporeal organ of the imagination; but intelligence alone understands, and when we say that a man understands, we are not speaking of man as a being composed of soul and body but only of his intellect.

In spite of the precautions taken by Siger, his teaching was judged dangerous by the ecclesiastical authority. In 1270 the Bishop of Paris, Étienne Tempier, condemned thirteen propositions in Aver-

[28] Cf. "La demande de consultation" and "La réponse d'Albert," in P. Mandonnet, *Siger de Brabant et l'Averroïsme latin au XIIIᵉ siècle,* II, 29.

roist teaching concerning the knowledge of God, the eternity of the world, the identity of human intellects, fatality—the very propositions that Giles of Lessines had submitted to Albert. In 1277, at the invitation of Pope John XXI, the Bishop of Paris conducted an inquiry that resulted in a new condemnation of 219 propositions. The condemnation starts by attributing to the Averroists the double-truth theory: "they say that things are true according to philosophy but not according to the Catholic faith, as if there were two opposite truths and as if there were in the words of the heathen who are damned a truth contrary to the truth of the Holy Scripture."[29] Siger, obliged to leave the University, was summoned before the Inquisitor of France. He appealed to the Holy See, but was sentenced to be interned for life. He died tragically in 1282, stabbed by the cleric who served as his secretary.

The Averroist movement, which was led not only by Siger but also by Boetius of Sweden and Bernier of Nivelles, who were condemned along with him, continued in spite of such harsh measures. John of Jandun, Master of Arts in Paris about 1325 (died in 1328), was excommunicated in 1327 by Pope John XXII. He nevertheless protested that he, too, was adhering to the faith: "It is certain that divine authority must be relied on to a greater degree than any reason of human invention."[30] He sought to support opinions of faith contrary to reason "by granting as possible with God that which our reasoning leads us to declare impossible." He therefore was led logically to a type of fideism. "I assert the truth of all these dogmas," he said, speaking of dogmas which contradicted Aristotle, "but I do not know how to demonstrate them; those who do know how have an advantage, but I possess them and confess them solely through faith." We shall see later that Averroism played an important role during the Renaissance.

[29] *Ibid.*, II, 175.
[30] Quoted by Gilson, *Études*, p. 71.

XIII *Polemics Relating to Thomism*

The condemnation directed by Tempier in 1277 came in the midst of a state of uneasiness brought about not only by Averroism but also by Peripateticism in general. Judged from his own viewpoint, St. Thomas was surely the adversary of the Averroists. His vast theory of the intellect is but a lengthy reply to Averroism, and the *De unitate intellectus contra Averroistas* was probably written in 1270 to refute Siger. Viewed from the outside, however, his philosophy was Peripatetic, and it was difficult to see exactly where the danger posed by Aristotelianism, which had been introduced into the University of Paris, would stop. Thus some of the 219 condemned propositions relate not to Siger himself but to the innovations of Thomism. Those that seemed suspect include: the impossibility of the plurality of worlds (27), individuation through matter alone (42, 43), and the necessity for the will to pursue that which is judged good by the intellect (163). St. Thomas found some contradictions in his own order: the Dominicans who had preceded him at the University of Paris, Roland of Cremona and Hugh of St. Cher, were Augustinians. One of his most ardent adversaries was the Dominican Robert Kilwardby who, as Master of Theology at Oxford from 1248 to 1261 and Archbishop of Canterbury in 1272, taught St. Bonaventure's ideas on matter and form. He held that matter contained the seminal reasons that explain the production of things; and, contrary to the thesis of the unity of form, he taught that the soul was not simple but composed of vegetative, sensitive, and intellectual parts. It is not surprising that he had the theory of the unity of form condemned at Oxford in 1277. The some theory was repeatedly condemned by his successor to the see of Canterbury, the Franciscan John Peckham. The latter condemned the new philosophy in its entirety in a letter of 1285 in which he criticized "the profane innovations in vocabulary introduced during the last twenty years into the very heart of theology, going against the true philosophy and offending the saints." And he called attention especially to the abandoning of the Augustinian doctrine "of eternal rules and immutable light, of the powers of the soul, of seminal reasons inserted into matter, and of a number of other doctrines." The passage evidently refers to the corresponding theses in Thomism: agent intellect, unity of forms, theory of the eduction of forms.

xiv *Henry of Ghent*

From these dry formulations emerge two opposing views of the universe. In the Augustinian universe reason is already an illumination, being already possesses form and aspires to new forms, matter is pregnant with determinations that will engender form; in the Peripatetic universe all intellectual knowledge is abstraction, the individual being is complete in itself, matter passively awaits form. A leading exponent of anti-Thomistic Augustinianism in Paris was the secular master Henry of Ghent, the *doctor solemnis*. Master of Theology in Paris in 1277, he died in 1293. Contrary to the Peripatetic principle which states that form gives being to matter, he held that matter exists independently and subsists in actuality. Its subsistence is, of course, imperfect and leaves it capable of receiving the form that complements it and makes it complete. In his view, contrary to the Thomistic principle, essence is not really distinct from being. According to St. Thomas each essence awaits its actualization from universal being and, as pure potentiality, has no independent right to it. Henry held that essence has its own being independently and that to diverse essences correspond an equal number of diverse beings—a principle which allows to each essence something of the power of God. His theory of individuation was equally anti-Thomistic: individuation is due not to matter but to negation. The individual being, the lower term in the division, becomes incapable of dividing in its turn; it is equally incapable of identifying itself with the other individual beings and of communicating with them. The theory of essences and individual beings led him, it would seem, to posit the objects of our intelligence in God himself, at least at their highest level. Thus he thought "that man, starting from natural things, cannot attain to the rules of eternal light that God gives to whomever he wills and withholds from whomever he wills." No other theory reveals more clearly the contrast between his view and Thomism, which outlines sharply the limits of reason and could be epitomized in these words: continuity in being *but* discontinuity in knowledge. The essence of Augustinianism, which views reason as a continuation of illumination, is this: continuity in being *and therefore* continuing in knowledge. From the two opposing views issue two strikingly different conceptions of the spiritual life. To Henry of Ghent, the end of this life is not knowledge of God, as in the case of St. Thomas, but union with God or love. Will, which is the faculty of desiring or loving, therefore has an end superior to that of intelligence and meritorious in its own right. Consequently intelligence does not, as St. Thomas holds, impose on will the end that it pursues.

xv *Giles of Lessines*

Thomism, following the condemnation of 1277, was not without its ardent defenders. Countless refutations were prompted by the appearance in 1278 of William of La Mare's *Correctorium fratris Thomae,* in particular a number of dissertations designed to show the inner coherence of Thomism. The Dominican Giles of Lessines (died in 1304) published such a treatise, the *De unitate formae* (1278), in which he presented the same argument from every possible viewpoint: "Although the forms abstracted by judgment (for instance, the line from the surface or the surface from the body) are really multiple and different as forms, yet in the unique subject of which they are parts and in which they have individual roles they constitute but one being, that has its source in the form through which they have their physical being and from which their functions derive, as secondary acts derive from the primary act." [31]

Furthermore, we find secular clerics like Godfrey of Fontaines

[31] Ed. De Wulf, p. 57.

(died in 1308), who sometimes takes a stand against his teacher, Henry of Ghent, and defends certain points in the Thomistic doctrine. Godfrey grants that St. Thomas is wrong in holding that being does not differ from essence. God is the cause of the essence of a thing just as he is the cause of its existence; before a thing is created both its essence and its existence are in potency; after the thing is created both its essence and its existence are in act; but it is patently false that essence is in potency with respect to its existence.[32] Godfrey also contradicts the Thomistic theory of individuation which, according to him, would make it impossible to posit anything but accidental differences between individual beings, "which is an obvious disadvantage." But he defends, against the doctrine of illuminism, the theory of intellectual knowledge by abstraction and, against the doctrine of voluntarism, the Thomistic thesis according to which will is subject to the understanding.

Finally, at the beginning of the fourteenth century Thomism pervaded some of the influential orders. Giles of Rome (died in 1316), a member of the Augustinian hermits order, defended the thesis of the unity of forms. Humbert introduced Thomism to the Cistercians, and Gerard of Bologna introduced it to the Carmelites. Thomas Aquinas was canonized by Pope John XXII in 1323, and we recall that Dante (1265–1316) reserved a place for him in *the Divine Comedy*: in the fourth heaven Dante meets the masters of philosophy and theology, of whom the greatest is St. Thomas. St. Thomas has on his left Siger of Brabant, and the poet has the saint eulogize the Averroist. The passage has caused his commentators considerable difficulty and may indicate that in the minds of his friends and enemies alike, St. Thomas has essentially the same aim as Siger: to bring together Aristotle and Christ, notwithstanding the ancient theological tradition.

[32] Ed. De Wulf and Pelzer, pp. 305–6.

XVI *The Oxonian Masters*

Augustinianism and Peripateticism are not the only philosophical currents of the thirteenth century. The third current, to which we now turn our attention, is harder to define. To a greater degree than the movements we have been studying, it is in some ways a continuation of twelfth-century thought and a clear anticipation of modern philosophy. The spirit of Chartres that freely assimilated the positive sciences, mathematics and the experimental sciences, classical erudition, and the pursuit of the metaphysical intuition of nature considered as a whole—an intuition that found its satisfaction in an attachment to Platonism—this spirit which is at the same time positive, naturalistic, and haunted by the desire for universal intuition appears once again in a group of thinkers to whom this brief *History* cannot give the space that they deserve.

First come the Oxonians. Their spirit appears vaguely in Alexander Neckham (died in 1217), who was familiar with the *De caelo* and the *De anima* of Aristotle; it appears more clearly in his contemporary, Alfred of Sereshel, who learned Arabic when traveling in Spain. Alfred translated from Arabic to Latin pseudo-Aristotle's *De vegetabilibus* and the *Liber de congelatis,* which is a supplement to the *Meteorology*; he wrote the *De motu cordis*; and he was acquainted with Hippocrates' *Aphorisms* and with Galen's *Medical Art*. Michael the Scot (died about 1235) translated from Arabic Al Bitrogi's *De sphaera,* works by Averroes and Avicenna (the astronomer and the alchemist who appear in Dante's *Inferno*), and Aristotle's *History of Animals,* which he dedicated to Emperor Frederick II.

Oxonianism finally flowered in Robert Grosseteste, Chancellor of the University of Oxford and Bishop of Lincoln from 1235 until his death in 1253. The twenty-nine treatises edited by Baur included mainly his scientific writings, particularly the treatises on optics (*On Light or the Delineation of Forms, On the Rainbow and the Mirror, On Color, On Corporeal Motion and Light*), but they also included treatises on acoustics, astronomy, and meteorology, as well as metaphysical writings on man as a microcosm, on intelligences, and on creations and the order of their emanation from God. In short, his is a conception of the physical universe predicated on the study of light, a metaphysical conception of the universe predicated on the idea of the emanation of forms from unity; it is the radical fusion of a system of physics describing the laws of diffusion of light and a system of metaphysics describing the emanation of beings.

Here light in some ways plays a role analogous to that of fire in the Stoic cosmogony. Through its expansion, its condensation, and its rarefaction, this "primary corporeal form" explains every body in the universe. It has the property of being immediately present in all places: "It is indeed propagated in every direction, with the result that from one luminous point is immediately engendered a sphere of light as large as desired, unless a shadow interferes." To explain the cosmos and its spheres, Grosseteste required only the spherical propagation and infinite swiftness of light, whose expansion is checked by darkness: "Everything is one, born of the perfection of a unique light, and multiple things are multiple only by virtue of the multiplication of light itself."

But we must discover what lies at the heart of his bold investigations. For in his metaphysics of light is the germ of a mathematical physics of nature: optics is inseparable from the study of the lines, angles, and figures that are to some degree realized in the propagation of light; and this outline of mathematical physics culminates in the affirmation of the existence of a precise order in nature, an order of which the mind can have a precise conception. "Any operation in nature is accomplished in the most definite (*finitissimo*), orderly, concise, and perfect manner possible." [33]

From the school of Robert Grosseteste comes a *Summa philosophiae* that includes nineteen treatises on subjects ranging from the history of philosophy to mineralogy. In spite of its fantastic features —among the earliest philosophers the author places not only Isidore,

[33] De luce, ed. Baur, p. 75.

Berossus, Josephus, and St. Augustine, but also Abraham, Atlas, and Mercury—the *Summa* evidences a critical spirit by pointing up the manner in which the Arab translators freely handled Aristotle's texts, having him cite Ptolemy in the *De caelo* and address himself to Emperor Hadrian in the *Meteorology*. The author also tells us that theologians may have erred in their treatment of natural things not related to salvation. On metaphysical issues he contradicts Thomism. He refuses, along with almost all the Augustinians, to acknowledge the existence of the intelligible species that St. Thomas declared indispensable to intellectual knowledge (*Summa philosophiae,* p. 298). The essence of a thing is joined to the intellect, in the absence of any intermediary, for "otherwise what would set the intellect in motion would be their images (*idola*) rather than essences themselves, and what we would apprehend would be their images rather than forms themselves." He also upholds the Augustinian tradition on the question of the intellect's knowledge of itself: "The soul as it acquires an understanding of itself does not receive its own species but rather has intuitive knowledge (*contueri*) of itself" (p. 436). He clings not only to the notion of the intuitive character of the intellectual knowledge of essences of things or of ourselves, but also to the idea that the intellectual soul is an individual being, unrelated to the body.

XVII *Roger Bacon*

The most remarkable of the Oxonian scholars was Roger Bacon, the *doctor mirabilis,* whose impetuous, ardent, and indomitable spirit was reflected in his life as well as in his writings. No one was more critical than he of the ignorance and stupidity of the "Parisian philosophers," and particularly of their negligence in the matter of studying languages, mathematics, and the natural sciences. Born between 1210 and 1214, he was first a pupil of Robert Grosseteste at Oxford, for whom he always evidenced profound admiration. He lived in Paris between 1244 and 1252. After entering the Franciscan order and returning to Oxford he wrote his *Opus majus* (1266–

1268). Divided into seven parts, the work discusses the causes of human ignorance; the relation of philosophy and theology to the science of languages; the utility of mathematics in physics, astronomy, the reform of the calendar, and geography; optics, experimental science, and moral philosophy. Begun at the request of Pope Clement IV, the *Opus majus* was accompanied by two other works which contained preliminary studies: the *Opus minus* and the *Opus tertium*. In 1278 Roger Bacon wrote the *Speculum astronomiae* (wrongly attributed to Albert the Great), a defense of judicial astrology. In it he called in question the condemnation of astrology pronounced in the one hundred and seventy-first proposition in the list condemned in 1277 by Bishop Tempier: "Through signs one can recognize the intentions of men and changes in their intentions." This text probably sealed his doom: the general of the Franciscans, who since 1277 had been following a policy that finally resulted in complete harmony between his order and the Dominican order, condemned him to prison in 1278.

The truth is that Bacon's massive work struck at the very roots of Thomism, a careful partitioning that prescribed for each thinker the limits beyond which he must not venture. Bacon was the foremost champion of the unity of wisdom; all writings constitute but one common body of wisdom. Philosophy and canon law merely "spread over the palm of the hand" (*velut in palmam*) what divine wisdom concentrates "in the fist" (*velut in pugnum*). He recalled the ancient manner of conceiving spiritual unity which had prevailed throughout the Middle Ages and which had been borrowed from St. Augustine and Bede: the liberal arts were to be used in interpreting Scripture, pagan philosophy in refuting the errors of the heathen; the result was that "philosophy considered independently" and apart from the general plan "has no utility." Aristotle himself, as interpreted by the Arabs, is called upon to guarantee spiritual unity; he grants that intellectual knowledge is impossible without the help of an agent intellect that contains all forms; in other words, the agent intellect knows everything, but "if it knows everything, then such knowledge befits not a soul, not an angel, but

God alone." And if Bacon did not go so far as to say, with certain Franciscans, that we see immediately the essences in God, he at least stated that we acquire knowledge intellectually only under the immediate influence of an agent intellect that is identical to the Word, the author of our salvation. Thus Christian philosophers, far from limiting and contracting the domain of their investigations, "ought to bring together in their treatises all the writings of the philosophers on the subject of divine truths, and even to go much farther, but without becoming theologians." Spiritual unity is proven, obviously, by recourse to the divine origin of wisdom. Its divine origin is also demonstrated, according to Bacon, by the fanciful history of philosophy which he borrows from the Church Fathers: philosophy, revealed to the patriarchs, was transmitted through different intermediaries to the pagan philosophers and, through them, to the Christians. And Scripture is also the summation of divine wisdom—Scripture "in which is found every creature or the image of every creature, in its universal type or in its singularity, from the height of the heavens to the ends of the earth, with the result that just as God made his creatures and Scripture, he saw fit to put his creatures in the scriptures, whether we understand this literally or in the spiritual sense."

His conception of wisdom leads, practically, to the most immoderate theocracy: "for by the light of wisdom the Church of God is organized and the Church of the faithful is laid out." Since it rules the world, "no other science is needed for the use of mankind." The Baconian city resembles the Platonic city: at the summit clerics, underneath scholars, underneath them soldiers, and finally artisans; ecclesiastical law grounded solely on Scripture and superior to civil law; popes and princes who choose as counselors wise men, who because they possess wisdom should be the only ones to possess power; finally, religious unity of the world achieved through an apostolate founded on wisdom.

There is a strange contrast between these features of Baconian thought and the points in his doctrine that are generally given primary attention and are of primary historical significance. Roger

Bacon extolled the experimental method in science as the only possible one: "We have three methods of knowing," he says, "authority, experience, and reason; but authority does not contribute to our knowledge if it does not give us the reason for what it states. . . . Reason, in turn, cannot separate sophistry from demonstration unless its conclusions are verified by experience. The truth is, however, that no one today shows concern over this method . . . and that is why all or almost all of the secrets, and the greatest secrets, of science are ignored by most of those who devote themselves to learning." An advocate of the experimental method, he had at the same time the idea of mathematical physics that is inseparable from it: physics linked, as in the case of Robert Grosseteste, to Ptolemaic optics as interpreted by the Arab mathematician Alhazen, to the geometric structure of optics in cases of reflection, refraction, and the theory of the rainbow. The mathematical structure of the point of combustion behind a convex lens lighted by the sun seemed to Bacon to provide "the proper and necessary cause of the phenemenon." At the same time that he was working with mathematics, Bacon also took up technical problems, ranging from the engineering techniques that caused him to imagine automotive machines and flying machines, and social techniques such as the problem of organizing work and providing for public welfare.

This experimental, mathematical, and technical spirit had indeed been present in the case of engineers, architects, and artisans throughout the Middle Ages, but, carried into speculative matters, it seems to make Bacon the true ancestor of modern philosophy. Still, we must not lose sight of his enlightened theocracy; he looked upon Clement IV as the pope destined by the stars to convert the world to Catholicism. Illuminism and positivism are the two features whose union constitutes the physiognomy of Bacon. The union would be inexplicable if we were dealing with the experimental method as it is understood today. But such is not the case; in him we find no precise method either for designing experiments or deducing laws from them.

The word *experimentum* was closely linked, for a thirteenth-century man, to ideas that it no longer suggests to us. An *expert* to Bacon is essentially the man who can release and utilize occult forces unknown to other men; the alchemist creates the elixir of life and the philosopher's stone; the astrologer knows the powers of the stars; the magician knows the formulas that control the wills of men. The image of the universe provided by *experiment* is quite different from that provided by the physics of the philosopher: the latter deduces natural phenomena from the properties of the four elements; experiment involves the acquisition of knowledge of hidden forces which are irreducible to the forces of the elements, such as those brought to light by Peter of Maricourt in connection with his studies of the magnet. When Bacon speaks of experimental science he is thinking of a secret, traditional science that consists in the investigation of occult forces and of the power that knowledge of these forces confers on the expert. The universe of the *experts* is essentially the universe described by Plotinus: a set of interpenetrating forces, enchantment, magic words, forces which have emanated from the stars and to which people are unwittingly subject. Bacon finds in perspective the typical illustration and example of the diffusion of each such force, starting from its point of origin; perspective, studied intensively during his time, provides in the diffusion of light an example of the "multiplication of species." This multiplication is like the general law of the forces that are intermingled in space.

Starting from there, Bacon attaches much less importance to control of facts than to the discovery of secrets or of astonishing facts that the experts transmit to each other from generation to generation. He welcomes with unbelievable credulity (*credulitas* is to him the first of the expert's virtues) Pliny the Elder's tales about the diamond that was attacked by the blood of a he-goat (Pliny 20. 1; 37. 15), the use of castor beans in medicine (Pliny 32. 13), and many other fabricated facts borrowed from the experiences of peasants and old women.

Corresponding to the experience of nature as defined here are inward experiences relating to spiritual things: the illuminations received by the patriarchs and the prophets. Such experiences, at their highest degree, are also shrouded in mystery: beyond virtues, beyond the gifts of the Holy Ghost and divine peace, are "states of ecstasy and their various forms, each of which in its own way reveals experiences impossible to convey in words." He who has the key to such spiritual secrets also possesses thereby the key to human sciences.

Bacon's doctrine, with all its shortcomings and even because of them, admirably points up the impatience with which certain men of the thirteenth century endured the limitations which the "philosophy of the Parisians" sought to impose on man and the universe. Their contention was that true reality is outside such limitations, in an abyss of miraculous powers where only a few rare men enlightened by a superior wisdom know what to do.

XVIII *Witelo and the Perspectivists*

A kindred spirit characterizes the works of Witelo, born in Poland between 1220 and 1230. He resided in Italy and was, at the same time as St. Thomas, a friend of William of Moerbeke, the Hellenist. It was at the request of the latter that he wrote the *Perspectiva,* a compilation of the works of Euclid and Apollonius of Perga, of the *Optics* of Ptolemy (which had been translated into Latin in the twelfth century), and especially of the *Optics* of Alhazen, the Arab scholar. He translated Alhazen's remarkable studies of acquired visual perceptions, the basis of all modern theories of the psychology of perception. He also wrote a treatise, *De intelligentiis,* in which, following the *Book of Causes,* he studied the three Neo-Platonic hypostases: the First Cause or the One, Intelligence, and Soul.

Like Robert Grosseteste he linked perspective to Neo-Platonic metaphysics. The symbolism of light marking the actions of the One was probably based on St. Augustine and the *Epistle to the Romans,* but he developed his symbolism through studies in perspective. Light is a simple body and is for this very reason capable of multiplying itself: "the simplest body is characterized by the greatest extension; water by a greater extension than earth, air by a greater extension than water, and fire by a greater extension than air." Light, the most subtle of bodies, therefore has the greatest extension; it has room for bodies; it allows models to be reflected in matter and in this way is the principle of knowledge. Neo-Platonic metaphysics has one trait which we have already noticed several times and which sets it apart from Thomism. That is the preponderance of love over knowledge: "In the same being love naturally precedes knowledge . . . and love is consummated through knowledge, not because knowledge is its complement but because knowledge makes it multiply and live independently. . . . Knowledge is not the perfection of love; but rather, quite the contrary, knowledge is conditioned by enjoyment and love."

Finally, we find the same link between experimental studies, especially optics, and Neo-Platonic metaphysics in Dietrich of Vriberg, who was born *ca.* 1250, became Master of Theology in Paris in 1297, and died after 1310. The author of a mathematical theory of the rainbow which explains the phenomenon by a double refraction followed by reflection on raindrops, he adhered to an Augustinian and Neo-Platonic philosophy quite different from the official doctrine of his order, the Dominicans. He adhered to the doctrine of the three hypostases in Proclus' *Elements of Theology* and he accepted the image of the production of things through emanation and their conversion, though he reconciled them with the theory of Creation. Against this, he borrowed from Aristotle the notion of the agent intellect and identified it with the hidden part of the mind (*abditum mentis*), the depths of memory (*profunditas memoriae nostrae*), and the image of God in which the eternal laws and immutable truths are immediately and effortlessly present (in contrast to abstraction, which involves only the faculty of cognition).

XIX *Ramon Lull*

The vast and still neglected work of Ramon Lull reveals the dominant preoccupations of the last years of the thirteenth century. His books, written in Catalan but translated for the most part into Latin, were all designed to serve a practical aim: to establish Catholicism, which he considered identical to reason, all over the world. His actions and an unrelenting flood of propaganda were motivated by this aim. Born in Majorca in 1235, he left his wife and children in 1265 to devote all his time to his mission. For nine years he studied the language and science of the Arabs in Majorca. In about 1288 he proposed to the popes a plan for a crusade and for missions in the land of the infidels. In 1298, and later in 1310 and 1311, he was in Paris, where he wrote a great number of treatises (still in manuscript) against the Averroists. In 1311 he attended the council of Vienna and proposed the adoption of his plan for teaching Arabic and Hebrew in Rome and in several universities in order to prepare missionaries. He himself departed for Tunis to convert the infidels and died there in 1315.

A man passionately committed to a practical task, and a mystic whose activity was motivated by a vision, Ramon Lull wrote *Dialogues and Canticles of the Lover and the Beloved* and a famous work on what he termed "the great art." In keeping with the general design of his life, his *Ars major* is practical rather than theoretical. Like all those who tried in the Middle Ages to combat infidels and heretics, Lull intended "to prove the articles of faith through necessary reasons." To this end he wrote his *Ars generalis* or *Ars magna,* the art of reasoning. He tried to make the work so appealing and so easy that even the common people would have the means of defending the faith: a universal religion based on an equally universal method of thinking. Such was Lull's idea of Catholicism.

Exactly what is his "great art"? We recall that Aristotle's logic could not resolve two problems: first, the discovery of the necessary premises or principles that could give to the conclusion of the syllogism a demonstrative or scientific character; second, given the extreme terms, the discovery of the middle term that could unite them. These are the two problems that Lull boasts of resolving in *Ars magna*. His is not, strictly speaking, an art of reasoning but rather an art of invention. This is shown by the titles of some of his treatises: De *venatione* medii inter subjectum et praedicatum; Ars compendiosa *inveniendi* veritatem, seu ars magna et major; ars *inveniendi* particularia in universalibus; quaestiones per artem demonstrativam seu *inventivam* solubiles: Ars *inventiva* veritatum.

"Each science has its own principles, and they are different from the principles of other sciences. For instance, judgment requires a general science with general principles in which are implied and contained the principles of particular sciences, just as the particular is implied by and contained in the universal." These are the opening words in the *Ars magna generalis et ultima*. We recall the method that Aristotle had indicated to discover the middle terms that makes possible the resolution of a question, that is, to determine whether a predicate is true of a given subject: by identifying for a given subject all possible predicates and for a given predicate all possible subjects, we of necessity discover every possible middle term between the subject and the predicate. Lull's *Ars magna* is a generalization of Aristotle's procedure. He thinks first of discovering every possible predicate of a given subject by enumerating the following attributes: *bonitas, magnitudo, aeternitas; potestas, sapentia, voluntas; virtus, veritas, gloria; differentia, concordia, contrarietas; principium, medium finis; majoritas, aequalitas, minoritas*. The first nine words designate divine attributes, the last nine, relations. Any predicate, according to him, can be related either to one of these attributes or to a combination of them, and the combination follows certain rules. With respect to a subject, he asks ten questions: whether it is, what it is, what it is made of, why it is, how it is, how big it is (*quantum*), what it is like (*quale*), when it is, where it is, with what it is.

The foregoing remarks are enough to show that Lull's *Ars magna* could not break through the circle of Aristotle's logic. His presumed art of invention is merely an art of classifying and combining certain concepts, not an art of discovering them. At times it seems that he confuses order with invention. For instance, he advises the "artist" who deals with physics "successively to apply the ten rules to the concept about which he is doubtful" (that of nature), in other words, to ask the ten questions enumerated above. And he adds (fol. 78 b.): "Just as a glass takes on the color of its red or green background, so an unknown term is colored or illuminated by the rules and species of rules to which it is exposed (*discurritur*)." His is obviously a purely formal explanation; it enables us to determine what we ought to ask of a thing and to examine the thing from different angles, but it will never enable us to discover the answers.

Such are the main currents of thirteenth-century thought. Against the background of their diversity one common trait stands out: the universal dream of a hierarchical organization and of spiritual unity. It is fitting that the period we have been studying should have been inaugurated by Innocent III, who, more than any other pope, defended the primacy of the spiritual power, and that the regular clergy, directly dependent on the pope, should have exercised an important role in the universities. The systems we have examined derived from the same force that gave birth to the crusades: the urge to spread Catholicism everywhere. This spiritual unity was projected upon metaphysical reality, and everyone, without exception, believed that Neo-Platonic metaphysics (easily reconciled with the idea of the Creation), with its unity and its hierarchy, was an exact representation of this reality. A political ideal was constructed in which temporal power was either absorbed completely by the spiritual power or subordinated to it. If reason and the terrestrial city were autonomous in the minds of some, it was in the sense that an office whose limits have been precisely delineated by a higher power is autonomous.

The thrust toward unity was decisively checked. In the fourteenth century, even as the throes of the Hundred Years' War were giving shape to the nationalism that was to destroy forever the dream of political and Christian unity, the image of the universe was being shattered. For the truth is that the very elements that the thirteenth-century thinkers had accepted for their edifice surreptitiously contributed to its collapse. Platonism, Aristotelianism, the experimental method, mathematics, ancient traditions—all these forces that seemed at the time to have had a part in the construction of a system of Christian thought were found in the light of day to be completely independent of the Christian belief in a supernatural destiny.

BIBLIOGRAPHY

I to III

Texts

Dominicus Gundissalinus. *De divisione philosophiae.* Edited by Baur.
   Beiträge, Vol. IV. Münster in Westfalen, 1903.
———. *De immortalite animae.* Edited by Bülow. *Ibid.,* Vol. II. 1897.
———. *De unitate.* Edited by Correna. *Ibid.,* Vol. I, 1891.
———. *De anima.* Edited by Loewenthal. Berlin, 1890.
William of Auvergne. *Opera omnia.* 2 vols. Paris, 1674.

Studies

Callus, D. "Introduction of Aristotelian Learning to Oxford," *Proceedings of
   the British Academy,* XXIX (1943).
Chroust, A. "The Definitions of Philosophy in the 'De divisione philosophiae'
   of Dominicus Gundissalinus," *The New Scholasticism,* XXV (1951), 253–
   81.
Denifle, H., and Chatelain, A. *Chartularium universitatis parisiensis.* Vol. I.
   4 vols. Paris, 1889–97.
Gilson, E. "La notion d'existence chez Guillaume d'Auvergne," *Archives
   d'histoire doctrinale et littéraire du moyen âge,* XV (1946), 55–91.
———. "La Servante de la théologie," *Études de philosophie médiévale* (Stras-
   bourg, 1921), pp. 30–50.
McKeon, R. "Aristotelianism in Western Christianity" in *Environmental
   Factors in Christian History.* Chicago, 1939. Pp. 206–31.
Rashdall, H. *The Universities of Europe in the Middle Ages.* 3 vols. Oxford,
   1936.
Van Steenberghen, F. *Aristotle in the West; The Origins of Latin Aris-
   totelianism.* Translated by L. Johnston. Louvain, 1955.
———. *The Philosophical Movement in the Thirteenth Century.* New York,
   1955.

IV to VI

Texts

Albert the Great. *Opera omnia*. Edited by A. Borgnet. 38 vols. Paris, 1890–99.
———. *On the Intellect and the Intelligible*. Book I. Translated by R. McKeon. *Selections*, I, 326–75.
Alexander of Hales. *Summa theologica*. 4 vols. Quaracchi, 1924–48.
St. Bonaventure. *Opera omnia*. 10 vols. Quaracchi, 1882–1902.
———. *Commentary on the Sentences*, I, 3, 1. Translated by R. McKeon. *Selections*, II, 118–48.
———. *De reductione artium ad theologiam*. Translated by Sr. Emma Therese Healy. St. Bonaventure, N.Y., 1939.
———. *The Mind's Road to God*. Translated by G. Boas. New York, 1953.

Studies

Boehner, Ph. "The System of Metaphysics of Alexander of Hales," *Franciscan Studies*, II (1951), 157–201.
Bourke, V. "The Provenance of the *De apprehensione* Attributed to Albertus Magnus," *Speculum*, XVIII (1943), 91–98.
Gilson, E. "L'Âme raisonnable chez Albert le Grand," *Archives d'histoire doctrinale et littéraire du moyen âge*, XIV (1943–45), 5–72.
———. "La philosophie franciscaine," in *Saint François d'Assise*. Paris, 1927. Pp. 148–75.
———. *The Philosophy of St. Bonaventure*. Translated by I. Trethowan and F. Sheed. London, 1938.
Grabmann, M. "Albertus Magnus Theologe Philosoph und Naturforsher," *Philosophisches Jahrbuch der Görresgesellschaft*, LXI (1951), 473–80.
Kennedy, L. "The Nature of the Human Intellect According to St. Albert the Great," *Modern Schoolman*, XXXVII (1960), 121–37.
Klubertanz, G. "*Esse* and *Existere* in the Philosophy of St. Bonaventure," *Mediaeval Studies*, VIII (1946), 169–88.
O'Donnell, C. *The Psychology of St. Bonaventure and St. Thomas Aquinas*. Washington, D.C., 1937.
Pegis, A. "St. Bonaventure and the Problem of the Soul as Substance." Chap. ii in *St. Thomas and the Problem of the Soul in the Thirteenth Century*. Toronto, 1934.

VII to XI

Texts

St. Thomas Aquinas. *Opera omnia*. Parma edition. 25 vols. Parma, 1852–73. Reprinted: New York, 1948.

St. Thomas Aquinas. *Summa theologica. Summa contra Gentiles. Quaestiones disputatae.* Translated by the English Dominican Fathers. London (B.O.W.)

——. *Basic Writings.* Edited by A. Pegis. 2 vols. New York, 1948.

Sources

De Wulf, M. *Études historiques sur l'esthétique de S. Thomas d'Aquin.* Louvain, 1896.

Finance, J. de. *Être et agir dans la philosophie de S. Thomas.* Bibliothèque des Archives de philosophie. Paris, 1945.

Forest, A. *La structure métaphysique du concret selon S. Thomas d'Aquin.* Paris, 1931.

Garrigou-Lagrange, R. *God: His Existence and His Nature.* 2 vols. Translated by B. Rose. London, 1934-36.

Gilson, E. *The Christian Philosophy of St. Thomas Aquinas.* Translated by L. K. Shook. New York, 1956.

——. *S. Thomas d'Aquin.* ("Les moralistes chrétiens.") Paris, 1941.

Grabmann, M. *Der göttliche Grund menschlicher Wahrheitserkenntnis nach Augustinus und Thomas von Aquin.* Cologne, 1924.

——. *Das Seelenleben des heilingen Thomas von Aquin.* Munich, 1924.

Lottin, O. *Le droit naturel chez S. Thomas et ses prédécesseurs.* Bruges, 1926.

——. *Psychologie et morale aux XIIe et XIIIe siècles.* Vol. I. *Problèmes de Psychologie.* Louvain, 1942.

Maritain, J. *St. Thomas Aquinas.* London, 1946.

Péghaire, J. *Intellectus et ratio selon S. Thomas d'Aquin.* Paris, 1936.

Roland-Gosselin, B. *La doctrine politique de S. Thomas d'Aquin.* Paris, 1928.

Sertillanges, A. *Foundations of Thomistic Philosophy.* Translated by G. Anstruther. London, 1931.

Tonquédec, J. de. *Les principes de la philsophie thomiste. La critique de la connaissance.* Paris, 1929.

XII to XV

Texts

Giles of Lessines. *Le traité "De unitate formae" de Gilles de Lessines: Texte inédit et étude.* M. De Wulf. Louvain, 1901.

Henry of Ghent. *Summa theologica.* 3 vols. Ferrara, 1646.

——. *Quodlibeta.* 2 vols. Venice, 1608.

Siger of Brabant. *Die Impossibilia des Siger von Brabant.* Edited by C. Baeumker. *Beiträge,* Vols. II, VI. Münster, 1898.

——. *L'Opuscule de Siger de Brabant "De Aeternitate Mundi."* Edited by W. Dwyer. Louvain, 1937.

Studies

Callus, D. *The Condemnation of St. Thomas at Oxford*. Westminster, Md., 1946.

Hocedez, E. "Gilles de Rome et Henri de Gand" *Gregorianum* (1927).

Kendzierski, L. "Eternal Matter and Former in Siger of Brabant," *The Modern Schoolman*, XXXII (1955), 223–41.

Mandonnet, P. *Siger de Brabant et l'averroïsme latin au XIIIe siècle*. 2 vols. "Les philosophes belges," Vols. VI, VII.) Louvain, 1908–11.

Maurer, A. *"Esse* and *Essentia* in the Metaphysics of Siger of Brabant," *Mediaeval Studies*, VIII (1946), 68–85.

———. "Another Redaction of the Metaphysics of Siger of Brabant?" *Mediaeval Studies*, XI (1949), 224–32.

Paulus, J. *Henri de Gand. Essai sur les tendances de sa métaphysique*. Paris, 1938.

Van Steenberghen. "Siger of Brabant," *The Modern Schoolman*, XXIX (1951), 11–27.

XVI to XIX

Texts

Alexander Neckham. *De naturis rerum*. Edited by T. Wright. London, 1863.

Alfred of Sareshel. *De motu cordis*. Text in C. Baeumker, *Des Alfred von Sareshel (Alfredus Anglicus) Schrift De motu cordis. Beiträge*, Vol. XXIII. Münster in Westfalen, 1923.

Dietrich of Vriberg. *De intellectu et intelligibili. De habitus*. In E. Krebs, *Meister Dietrich, sein Leben, seine Wissenschaft. Beiträge*, Vol. V. Münster in Westfalen, 1906.

———. *De esse et essentia*. In E. Krebs, "Le traité 'De esse et essentia' de Thierry de Fribourg," *Revue Néo-Scolastique de philosophie*, XVIII (1911), 511–36.

Ramon Lull. *Opera omnia*. Edited by I. Salzimger. 8 vols. Mainz, 1721–42.

Robert Grosseteste. Shorter philosophical treatises in L. Baur, *Die philosophische Werke des Robert Grosseteste. Beiträge*, Vol. IX. Münster in Westfalen, 1912. (The last part contains the *Summa philosophica*, erroneously attributed to Robert.)

———. *On Truth. On the Truth of Propositions. On the Knowledge of God*. Translated by R. McKeon. *Selections*, I, 263–87.

———. *On Light or the Beginning of Forms*. Translated by C. Riedl. Milwaukee, 1942.

Roger Bacon. *Opus Maius*. Edited by J. Bridges. 2 vols. Oxford, 1897–1900.

———. *Opus Maius*. Translated by R. Burke. 2 vols. Philadelphia, 1928.

Witelo. *De intelligentiis.* Extracts from the *Perspectiva* in C. Baeumker, *Witelo, ein Philosoph und Naturforscher des XIII Jahrhunderts. Beiträge,* Vol. III. Münster in Westfalen, 1908.

Studies

Callus, D. (ed.). *Robert Grosseteste: Scholar and Bishop.* Oxford, 1955.

Carton, R. *L'expérience physique chez Roger Bacon, contribution à l'étude de la méthode et de la science expérimentale au XIII*e *siècle.* Paris, 1924.

Crombie, A. *Robert Grosseteste and the Origins of Experimental Science, 1100–1700.* Oxford, 1953.

Crowley, T. *Roger Bacon: the Problem of the Soul in His Philosophical Commentaries.* Louvain, 1950.

Easton, S. *Roger Bacon and His Search for a Universal Science.* Oxford, 1952.

Gauthier, L. "Un psychologue de la fin du XIIIe siècle: Thierry de Fribourg," *Revue Augustinienne,* XV (1909), 657–73; XVI (1910), 178–206, 541–66.

Hunt, R. "Alexander Neckham." Unpublished thesis. Cf. F. Ueberweg, *Grundiss der Geschichte der Philosophie,* p. 731.

Lacombe, G. "Alfredus Anglicus in Metheora," *Aus der Geisteswelt des Mittelalters, Festgabe M. Grabmann.* Münster in Westfalen, 1935.

Little, A. (ed.). *Roger Bacon.* Essays contributed by various writers. Oxford, 1914.

Lynch, L. "The Doctrine of Divine Ideas and Illumination in Robert Grosseteste," *Mediaeval Studies,* III (1941), 161–73.

Peers, E. *Fool of Love: The Life of Ramon Lull.* London, 1946.

Sharp, D. *Franciscan Philosophy at Oxford in the Thirteenth Century.* Oxford, 1930.

THE FOURTEENTH CENTURY

1 *Duns Scotus*

The first symptom of collapse is found in the trend inaugurated by Duns Scotus, the "Subtle Doctor." His career was very brief. Born in England before 1270, he was educated at Oxford, where he acquired the traditional taste for mathematics, which was supposed to provide a model of certainty. From 1305 until his death in 1308 he taught in Paris. In England he wrote his commentaries on Aristotle and his *Questions on the Sentences of Peter Lombard* (the *De rerum principio,* attributed to this period, has been proven inauthentic); and in Paris, the *Reportata parisiensia* and the *Collationes.* In the *De perfectione statuum* he shows the religious superiority of the mendicant monks over the regulars.

Duns Scotus has no place in any of the currents that we have followed. Those who would make him an Augustinian are unable to account for his sharp criticism of the school's most precious theories: those of intellectual knowledge as illumination, of seminal reasons contained in matter, and of innate knowledge contained in the soul. But he is even less a Thomist, for his most celebrated doctrines—the actual existence of matter, individuation through form (*haecceity*), the priority of the will—are deliberately and consciously opposed to those of St. Thomas.

One of the essential traits that isolates him and gives him distinction is the outright affirmation of what might be called the historical character of the Christian vision of the universe. Creation, incarnation, the attribution of the merits of Christ—these are free acts on the part of God, in the fullest sense of the word; that is, they are acts which might not have occurred and which are dependent on the initiative of God, who has no reason other than his own will. St. Anselm's *credo ut intelligam* and the attempt to examine the motives of God are diametrically opposed to this new spirit. And that is why he lengthened in a singular way the list of pure objects of faith, the *credibilia,* "which are all the more certain to Catholics because they are not based on our blind and often vacillating judgment but find firm support in the most solid of verities." Omnipotence, incommensurability, infinity, life, will, omnipresence, truth, justice, providence—almost all the divine attributes that St. Thomas deduced from the notion of God as the cause of the world —are to Duns Scotus objects of faith. He nevertheless acknowledges a rational proof of the existence of God, the proof *a contingentia mundi* that forces us to pass from the changing being of our experience to necessary being that has its own reason for being. This proof could not have as its starting point, as St. Anselm insists that it has, the notion of "the being greater than which no other being can be conceived to exist"; for this notion is not a simple, innate idea, but one we have fashioned for ourselves on the basis of finite beings, and the first step is to show that it is not contradictory.

These views could be summarized in one statement: Duns Scotus exhibits hardly a trace of Neo-Platonism. The concept of the continuity of all things, of a hierarchy of grades of living beings, has almost disappeared. If Augustinianism affirmed continuity in being *and therefore* continuity in knowledge, and Thomism continuity in being *but* discontinuity in knowledge, the doctrine of Scotus might be formulated: discontinuity in being *and* discontinuity in knowledge.[1] As a matter of fact, Duns Scotus used every concept that had gained ascendancy during the thirteenth century: possible intellect and agent intellect, matter and form, universal and individual, will

[1] The affirmation of the continuity of forms is found only in *De rerum principio,* the authenticity of which is dubious.

and understanding. But whereas in the case of earlier thinkers these concepts evoked each other, were associated with each other, fitted into a hierarchy, and formed a coherent pattern, the aim of Duns Scotus seems to have been to exhibit independent terms, each of which has full and sufficient reality: terms which can, of course, be added to each other but which do not require each other.

Duns Scotus seems to abandon the principle of universal analogy which was the moving force behind continuity for Bonaventure and even for St. Thomas. By declaring that the being has a univocal and not an equivocal sense with respect to God and his creatures (that is, that it signifies the same thing), he removes the whole basis of the analogical relation that allows passage from one term (the creature), being in a derived sense, to another—God—who is being in a nobler sense. For the creature and God are related by the same title and in the same way to the notion of being, which consequently provides no means of separating them by comparing them.

The discontinuity is manifested first in the theory of matter. Here Duns Scotus contradicts both Augustinianism and Thomism: the former because he denies the existence of seminal reasons in matter, and the latter because he denies the Peripatetic principle that there is no potency which can make matter exist without form. In short, he denies what the two theories, which contrast so sharply in other ways, have in common: the link between matter and form which (in Augustinianism) causes matter to contain an inner principle that makes it aspire to form and which (in Thomism) causes matter to exist only relative to the form that makes it an actuality.[2] Duns Scotus (like Henry of Ghent) thinks that matter, since it has a distinct idea, has its own actuality. He is not stopped by Aristotle's objection that if this is true a composite being made of form and matter consists of two actual beings that are added to each other, and that the composite being no longer has unity.

Duns Scotus' theory of haecceity solves the problem of individuation in a manner that obviously runs counter to both Thomism and

[2] *In II Sententiarum*, dist., xii, ed. Wadding, VI, 664–99.

Augustinianism. We recall that the Peripatetics extended their lowest classification of genera and species to the lowest or most specialized species, and that they refused to attribute anything intelligible to the individual beings in which specific form was distributed; they attributed purely numerical division to matter, to the addition of accidents to specific form. We also recall that the Augustinians, contemplating the supernatural destiny of the individual soul, conferred on it independent self-knowledge, making it intelligible to itself even though singular, and repudiated in the name of faith the theory of individuation through matter. Traces of Augustinianism are undoubtedly found in the thinking of the Franciscan Duns Scotus: to acknowledge the Thomistic thesis, to believe that nature or specific form is the same in every individual in the same species, would be to revert to "the accursed Averroes"[3] and to believe that human nature, intrinsically undivided, can be divided only quantitatively, as homogeneous water might be distributed in different vessels. But Duns Scotus had a much more general aim: to give to every individual being as such an intelligibility analogous to that which the Peripatetics give to species, that is, a determination through positive and essential characteristics and not through negative and accidental ones. "Socraticity" is something positive even before the existence of Socrates in matter, and it persists in spite of changes in quantity and accidents affecting the real Socrates. It is the unity of the individual being, universally accepted, that forces Duns Scotus to posit a determinate entity, haecceity. Since this entity is included neither in specific form (equinity) nor in the matter to which it is linked (the corporeal structure common to the body of every horse, for instance), we must look for it outside form, outside matter, and consequently outside the composite being formed by them. We must look for haecceity in an ultimate reality. But we must bear in mind that passing from species to individual beings is not the same as passing from genus to species:[4] in passing from genus to species, the genus is to the difference as a

[3] Vol. VI, p. 405.
[4] Vol. VI, p. 413

potential being is to the form that determines it, and that is why genus and difference are fused in a unique reality. Against this, the most specialized species is quite definite: it does not require individuality for its perfection. It follows that in one and the same individual being (a horse) "the singular entity (the haecceity of the horse) and the specific entity are formally distinct realities." This means that individuality is simply added to the species without there being any intelligible bond of continuity between the two. The importance of this trait is obvious in Duns Scotus' criticism of St. Thomas' conception of angelic knowledge. Following in the Neo-Platonic tradition, St. Thomas held that the angels know singular things, not as we do, but because they possess an intellect superior to ours, in which knowledge of singulars is contained in knowledge of universals. In the thinking of Duns Scotus such continuity is forever impossible.

Duns Scotus makes matter an actual reality even without form, and he makes the individual being a positive reality distinct from species. In the same way he attributes to the possible intellect an activity that is to a certain degree autonomous with respect to the agent intellect: the distinctive role of the agent intellect is to separate the specific form from the sensible image wherever it may exist potentially; but the distinctive role of the possible intellect is the act of understanding, and it is the total cause of this act. The intelligible species, a product of abstraction, is necessary not for producing the act of understanding, which derives solely from the possible intellect, but for relating the act to this or that object.[5] He also believes that the distinction between acts is made obvious only by that between objects even though the distinction itself derives solely from the intellectual powers. The contrast between his theory and Augustinian illuminism is also obvious. He counters the thesis of Henry of Ghent that sensible objects cannot illuminate the soul and that divine enlightenment is necessary by citing the certainty of first principles which are clearly apprehended as soon as their terms are apprehended, the certainty of experience, and the inner

[5] Vol. III, pp. 362, 365.

certainty of the data of consciousness—all examples of direct, autonomous certainty.

In the same spirit and in direct contrast to Thomism, he asserts the primacy of the will over understanding. No matter how far it trails behind the good known by understanding, the will "commands understanding" by directing it to consider this or that object; it follows that "understanding, if it is the cause of volition, is a cause dominated by the will." The aim of Duns Scotus is not to offer as a substitute for Thomism the Augustinian view that makes love rather than knowledge the final end of things, but to free will from understanding just as he freed matter from form, the individual being from the species, the intellect from divine illumination. For these considerations all point mainly to the conclusion that the will is wholly free: "Nothing other than the will is the total cause of volition in the will."

Duns Scotus carries his psychological views over into theology. There can be no subjugation of God's will to a good conceived by his understanding. To be sure, the possibles rationally conceived by God are not in any way creations of his will, and nowhere in the writings of Scotus do we find a theory of the primacy of will and of the creation of eternal verities. The will cannot will what is impossible and contradictory. But the possibles conceived by God's reason impose no restrictions on his creative will: "There is no cause for the divine will to have willed this or that, other than the fact that the divine will is the divine will." Thus will does not depend on the rule of goodness; instead, the will is the first rule, and "no rule is right unless accepted by the divine will."

The thesis of the relation between the good and the divine will strongly influenced the moral philosophy of Duns Scotus. The moral precepts that cause us to know the good depend on a divine law; but the good derives solely from the fact that these precepts have been willed by God; and since his will is arbitrary, it is conceivable that God might have given commandments other than those in the Decalogue.

The arbitrariness and radical discontinuity that Duns Scotus introduced into even the divine reality dominated his conception of politics. A fusion of social atomism and unbridled authoritarianism, this conception was the reflection in society of the vision of the universe that we have been examining: men were at first equal, but they willingly sacrificed their independence to an authority established by them in order to limit the dangers to which they subjected each other on account of their egoism; since that time the authority that they set up has become omnipotent and absolute, the chief establishing, distributing, and revoking properties as he sees fit; there are no laws other than the positive laws instituted by him; there are no duties other than duties to God, and among such duties is the forcible conversion of Jews (who were being persecuted and banished at the beginning of the thirteenth century by a Capetian monarchy that had arrogated to itself the absolute power accorded to it by the Franciscan's theory).[6]

The voluntarism of Duns Scotus found its fullest expression in the work of a fourteenth-century Oxonian, Thomas Bradwardine. Born before 1290, he died Archbishop of Canterbury in 1349. A mathematician who found the Anselmian proof of the existence of God appealing, he wished only to demonstrate that the concept of the most perfect being does not imply a contradiction; but he is remembered mainly as the anti-Pelagian who almost went so far as to deny outright any causality other than divine causality. In his thinking there is "no reason or necessary law in God prior to his will." Furthermore, "divine will is the efficient cause of every thing, of every motion," and the freest act that can be accomplished by man is necessitated by God.

His theory of the enthralled will was widely accepted during the fourteenth century. It is a dry theory, far removed from mysticism since, instead of joining God to man through meditation and love, it makes man's dependence on God something external, like a thrall's dependence on his lord: "Man is the thrall of God, but by

[6] Cf. B. Landry, *Duns Scot*, pp. 233–45.

his own free will and not by constraint." The theory was represented at the University of Paris by the Cistercian John of Mirecourt, who saw forty of his theses condemned in 1347. Among the condemned theses were those which said that "God wills that a man should sin and be a sinner, that he is the cause of sin as sin, of the evil of guilt as evil of guilt, the author of sin as sin." His theological determinism, through the Englishman John Wycliffe, influenced Luther. Thus the doctrine of Duns Scotus, which attracted many commentators and was even taught in the leading universities of Europe, was a fountainhead of the new spirit.

II *The Universities in the Fourteenth and Fifteenth Centuries*

The social importance of the universities during the fourteenth century and the first part of the fifteenth century can hardly be exaggerated. By pragmatic sanction, reconfirmed by a decree issued by Louis XII in 1499, privileges were granted to the graduates of the universities in the conferring of benefices. Long years of university study (three years in theology and canon law) were a prerequisite to appointment to the office of curate in a city parish. But the freedom that existed within the university had no counterpart elsewhere. The university was "the oracle of the mind and the guide to European thought, the most redoubtable power that ever confronted the legal powers. No body is freer, no organization more democratic. Meetings of societies, faculties or nations, and general meetings; the right to legislate on all matters—administration, teaching, justice; in some of them, students are even accorded representation . . . and professors are recruited by professors; authorities are elected and for a specified time (rector and proctor for three, four, or six months, or for one year at most); against the meddling of the central authority or local powers, the solid armature of uncontested privileges; fiscal exemption, the right to be judged by one's peers and, to enforce these guarantees, the power to suspend instruction

. . . such is the charter recognized and consecrated by popes and kings."[7]

The universities continued to flourish until the middle of the fifteenth century, when diverse circumstances weakened their power and influence even as they reinforced the central authority, when speculation was abandoned, and when preparation for degrees became their sole concern. Then the universities ceased for a long time to be the centers of activity they had once been, and the spiritual life continued under different conditions.

But in the fourteenth and fifteenth centuries the spirit of independence was manifested in bold, new speculations much more closely related to the tradition of the twelfth century than to that of the thirteenth. The whole era was dominated by the conflict between the *antiqui* and the *moderni*. The ancients were in reality the innovators of the thirteenth century, deeply immersed in discussions motivated by the concepts of Aristotle and his Arab commentators: form and matter, the principle of individuation, agent intellect and possible intellect, intelligible and sensible species, the moving intelligences of the heavens. The moderns were those who, far from providing contradictory or supporting evidence on the issues, rejected them as senseless and turned back to the free and uncluttered vision of the universe that we saw outlined in the eleventh and twelfth centuries: the nominalism of Roscelin and Abelard and the atomistic theory of William of Conches. There was no longer an attempt to rationalize faith, as in the case of St. Anselm, or to illuminate reason, as in the case of St. Bonaventure, or to prescribe the limits of reason, as in the case of St. Thomas. Philosophical speculation unfolded freely and independently.

In the midst of such agitations no part of the old system of Christianity could survive. The power of the emperor was annihilated by the splintering of the empire into more than three hundred principalities that eroded the central power. "As the princes devour the empire, so the people will devour the princes," predicted Nicho-

[7] Imbart de la Tour, *Les origines de la réforme,* I, 347, 527 ff.

las of Cusa in 1433.[8] The power of the popes was not enhanced thereby, and it was seriously impaired by the great schism (1348) that resulted in the Council of Constance (1414–1418) and the Council of Basel (1433), both of which simply intensified the conflict between the advocates of Conciliarism, who believed in the supremacy of the council over the pope (whom they considered an administrator of the Church), and the Ultramontanists, who believed that the pope had unlimited power. As the traditional powers declined, national royalties gained incomparable strength.

The masters of the fourteenth and fifteenth centuries took an active part in the diverse conflicts that involved so many practical interests and focused attention on so many judicial concepts. Most of them were active politically and were jurists as well as philosophers. The great initiator of nominalism, William of Ockham, was also one of the opponents of John XXII. Excommunicated in 1328, he was received at the court of Emperor Louis of Bavaria, where he found John of Jandun, another enemy of the pope. In his *Defensor pacis,* John of Jandun had maintained that "the universality of the citizens was the only human legislator" (he was excommunicated in 1327). William remained there for more than twenty years and wrote pamphlets against the pope, among them the *Compendium errorum papae Johannis XXII* and a vast political work, the *Dialogus inter magistrum et discipulum de imperatorum et pontificum potestate*. Another nominalist, Durand of Saint Pourçain, was the author of the treatise *De jurisdictione ecclesiastica et de legibus*. The great schism caused Henry of Hainbuch, the mathematician and astronomer, to write after 1378 numerous works on the requirements for peace in the Church; but he also wrote works on economics and politics. In the fifteenth century Cardinal Peter of Ailly defended Conciliarism at Basel. Nicholas of Cusa, on the other hand, went over to the pope's side at the Council of Constance and, after becoming a cardinal, took a leading role in all of the ecclesiastical affairs of his time: the internal reform of the clergy in Ger-

[8] Quoted by Vansteenberghe, *Le Cardinal Nicolas de Cues* (Paris, 1920), p. 47.

many, the refutation of the Hussites, and preparations for a crusade against the Turks in 1454.

III *The Beginnings of Nominalism*

A study of the fourteenth and fifteenth centuries brings us face to face with a generation of men whose minds were cold and sober, who had lost the religious enthusiasm that animated the generations of the great crusades, and who had acquired, through the complicated diplomacy necessitated by the most trivial issue during this era, the clear and positive outlook that characterized their doctrine. For under the blows of the nominalists, the metaphysical structure erected during the thirteenth century collapsed. The nominalism of this period was not simply a particular solution to the special problem of universals. It was a new spirit which treated as fictitious all the metaphysical realities that the Peripatetics and the Platonists thought they had discovered, which stressed experience and relegated the affirmations of religion to the domain of pure faith where any communication with reason was impossible.

The first of the nominalists was the Dominican Durand of Saint Pourçain (in the Auvergne), Bishop of Meaux, who died in 1334. He refused to accept the authority of any doctor "no matter how celebrated or solemn he may be." And he viewed as fictitious the sensible and intelligible species which St. Thomas deemed necessary but which no one has ever seen. Also fictitious is the agent intellect whose abstractive operation, rightly understood, in no way implies existence. The agent intellect is indeed necessary when the universal is taken for the specific form which is the fundamental reality of things; the fundamental reality, since it is not given in sensible images, must be apprehended through a higher operation. But everything is reversed if the universal springs from nothing more than a certain manner of considering the sensible image without paying attention to its individual properties; the universal does not exist prior to such consideration, and it differs from the individual being as the indeterminate differs from the determinate. Consequently the problem of individuation is fictitious; it assumes that the species exists prior to the individual being, since it asks what individualizes it; and the truth is that nothing exists but the individual being, which is the first object of our knowledge.

In the same way the Franciscan Peter Auriol, who became Master of Theology at Paris in 1318 and died at Avignon in 1322 at the court of Pope John XXII, his protector, shows a definite preference for nominalism in his *Commentary on the Sentences*. Knowledge of universals goes no deeper than knowledge of individual realities; indeed, "it is nobler to know an individual, designated reality (*demonstratum*) than to know it in an abstract, universal manner." [9] This formula is illuminated by Peter Auriol's attempted analysis of knowledge: things produce in the intellect "impressions" that may differ in strength and precision; consequently they produce in the intellect an "appearance" which Peter also calls an intentional being (*esse intentionale*), a reflection (*forma specularis*), a concept or a conception, or an objective appearance—all synonyms designating, not the Thomistic *species* or intermediary through which the soul knows a thing, but the true object of knowledge. We should also note that his semblance is in no way an image of the thing with a reality distinct from what it represents; it is the thing itself, "present" in the mind, but only to the extent that it is actually visible to the mind. He adds that there is knowledge of genus when the "conception" is wholly imperfect and indistinct, knowledge of species when it becomes more perfect and more distinct. The progression of knowledge is therefore from the universal to the singular, which means from confusion to clarity and distinction.

IV   *William of Ockham*

The greatest of the nominalists was the English Franciscan William of Ockham, who deduced all the consequences of the theory. He was born between 1280 and 1290, studied at Oxford, and died in

[9] Vol. I, p. 816b

1349 or 1350. In the fourteenth and fifteenth centuries he was called the venerable initiator (*venerabilis inceptor*) of nominalism, the monarch or standard-bearer (*antesignanus*) of the nominalists, and his associates were called indifferently nominalists (*nominales*), terminists, or conceptists.

William's arguments against the existence of universals were not new. They were used in the eleventh and twelfth centuries and go back through Boethius to Aristotle's discussion of Plato's ideas: since the universal is supposed to exist independently it must be an individual being, which is contradictory; to posit universals to explain singulars is not to explain but to double beings (application of the celebrated principle of economy previously employed by Peter Auriol and stated by William in this way: *nunquam ponenda est pluralitas sine necessitate*); finally, to put universals in singular things from which the mind would extricate them through abstraction is also to make them individual beings.

But neither does William, still faithful on this point to Boethius and to all the ancient commentators of the *Categories,* place universals in words themselves. He attributes them instead either to the significations of a word (*intentio animae, conceptus animae, passio animae*) or to words as signifiers of something. In the second sense they are conventional since words are a human institution; but in the first sense they are natural universals (*universalia naturalia*).

By designating universals as signs or significations, William (as Abelard had done before him) transposed the question of the nature of universals into that of their use in knowledge. They are used— and this accounts in full for their existence—in propositions to replace the very things that they designate (*supponere pro ipsis rebus*). Far from being a fiction or a chimera, they are images which can represent equally any of the singular things contained in their extension, and which can replace them as the sign replaces the thing signified. One must never lose sight of their reference to things; the universal is never anything more than a predicate that can refer to several things; it is not a thing, by virtue of the axiom: *res de re non praedicatur.*

Ockham teaches that primary knowledge is intuition of singular things, "the apprehensive act" which, as in Stoicism, always includes a judgment of existence. Such intuition is either external and attains to sensible things, or internal, in which case "our intellect acquires particular, intuitive knowledge of certain intelligibles that are in no way dependent on the senses, such as intellection, volition, joy, or sadness, and of other things that man can experience directly." [10] Thus the contrast between the sensible and the intelligible persists in the thinking of this nominalist, but no longer is it a contrast between the concrete and the abstract or between sense data and the metaphysical realities on which they are based or modeled; it is the contrast between two types of experience, the external and the internal. It follows that the contrast provides us with no basis for positing a metaphysical reality to which the data of experience would have to relate. Thus neither reason nor experience enables us to know whether the soul is an incorruptible and immaterial form, whether the act of comprehending implies such a form, or whether the soul is the form of the body.[11] Instead, the contrast between sensibility and reason inclines Ockham, following the practice of Aristotle but in opposition to St. Thomas, to separate intellect and the sensible soul and to add to them a third form, the *forma corporeitatis*. Nor are we provided with knowledge of God and his attributes. Since we do not know him intuitively, we persist in formulating our own idea of God. But such an idea, built on features borrowed from things within the range of our experience, will not enable us to penetrate to his existence as St. Anselm wished to do. The same is true of any attempt to go back, like St. Thomas, from effects to the cause. The principle of the demonstration "Everything that is moved is moved by something else" is neither self-evident nor demonstrated (we shall see the attacks to which it was subjected by the Ockhamists); the other principle—that in tracing the series of causes one must eventually come to a stopping point, the first cause—is probable but cannot be conclusively proven. Here

[10] *In sententias* Prolegomena, qu. 1.
[11] *Quodlibet* I. qu. 10.

we have one more reason to conclude that the unity of God, his infinity, and the trinity of persons are pure articles of faith.

Such a faith, wholly external and impervious to reason, favors the view that the moral precepts that come from God are arbitrary as well as obligatory: the commandments of the Decalogue are pure acts of volition on the part of God, to whom we owe obedience for no other reason. "God is not obliged to perform any act; it is therefore right for us to do that which he wills."

v The Parisian Nominalists of the Fourteenth Century: Criticism of Peripateticism

The teaching of the theories of William of Ockham was prohibited in the faculty of arts of the University of Paris in 1339 and 1340. More than a century later, in 1473, an edict of Louis XI again prohibited the teaching of Ockhamism, and the masters had to take an oath to teach realism. Between the two dates, while the Oxford science languished, there arose at the University of Paris a nominalistic movement which was very important in the history of science and philosophy, and which P. Duhem is the first to have studied and evaluated properly. Pope Clement VI watched uneasily in 1346 as the Masters of Arts turned to "sophistical doctrines." [12] During the following year he condemned the theses of the Cistercian John of Mirecourt who, inspired by Duns Scotus, declared that God was the only real cause, and, with Ockham, that hate for others was demeritorious only because prohibited by God.

In 1346 he condemned the theses of another master, Nicholas of Autrecourt, a Master of Arts. The next year Nicholas had to abjure his theses publicly at a convocation of the university. A corpuscular physics in which all change is reduced to local motion, a world in which the only efficient cause is God and in which any natural causality is denied—such was the simple image of the universe that Nicholas wanted to substitute for Aristotelian physics and metaphysics which, in his opinion, contained not a single demonstration

[12] *Chartularium Universitatis parisiensis* II. i, p. 588.

and should be abandoned in favor of the study of Aristotle's *Ethics* and *Politics*.

He advanced his theses by attacking the two great notions at the heart of physics and metaphysics, namely causality and substance. His method of criticism, which has been compared to that of Hume but which was closer to that used by Sextus Empiricus in his tropes on causes, known through William of Moerbeke's translation of the *Outlines of Pyrrhonism,* consisted essentially in applying as the criterion of truth the principle of contradiction as it is stated in metaphysics. Then he could easily show that "from the fact that one thing is known to exist, it cannot be inferred through evidence (through evidence that can be reduced to the first principle or to the certainty of the first principle) that another thing exists." From the fact that a flame is placed near oakum, I cannot infer positively that it will be burned. I can only conclude with probability that since my hand grew warm whenever I placed it near a flame, oakum will grow warm under the same conditions. Such criticism destroyed Peripatetic physics, which related the bond of causality to the bond of identity (any causality being in principle the production of like by like), and in this way insured the unity of becoming, the unity of the world, and consequently the unity of monotheism; in contrast, Nicholas' viewed becoming as a succession of disconnected moments.

The same criticism applies to the notion of substance. The substance posited by Aristotle as the basis for the likenesses provided by the senses is known neither intuitively (since everyone would know it) nor through discursive reasoning, since likenesses are one thing and substance another, and it is not permissible to draw conclusions from one thing and apply them to another. It follows that "I am absolutely certain only of the objects (*objectis*) of my senses and of my acts." Among the *impossibilia* which Siger of Brabant offered to demonstrate through a play on logic was the following proposition: "Everything that appears to us is but semblance and dream, with the result that we are not certain of the existence of anything." [13] And Siger stressed the following argument: likenesses are provided not by our senses but by another faculty that alone can judge whether they are true likenesses. Nicholas simply carried the argument to its logical conclusion by showing that the principle of contradiction cannot enable us to go beyond appearances to reality. In the same way he attacked the notion of the faculties of the soul, asserting that there is no basis for inferring the existence of will from the act of volition.

VI *The Parisian Nominalists and Aristotle's Dynamics*

The world of Aristotle had been torn apart. Still to be attacked was the very basis of his system, namely his dynamics: "Everything that is moved is moved by something else." The principle must be interpreted to mean: not only at the initial moment, but also at each successive moment, motion is produced by a mover that contains *in actu* that which is in the process of being realized in the moving body. This is the source of two of the most singular theories that we have yet examined: the theory of the motion of projectiles which can continue only by virtue of a thrust that is constantly being renewed; and the theory of the motion of the heavens which is possible only by virtue of moving intelligences that exist eternally. The theory of moving intelligences in the heavens had been linked by the Arabs and by thirteenth-century philosophers to a theological conception of the universe to which it contributed indispensable support: the angelical hierarchy of Dionysius the Areopagite was realized in the separate intelligences whose nature stimulated endless speculation. Furthermore, Aristotle's dynamic principle also served to support Thomism since it was the major premise of his first proof of the existence of God.

We see, then, what strong interests were linked to the principle. It was attacked by the Parisian nominalists who in this way cleared the ground for the development of modern physics,

---

[13] Mandonnet, *Siger de Brabant*, II, 77.

founded mechanics, substituted for the mythology of moving intelligences a celestial mechanics whose principles were identical to
those of terrestrial mechanics, and at the same time broke the bond
of continuity that the old dynamics established between the physical
theory of things and the metaphysical structure of the universe.

John Buridan was born at Béthune around 1300; he served as
Rector of the University of Paris (*ca.* 1348) and died not long after
1358. He introduced the notion of impetus, which must be understood as the antithesis of Aristotle's dynamic principle. The idea is
borrowed from the motion of projectiles, which was the crux of
Aristotle's physics: if a stone is thrown into the air, the mover im-
parts to the moved object a certain power that makes it capable of
continuing the move by itself in the same direction; the force of the
impetus is proportional to the speed of the stone; and the motion
would last indefinitely if not weakened by the resistance of the air
and its weight. But if we posited circumstances under which such
weakening would not occur, its motion would not cease. Such is
conceivably true of the heavens: God at the very beginning imparted
to the heavens a uniform and regular motion that continues endlessly. This thesis nullifies moving intelligences and even any special
concurrence on the part of God, likens the motions of the heavens
to the motion of projectiles, and together with the principle of
inertia, establishes the unity of mechanics. It also relegates to the
past not only the theory of natural places but also the finitude of
the world and geocentrism. But the new principle did not disclose
the full measure of its fruits at the outset, and Buridan himself was
applying it incorrectly when he assumed that the circular and uniform motion of a sphere could continue independently, just as
rectilinear motion could, by virtue of an initial impetus.

The same mistake was made by Albert of Saxony, Rector of the
University of Paris (1353) and Bishop of Halberstadt from 1366 until his death in 1390. But at the same time he enunciated a hypothesis
that posed the problem of celestial mechanics in a completely different way: "The earth moves and the heavens are at rest." For
since there was no longer any physical reason for the immobility of

the earth, as there had been in the case of Aristotle, it remained only to determine whether the new hypothesis "will save phenomena." Here we find a resurgence of the old Pythagorean vision of the immobility of the heavens (never wholly absent during the Middle Ages since some of Plato's interpreters saw it in the *Timaeus*). Erigena and Albert the Great referred to it, and the Scotist Francis of Meyronnes indicated a preference for it around 1320; but now the old image had the support of new notions of general mechanics capable of bringing out its full significance. Furthermore, and in the same spirit, Albert of Saxony investigated the problem of gravity apart from any hypothesis concerning natural places; and he defined, though not yet accurately, the relation between speed, time, and the space traversed by falling bodies.

Nicole Oresme, who studied theology in Paris in 1348 and served as Bishop of Lisieux from 1378 until his death in 1382, was one of the disseminators of the new celestial mechanics. In his *Commentary on the Books of the Sky and the World* (written in the vernacular like a number of his other works), he showed that neither experiment nor reason proves the motion of the heavens, and he cited "several persuasive arguments to show that the earth has a diurnal motion while the heavens do not." He did not forget to draw the conclusion that "such considerations can be used to advantage in defense of our Faith." The same man discovered, before Descartes, the use of geometrical co-ordinates, and before Galileo, the exact formula for the distance covered by a body falling with uniformly accelerated motion. His ideas were propagated by Marsilius of Inghen (died in 1396) and by Henry of Hainbuch, who served as Rector of the University of Vienna in 1393 (died in 1397), and whose works on astronomy and physics are still unpublished.

Ockhamism was continued by Cardinal Peter of Ailly (1350–1420), who became Chancellor of the University of Paris in 1389, and later, during the last years of his life, served as legate for Martin V in Avignon. Like Nicholas of Autrecourt, he was convinced that the existence of the external world could not be proved since "if every sensible external thing were destroyed, God could still preserve the same sensations in our souls." Nor is the existence of God demonstrable; the existence of both the external world and God remains merely probable. Like William of Ockham, he stated that the divine will is in no way subject to the rationality of the good, but that the natural order and the moral order willed by God derive from a "will that is not directed by any reason to will as it does." God is not just because he loves justice but, inversely, a thing is just because God loves it, that is, because it pleases him.

VII *Ockhamism, Scotism, and Thomism*

The history of the universities of the fourteenth century is mainly the history of the struggle between the ancients and the moderns. Ockhamism spread, particularly in Germany, where it was popularized by a faithful but not very original advocate, Gabriel Biel, who taught at the University of Tübingen in 1484 and died in 1495. It was Biel's pupils, Gabrielists such as Staupitz and Nathin, who in the Augustinian convent introduced Luther to nominalist theology, in which God seems more like a capricious and arbitrary Jehovah than a God who submits his will to the law of order and the good as conceived by his understanding.

The ancients were, of course, represented in the universities, especially by commentators: Johannes Capreolus (1380–1444) in Paris and Toulouse; St. Antoninus (1389–1459) in Florence; and Dionysius the Carthusian (1402–1471) in Cologne, which was still a purely Thomist university. At the beginning of the sixteenth century, from 1505 to 1522, Cajetan wrote a commentary on the *Summa theologica,* and Francis Silvester of Ferrara wrote one on the *Summa contra gentiles* in 1516. A Franciscan Scotist of the first half of the fourteenth century, John of Ripa, exercised a strong influence at the University of Paris until the end of the century. In Paris one of his disciples, Louis of Padua, witnessed the condemnation in 1362 of propositions on change and contingence in the will of God which he had extracted from his master's teaching. It was mainly on account of him, it seems, that nominalism did not invade every center of instruction.

VIII *German Mysticism in the Fourteenth Century: Eckhart*

The counterpart of the nominalist movement was the mystical movement that developed during the same era, especially in Germany. Toward the end of the fourteenth century, Gerson defined mystical theology as "clear and savory knowledge of things that are believed on the basis of the Gospel." [14] Mystical theology "must be acquired through penitence rather than through human investigation," and it would seem that "God is better known through a feeling of penitence than through rational study." We see in this French mystic who was a friend of Peter of Ailly the influence of the Victorines, for whom mysticism was mainly a method of meditation linked to spiritual advancement. Scholastic theology proves and demonstrates, and it leads to a system of well-ordered ideas; mystical theology sees and savors, and it leads to an ineffable union with God.

Mysticism was profoundly separated from the philosophy of the universities by the setting and the conditions under which it developed in Germany, as well as by the literary forms that it assumed. It was inseparable from the cloistered life, with all the training in spiritual meditation associated with the monastic organization, from sermons in the vernacular that appealed to sentiment rather than to the intellect, and from a general mood that extended to the lower classes and was manifested particularly in a belief in the millennium. There had been many instances of millenarianism in the twelfth century, and in the fourteenth it led to the sudden ap-

[14] *Contra vanam curiositatem,* ed. Dulin (1706), I, 106. Of course, Gersonian mysticism, which links the Chancellor of the University of Paris more closely to St. Bonaventure and to St. Bernard than to the Areopagite and Erigena, has none of the specific traits that are found among the German mystics (cf. A. Combes, *Jean Gerson* [1940], p. 469).

pearance of a great number of prophets and prophetesses who announced that the cycle was coming to an end and that the antichrist was about to appear. Mysticism,[15] even when doctrinal, retained many of the features that linked it to the common people: the German mystics of the fourteenth century favored the vulgar language; they explained through affirmation, through visions, but they never discussed or tried to provide proofs; according to Eckhart, the most speculative of them all, their aim was always to help the soul break away from the body and seek God, to become convinced of its nobility and of the purity of the divine nature.[16]

He was saying the same thing as Plotinus, whose doctrine had close affinities with his own even though Eckhart was not directly indebted to his predecessor. The Dominican John Eckhart, born in 1260, was at the University of Paris in 1300, but from 1304 until his death in 1327—except for a stay in Paris in 1311—he lived in Germany, where he served as Vicar General of his order after 1307 and acquired a good reputation as a teacher, preacher, and reformer of the Dominican convents of his order in Bohemia. The last two years of his life were darkened by the attacks of the Franciscans, who caused twenty-eight of his theses to be condemned in Rome in 1329.

It would be difficult to understand how this Dominican, who was in his own way a man of action, carried metaphysical speculation to such a point that he is rightly credited with originating German philosophy, if we did not first examine his conception of the Christian life. First, comes a whole system of spiritual interpretation of evangelical precepts and monastic rules derived from them: poverty, love, humility, good works, prayers. All these rules, intended to turn man away from himself and the world and to bring him nearer to God, are given a purely spiritual interpretation by Eckhart: poverty is the state of a man who knows nothing, who wants

[15] Pastor, *Histoire des Papes,* I, 166, cited by Vansteenberghe, *Le Cardinal Nicolas de Cues,* p. 33.
[16] Ed. Pfeiffer, p. 191; compare Plotius *Enneads* iv. 3. 1.

nothing, and who has nothing. Completely severed from himself and from all creatures, the man who is truly poor lacks even the will to accomplish the will of God; he is in a state of complete passivity; he allows God to accomplish his work in him; he is ready to suffer the torments of Hell or to partake of the joys of beatitude. The union of love is as complete as possible and has its end only in itself. In keeping with an enduring feature of mysticism, love is no longer a permanent deficiency as in Plato's description, but a plenitude identical to God himself. The action of the amorous soul therefore is characterized by no deficiency and is subservient to no end. Love and all the virtues that issue from love, far from being acquisitions of the soul, are therefore (as Eckhart expresses the Plotinian view) the very being of the soul. They are the profound unity in which are indissolubly fused all the virtues that thereafter are accomplished effortlessly and even involuntarily and unconsciously, and that exhibit no gradation; good works, almsgiving, and fasting are worthless unless the will that motivates them is taken into consideration. The will, indifferent to any external success and superior for this very reason to any temporal or spatial circumstance, brooks no obstruction and is the true work, the internal work which alone draws us to God. Nor is true prayer something external and limited to a definite, momentary end; it is constant submission to the will of God.

Here we see the resurgence in full force of a means of understanding the inner life which, since the time of Plotinus, had never been formulated with such clarity and completeness: love as the end of the spiritual life, the fusing of all virtues into one, the attainment of complete freedom by placing the soul once again at its proper depth, that is, beyond the states in which its activity is restricted and circumscribed. That is indeed the Plotinian tradition that has often appeared as the counterpart to another tradition: the tradition according to which virtue, instead of being withdrawal and return to self, is a voluntary acquisition involving multiple and repeated exposure to external, social conditions. But it is worth noting that Eckhart's doctrine, like Plotinism, does not lead to the kind of abstention from overt activity that in the seventeenth century was called quietism. The lower activities of the soul—those that lead to action, will, reason, understanding, external perception —are not eliminated by the soul's withdrawal into itself but are on the contrary ordered and directed. The problem that tormented the Stoics so much is here resolved: when one possesses the right principle, right actions independently follow.

The rhythm of this mystical conception of the spiritual life predominates in Eckhart's theology and metaphysics. Fourteenth-century thinkers had long been familiar with this rhythm: original unity of beings, division, return to unity. Since the time of the Stoics this pattern, modified somewhat by diverse considerations, had been the substructure of every single vision of the universe. Whether passage from one to many was envisioned as an emanation or a creation, the general conception of things had always been dominated by the idea that the consummation of things was a return to unity with God, a veritable deification.

Eckhart advanced the view that the return to unity would be impossible, even senseless, if finite individual creatures remote from God were thought to be endowed with true reality in the same sense as the divine reality. His whole system of metaphysics is therefore summed up in this negation: "Individuality is a mere accident, nothing (*unum purum nihil*); eliminate this nothing and all creatures are one." What he means is that unification with God, which is the consummation of destiny, simultaneously discloses to us the reality of things. It is in this sense that his mysticism is a speculative mysticism and that his doctrine of destiny is at the same time a doctrine of being.

The unity of God is not destroyed if we conceive of things in the fullness of their diversity as the *manifestation* or *revelation* of a deeper unity. If a word expresses an inner thought, it unites with the thought that it expresses; and it is enough for the many to appear to us as such in order for us to deny their diversity and their independent being and to relate them to God from whom they issued. Thus as soon as I conceive of things as revelations of God I know that they issue from God.

Eckhart applies his method to the diversity of God as revealed in the Trinity. Many Augustinian views of the Trinity are appropriate: is not the Son the *Verbum,* the Word or Intelligence through which the Father is expressed? And is not the Spirit the bond of love that unites the Son and the Father? Basing his analogy on the triads (which he modeled after those in William of Moerbecke's translation of Proclus' *Elements of Theology*), however, above the Trinity he first posits divinity (*Gottheit*) as a non-participated unity, an "unnatured nature" that remains intact while underneath the three persons constitute the "natured nature." The first, the Father, corresponds to Proclus' participated unity, the absolute unity in which the known and the knower are identified; the Son expresses the thought of the Father; and the Spirit unites them.

The creation of the world, or the procession of created things outside God, is essentially no different from the generation of the Son by the Father, for the created world is nothing but an expression of God. Each thing has in God its eternal being, included in the Word: the Creation is a non-temporal act through which God expressed himself in his Son. And that is why, since Eckhart acknowledges no divine causality other than immanent causality, it is not permissible to conceive of the individual existence of each creature in a determinate time and space as the result of a positive act of God. It is wrong to say that at a certain moment God created heaven and earth, for the finite existence of things apart from God, the diversity that separates them, can only be viewed as nothingness and privation. Eckhart obviously clings tenaciously to the Plotinian and Augustinian theory of evil, which makes evil a simple privation and a defect associated with diversity.

But it is nothing less than the knowledge of the primitive unity of all creatures that brings the world back to the point of its origin. The soul has no other function than this knowledge. We would expect Eckhart willingly to accept the Aristotelian statement that "the soul is in some way all things" and that in the active intellect the object is identical to the subject. We would also expect him to accept the Neo-Platonic thesis that each hypostasis, soul as well as intellect, includes all things in its own way. That is the true basis of his theory of the soul, which cannot be considered (as it sometimes is) as the starting point of his doctrine, but instead, as in the case of Plotinus, as the outcome. The depth of the soul, what he calls the "spark of the soul" (*Funke*) or synderesis, is the place where every creature rediscovers its unity. Consequently, knowledge in the highest sense (suprarational knowledge of this unity or faith) is not the representation of things that would be and would remain external to it; such knowledge is rather a transmutation of things themselves in their return to God. We might say that it is the spiritual aspect of the universal conflagration in which certain Stoics already saw a purification rather than a material conflagration.

In Eckhart's Christianity, Christ, incarnate in Jesus, acts less as the redeemer of the sin of Adam than as a paragon, as the man in whom is consummated all that which the human soul endeavors to attain: the perfect union of God and his creature. Hardly a trace of the historical, judicial, and sacramental aspect of the Christian doctrine remains. The incarnation of Christ, which would have occurred even in the absence of Adam's sin, is not explained primarily on the basis of atoning for original sin. Christ is rather the guide for souls through whom the universe returns to God.

From Eckhart's thought the German mystics of the fourteenth century drew not so much a metaphysical theory as a guide to the cultivation of the inner life. John Tauler (1300–1361) and Henry Suso (1300–1365) were primarily preachers. The Flemish mystic John Ruysbroeck (1293–1381), Prior of the convent of Grünthal near Brussels, through his predilection for the allegorical interpretation of Scripture, brings to mind Philo's piety more often than Plotinus' talent for speculation. "The soul must understand God through God," he says in *The Adornment of the Spiritual Nuptials,* "but those who wish to know what God is and to study him should understand that this is prohibited. They would become insane. All created light must fail here; the quiddity of God transcends all creatures; one must believe the articles of faith and not try to penetrate them . . . that is true sobriety." [17]

His interesting statement reveals the profound intellectual cleavage which characterized the last part of the fourteenth century. Gone is the universe in which the world leads to God and reason is perfected by faith. These are two choices: nominalism, in which reason under the guidance of experience begins to become acquainted with the natural laws of things, and in which faith cannot be superadded to reason unless by an arbitrary decree or yield knowledge of God other than that of his absolute, unaccountable power; and mysticism, which goes directly to God without passing through nature and subsequently rediscovers nature only as something permeated by God and in some way reabsorbed in him. More serious, perhaps, is the fact that this cleavage reflected the contrast between two intellectual settings: the universities,[18] where a true intellectual aristocracy was coming into existence and where the methods of science were being elaborated, and the monasteries, where the spiritual life was much more closely linked to the spiritual life of the masses and included not only the speculations of the profound mystics but also vast popular movements that were more social than intellectual.

[17] Trans. Hello, p. 61.
[18] But not because there were no mystics in the universities (as A. Combes notes in *Jean Gerson*, p. 469); Gerson was Chancellor of the University of Paris from 1395 to 1429.

BIBLIOGRAPHY

I

Texts

Duns Scotus. *Opera omnia*. Edited by L. Wadding. 26 vols. Paris (Vivès), 1891–95.
———. *De primo principio*. Translated by E. Roche. St. Bonaventure, N.Y., 1949.
———. *Philosophical Writings*. Selections translated by A. Wolter. London, 1962.
———. *The Oxford Commentary on the Four Books of the Master of the Sentences*. I, III, 4. Translated by R. McKeon in *Selections*, II, 313–50.
Thomas Bradwardine. *De causa Dei adversus Pelagium et de virtute causarum ad suos Mertonenses Libri tres*. London, 1618.

Studies

Gilson, E. "Avicenne et le point de départ de Duns Scot," *Archives d'histoire doctrinale et littéraire du moyen âge,* II (1927).
———. *Jean Duns Scot*. Paris, 1952.
Grajewski, M. *The Formal Distinction of Duns Scotus*. Washington, D.C., 1944.
Heidegger, M. *Die Kategorien—und Bedeutungslehre des Duns Scotus*. Tübingen, 1916.
Laun, J. "Recherches sur Thomas de Bradwardin précurseur de Wiclif," *Revue d'Histoire et de philosophie religieuse* (Strasbourg), IX (1929), 217–33.
Moody, E. *The Medieval Science of Weight*. Madison, Wisc., 1952. Pp. 285–91 on Thomas Bradwardine.
Shircel, C. L. *The Univocity of the Concept of Being in the Philosophy of Duns Scotus*. Washington, D.C., 1942.
Wolter, A. *The Transcendentals and Their Function in the Metaphysics of Duns Scotus*. St. Bonaventure, N.Y., 1946.

IV

Texts

William of Ockham. *Super quatuor libros sententiarum subtilissimae quaestiones earumdemque decisiones.* Lyons, 1495.

———. *Quodlibeta septem. Paris,* 1487. Strasbourg, 1491.

———. *Breviloquium de potestate papae.* 1937.

———. Critical edition of Ockham's non-political works in 25 vols. is in
preparation by the Franciscan Institute, St. Bonaventure, N.Y. (Vol. I,
1956).

———. *Selected Quodibetal Questions.* Translated by R. McKeon, *Selections,*
II, 360–421.

———. *Ockham: Philosophical Writings.* Translated by Ph. Boehner. New
York, 1957.

Studies

Boehner, P. *Collected Articles on Ockham.* St. Bonaventure, N.Y., 1958.

Maurer, A. "Ockham's Conception of the Unity of Science," *Mediaeval
Studies,* XX (1958), 98–112.

Moody, E. *The Logic of William of Ockham.* New York, 1935.

Pegis, A. "Some Recent Interpretations of Ockham," *Speculum,* XXIII (1948),
458–63.

Pelzer, A. "Les 51 articles de Guillaume Occam censurés en Avignon, en
1326," *Revue d'histoire ecclésiastique,* XVIII (1922), 240–70.

Shapiro, H. *Motion, Time, and Place According to William Ockham.* St.
Bonaventure, N.Y., 1957.

Vignaux, P. "Nominalisme," *Dictionnaire de théologie catholique,* XI (1931),
733–84.

Webering, D. *Theory of Demonstration According to William Ockham.* St.
Bonaventure, N.Y., 1953.

II, III, V, VI

Texts

Albert of Saxony. *Quaestiones super octo physicorum libros.* Padua, 1493.
Venice, 1504 and 1516.

———. *Quaestiones in libros de caelo et mundo.* Pavia, 1481. Venice, 1520.

Durand of Saint Pourçain. *In Sententias commentariorum libri quatuor*
(third and last redaction of his commentary on Lombard's *Sentences*).
Paris, 1508. Fifteen editions were published during the sixteenth century.

———. *Quaestio de natura cogitationis.* Edited by Koch. Münster in Westfalen, 1929. 2d edition, 1935.

John Buridan. *Quaestiones super octo physicorum libros.* Paris, 1509 and 1516.

John of Jandun. *Quaestiones in XII libros metaphysicorum.* Venice, 1586.

John of Mirecourt. Condemned propositions are in Denifle, *Cartularium universitatis parisiensis.* Paris, 1891. Pp. 610–14.

Nicholas of Autrecourt. *Exigit ordo executionis.* Edited by J. O'Donnell. "Nicholas of Autrecourt," *Mediaeval Studies,* I (1939), 179–280.

Nicholas Oresme. "Maistre Nicole Oresme, le Livre du Ciel et du Monde, Text and Commentary," *Mediaeval Studies,* III (1941), 185–280; IV (1942), 159–297; V (1943), 167–333.

———. *De difformitate qualitatum* (unpublished, cf. P. Duhem, *Études sur Léonard de Vinci,* 3d series, Paris, 1913, p. 373).

Peter Auriol. *Commentariorum in I Sententiarum.* Rome, 1596.

———. *Commentariorum in II Sententiarum.* Rome, 1605.

———. *Peter Auroli Scriptum super primum Sententiarum.* Edited by E. Buytaert. St. Bonaventure, N.Y., 1953.

Peter of Ailly. *Quaestiones super primum, tertium et quartum Sententiarum.* Venice, 1478, 1490, 1500.

Studies

Borchert, E. *Der Einfluss des Nominalismus auf die Christologie der Spätscholastik nach dem Traktat "De communicatione idiomatum" des Nicolaus Oresme.* Münster in Westfalen, 1940.

Dreiling, E. *Der Konzeptualismus in der Universalienlehre des Petrus Aureoli. Beiträge,* Vol. XI. Münster in Westfalen, 1913.

Duhem, P. *Études sur Léonard de Vinci.* 2d series. Paris, 1909. Pp. 379–441. 3d series. Paris, 1913. Pp. 1–492.

Gilson, E. "La doctrine de la double vérité," *Études de philosophie médiévale.* Strasbourg, 1921. Pp. 51–75 on John of Jandun.

Koch, J. *Durandus de S. Porciano, O.P., Forschungen zum Streit um Thomas von Aquin zu Beginn des 14. Jahrhunderts; I Teil, Literargeschichtliche Grundlegung. (Beiträge,* 26, I.) Münster in Westfalen, 1927.

Michalski, C. "Le criticisme et le scepticisme dans la philosophie du XIVe siècle," *Bulletin de l'académie polonaise* (1925), pp. 41–122. Cracow, 1926.

O'Donnell. "The Philosophy of Nicholas of Autrecourt and His Appraisal of Aristotle," *Mediaeval Studies,* IV (1942), 97–125.

Vansteenberghe, E. "Un 'programme de vie' de la fin du moyen âge" and "Le 'De exercitato proficiencium' de Pierre d'Ailly," *Aus der Geisteswelt des Mittelalters, Festgabe M. Grabmann.* Münster in Westfalen, 1935. Pp. 1231–1246.

Weinberg, J. *Nicholas of Autrecourt: A Study in Fourteenth Century Thought.* Princeton, 1948.

VII

Texts

Cajetan. *Commentary on the Summa theologica of St. Thomas.* Printed in the Leonine edition of St. Thomas.

Gabriel Biel. *Epitome et collectorium ex Occamo super quatuor libros sententiarum.* Tübingen, 1512.

Johannes Capreolis. *Defensiones. Libri IV Defensionum theologiae divi Thomas de Aquino,* Book IV. 7 vols. Tours, 1889–1908.

Studies

Carré, M. *Realists and Nominalists.* New York, 1945.

Feckes, C. *Die Rechtfertigungslehre des Gabriel Biel und ihre Stellung innerhalb der nominalistische Schule.* Münster in Westfalen, 1925.

Gilson, E. "Cajétan et l'existence," *Tÿdschrift voor Philosophie,* XV (1953), 267–86.

Grabmann, M. "Johannes Capreolus, O.P., der Princeps Thomistarum," *Divus Thomas* (Fribourg [Switzerland]), XXII (1944), 85–109, 145–70.

Penido, T. "Cajétan et notre connaissance analogique de Dieu," *Revue Thomiste,* XVII (1934–35), 149–92.

Schwamm, H. *Magistri Johannis de Ripa O.F.M. doctrina de praescientia divina.* Rome, 1930.

VIII

Texts

Henry Suso. *Little Book of Eternal Wisdom: Little Book of Truth.* Translated by J. Clark. London, 1953.

John Gerson. *Opera omnia.* Edited by M. Ellies du Pin. 5 vols. Antwerp, 1706.

John Ruysbroeck. *The Adornment of the Spiritual Marriage. The Sparkling Stone. The Book of Supreme Truth.* Translated by C. Wynschenk. New York, 1916.

John Tauler. *Opera omnia.* Paris, 1623.

Meister Eckhart. *Sermons and tractates in Meister Eckhart.* Translated by C. deB. Evans. 2 vols. London, 1931.

———. *Talks of Instruction, The Book of Divine Comfort, The Aristocrat, About Disinterest and Sermons, in Meister Eckhard.* Translated by R. Blakney. New York, 1941.

Studies

Ancelot-Hustache, J. *Master Eckhart and the Rhineland Mystics*. Translated by Hilda Graef. New York, 1957.

Clark, J. *Meister Eckhart: An Introduction to the Study of His Works*. London, 1957.

———. *The Great German Mystics: Eckhart, Tauler, and Suso*. Oxford, 1949.

Combes, A. *John Gerson: Commentateur dionysien*. Paris, 1940.

———. *Jean de Montreuil et le Chancelier Gerson*. Paris, 1942.

Connolly, J. *John Gerson: Reformer and Mystic*. Louvain, 1928.

De Hornstein, X. *Les grands mystiques allemands du XIVe siècle: Eckhart, Tauler, Suso*. Lucerne, 1929.

Delacroix, H. *Le mysticisme spéculatif en Allemagne au XIVe siècle*. Paris, 1900.

Lavand, B. *L'œuvre mystique de Henri Suso*. 4 vols. Fribourg, Switzerland, 1946–47.

Muller-Thym. *The Establishment of the University of Being in the Doctrine of Meister Eckhart of Hochheim*. New York, 1939.

Wauthier D'Aygalliers, A. *Rusybroeck the Admirable*. Translated by F. Rothwell. London, 1925.

THE RENAISSANCE

DURING THE FIFTEENTH CENTURY there was a sharp contrast between the universities and the humanistic circles where laymen and clerics mingled freely under the protection of princes and popes: for instance, at the Platonic Academy in Lorenzo the Magnificent's Florence and at the Aldine Academy in Venice. In these new settings no practical consideration took precedence over the desire for knowledge for its own sake. Human minds, completely liberated, were no longer forced, as in the universities, to meet the need of providing training for clerics. The following century witnessed the founding of the College of France which, unlike the University of Paris, had as its aim the advancement of knowledge rather than the classification of accumulated and traditional materials.

The new freedom produced a multiplication of doctrines and thoughts which had been incubating throughout the Middle Ages but which had previously been repressed. This confused mixture might be called naturalism, for generally it subjected neither the universe nor human conduct to a transcendental rule, but simply sought to identify their immanent laws. It contained, alongside the most viable and fruitful ideas, the worst monstrosities; above all, it turned away from all that had been previously accomplished. "Laurentius Valla finds fault with Aristotle's physics," wrote Poggio, who was as much a humanist and Epicurean as was his friend. "He finds Boethius' Latin barbaric, destroys religion, professes heretical ideas, scorns the Bible. . . . And has he not taught that the Christian religion is based not on proofs but on belief which is superior to any proof!"[1] But Poggio was in the service of the Roman Curia, and as for Laurentius Valla, the Cardinal of Cusa recommended him to the pope in 1450 and wanted him to enter its service.

This intense desire for a new, different, dangerous life was provoked or at least accentuated by an enormous expansion in the possible range of experience and in technology.[2] In one century the whole pattern of the material and intellectual life of Europe had changed. Temporal expansion of the range of experience occurred when humanists (who took up the study of oriental languages in the sixteenth century) read the Greek and Latin texts. Less important than the discovery of new texts was the manner in which the old were read: Cicero's *De officiis* was the same text for both St. Ambrose and Erasmus, but St. Ambrose was seeking rules for his clerics whereas Erasmus found in it a moral philosophy, autonomous and independent of Christianity; and the emphasis was no longer on utilizing the ancient texts to explain Scripture, but on understanding the texts themselves. Spatial expansion of the range of experience occurred when explorers went beyond the confines of the οἰκονμέγα set by Christianity (following the Greeks) as the boundaries of the habitable earth, and discovered not only new lands that caused people to look beyond the Mediterranean, but also new human types, whose religion and customs were unfamiliar. Technological expansion was made possible not only by the compass, gunpowder, and printing, but also by industrial or mechanical inventions, several of which are to be credited to Italian artists who were at the same time artisans. The men of the fifteenth century, although bound by tradition, sensed that life that had long been in a state of suspension was stirring once again and that the destiny of mankind was recommencing. "Everywhere," wrote the Cardinal

---

[1] Quoted by H. Busson, *Les Sources et le développement du rationalisme,* p. 55.

[2] In *Un nouveau moyen âge* (1927), N. Berdiaeff is struck by the individualism of the Renaissance: "Man cannot endure the isolation into which the humanistic age has plunged him."

of Cusa around 1433, "we see the minds of men most devoted to the study of the liberal and mechanical arts turn back to antiquity, and with extreme avidity, as if the full cycle of a revolution were about to be completed." [3]

Men were naturally inclined to contrast with the new developments the traditional conceptions of man and life based on a much more limited range of experience. In spite of a vast number of divergences and diversities there was throughout the Middle Ages but one image, or rather one single frame into which could be fitted every possible image of the universe: the frame that we have called theocentrism. From God as the principle to God as the end and consummation, following the passage through finite beings— this formula could be made to fit the most orthodox of the *Summae* as well as the most heterodox of the mystics, for the order of nature and the order of human conduct take their place as if by necessity between the principle and the end.

Such a synthesis was possible only so long as men saw everything in the universe in relation to its origin or its end, all finite beings as creatures or manifestations of God, all finite spirits as being engaged in moving toward or away from God. But the concept of theocentrism was gradually abandoned: as early as the twelfth century humanistic naturalism emerged and focused attention on the study of the structure and forces of society; in the fourteenth century the Ockhamists, deliberately neglecting everything that related to the origin or end of things and even demonstrating the fallacy of believing that something of the divine plan could be apprehended in the contrast between the immutable heaven and the sublunary region, studied nature in and for itself. It was the next two centuries, however, that offered every reason for abandoning the concept of theocentrism. Strange mysterious depths in history and in nature, hardly suspected previously, now began to appear: philology on the one hand and experimental physics on the other yielded new data on man and the universe. The Christian drama with its historical moments—creation, sin, redemption—could no

---

[3] Quoted by Vansteenberghe, *Le Cardinal Nicolas de Cues*, p. 17.

longer circumscribe a nature whose laws were completely indifferent to it, a humanity one segment of which was totally ignorant of it, an era in which Christians themselves threw off the shackles of spiritual power and won acceptance in their politics of goals totally alien to the supernatural ends of the Christian life or even deliberately opposed to the idea of Christian unity.

Such a vital change entailed an infinite number of repercussions. The most important was that practical men, men of action, artists and artisans, technicians of every kind were brought to the foreground at the expense of meditative and speculative men. The new conception of man and nature was a conception that was realized rather than conceived, and the names of true philosophers, from Nicholas of Cusa to Campanella, are overshadowed by those of great captains and artists. Technique, no matter what sense is attributed to the word, was all that mattered. The consummate technician was Leonardo da Vinci, painter, engineer, mathematician, and physicist all in one: but there was hardly a philosopher who was not at the same time a doctor or at least an astrologer and an occultist. Machiavellian politics was a technique intended for the Italian princes. The humanists were thinkers, but before this they were practitioners of philology, concerned with the methods that would allow them to restore the forms and thoughts of the ancients.

Yet—and this is perhaps the great paradox of the era—the philosophers of the Renaissance, from Nicholas of Cusa to Campanella, took pains to organize their thought around the ancient design of the universe. The return to Platonism, as we observe it in many of these philosophers, far from leading them to new ideas, simply convinced them all the more that the great task of philosophy was to organize everything in the material world and in the world of the spirit in terms of God as the principle and God as the end. The contrast between this ancient scheme and the new philosophy of nature that they integrated into their system accounts for the extreme difficulty of their doctrine.

1 *The Diverse Currents of Thought*

In spite of the general confusion that marks the Renaissance, the foregoing considerations allow us to separate several fairly distinct philosophical currents, the first of which is the Platonic current. Platonism had been warmly received by the new religion since the early centuries of Christianity, and fifteenth-century Platonic humanists such as Marsilio Ficino still entertained a sincere hope of finding in Platonism a philosophical synthesis favorable to Christianity, thus unwittingly continuing the tradition of Chartres and of Abelard. The second current is that of the Averroists of the University of Padua: they followed a tradition uninterrupted from the time of Siger of Brabant and transmitted to Padua at the beginning of the fourteenth century by Peter of Abano. The tradition rests on an Aristotelian interpretation opposed to that of the Christian Peripatetics; it reveals a naturalistic Aristotle, an Aristotle who denies Providence and the immortality of the soul but proclaims a rigorous determinism; it is not to be linked to the dawn of modern science since the Paduan reactionaries upheld the spirit of Aristotle's physics. The third current is that of the true scholars whose model is neither Plato nor Aristotle but Archimedes, the man who first discovered how to join mathematics to experience; completely ignored during the Middle Ages, Archimedes brings us suddenly to a state of science much more advanced than anything that tradition could teach. A fourth current, which is no less original than the third and leads to no fixed, definite formula, is that of moralists who, like the scholar who studies nature independently of its origin and its end, set out to describe the natural man without taking into account his supernatural destiny. Their description of human nature is actually rooted deep in the ancient systems of moral philosophy, especially the Stoic.

It seems that Ockhamism enunciated the supposition implicit in the doctrines of each current (with the exception of the first) after the fourteenth century: nothing in nature can bring us to the objects of faith; faith is a sealed domain, one circumscribed and inaccessible except by virtue of a gracious gift of God. But was that not also the fundamental idea of the Reformation? Neither our intelligence nor our will can help us through natural means to lay the slightest basis for faith. The Reformation was equally opposed to both scholastic theology and humanism; it denied scholastic theology because it denied with Ockham that our rational faculties can lead us from nature to God; and it repudiated humanism less for its errors than for its dangers since natural forces can impart no religious meaning.

But the Reformation was as hostile as humanism to the theocentric conception of the universe and to all the moral and political theses associated with it. Both chose to ignore the synthesis of the natural and the divine, of the sensible world and its principle, along with all the consequences that had been imagined during the thirteenth century.

Thus there were two ways, each contrasting with the other, of trying to rediscover the intellectual unity destroyed by the apparently definitive cleavage between knowledge of nature and divine reality: by taking pains to organize an autonomous moral life that has nature as its standard, or by denying man the possibility of justifying himself other than through grace.

ii Platonism: Nicholas of Cusa (Nicolaus Cusanus)

The intestine struggle between the ancient theocentric scheme of the universe and the humanistic method stands out clearly in the greatest of the fifteenth-century thinkers, Cardinal Nicholas of Cusa (1401–1464). We find in his work a strange blend of Ockhamism, transmitted to him by his teachers in Heidelberg, and of Neo-Platonism, thoroughly assimilated through the reading not only of Dionysius the Areopagite but especially of the great works of Proclus: the *Elements of Theology,* the *Commentary on the Parmenides,* and *Platonic Theology.* In spite of his extremely imperfect knowledge of the Greek language, his direct and sustained contact with the roots of Platonism was of capital importance. The Neo-Platonism of the Arabs and even of Dionysius the Areopagite was totally different; totally different also was the Neo-Platonism of Plotinus and of Proclus. The first was concerned mainly with describing the hierarchy of beings, from the angels or intelligences to the lower spirits, in order to determine in some way the metaphysical position of each being. The second, much closer to Plato, notwithstanding their differences, sought to show how each degree in the scale of the hierarchy of living beings contains the fullness of reality but reveals it from a different angle: the One contains all things, as do Intelligence, Soul, and the sensible world, but each hypostasis contains it in its own way. In the One all things are indistinct; in Intelligence they interpenetrate, thanks to an intuitive vision that sees all things in each thing; in Soul they are no longer bound by anything but the bonds of discursive reason; in the world they remain external to each other, with the result that their difference can be expressed in terms of knowledge rather than in terms of being. The Neo-Platonist conceived the passage from one hypostasis to the next highest, less as the passage from one reality to the next than as the ever deepening, ever unifying vision of one and the same universe.

The Neo-Platonic idea, expressed in myriad ways in the *De docta ignorantia* (1440) and in the other works of the cardinal, was the very heart of his thought. He was searching for a method that would allow him to reach a higher plane for viewing the universe than that of reason or the senses: to see all things *intellectualiter* rather than *rationaliter* was his aim.

Take his conception of mathematics. Though it failed to produce good results in this sphere, his thought is nevertheless of interest because of its orientation. First let us recall briefly what mathematics meant to Aristotle: for him the geometrical characteristics of a natural being, such as the stature of man or the physical configuration of the sky, depended on the essence of this being; consequently geometry, the study of such configurations, could be nothing more than a science of abstract realities that do not have their causes within them. Mathematical reasoning linked the properties of forms, statically given by definition, to each other. Geometry had long occupied the inferior position that many Renaissance thinkers were disposed to accord to it. Fracastoro, for example, noted that mathematics, though certain, deals with objects that are too humble and too lowly, and his thought was echoed in the *Discourse on Method*. Nicholas of Cusa would have liked to see instituted, alongside visual mathematics as represented by the surveyor's art and rational mathematics as represented by Euclid, an "intellectual mathematics." It is what he picturesquely labeled the art of "geometric transmutations" (1450), which deals with problems that modern mathematicians call problems of limit: the coincidence of forms that the geometrician considers distinct. For example, we see intuitively that an arc of a circle coincides with the chord when the arc is minimum.

The coincidence of the arc and the chord is but one application of the general principle of the coincidence of opposites that accounts for intellectual knowledge of things; the principle of contradiction, on the other hand, accounts for rational knowledge. Intelligence sees the unity behind contraries that reason contrasts and declares mutually exclusive. Thus knowledge tends toward the irrational, that is, toward the intellectual as toward a limit; "learned ignorance" is the mental state of the man who, not satisfied with rational knowledge, knows how far he is from intellectual knowledge and tries to shorten the distance. The coincidence of opposites, as interpreted here, is but one aspect of the state of unity of all things in which the Platonists saw the explanation of being and of knowledge; but it is an aspect that can introduce a multiplicity of problems—as many concrete problems as there are pairs of opposites. Thus the curve coincides with the straight line, a state of rest with motion; "motion is merely seriate rest (*quies seriatim ordinata*)." [4] Condemned are all the great contrasts on which Aristotelian physics was based.

We need not dwell on the metaphysics of Nicholas of Cusa, which simply projects these diverse states of unities on the plane of reality. To what the Platonists called state of unity he applies the term

[4] *De docta ignorantia* ii. 3.

complicatio, and to what they called state of dispersion he applies the term *explicatio.* "God is all things" in the state of *complicatio,* and the world is all things in the state of *explicatio.* Both God and the universe constitute a maximum containing all possible being, but God is the absolute maximum, the *possest* in which all power (*posse*) has already attained to being (*est*). Here, however, maximum does not signify the greatest of beings, which would imply that it is being compared with finite beings. Furthermore, to conceive of the excess that makes it disproportionate to things, we must say that it is also the minimum, that is, that it is apart from any opposition. The universe is the maximum "contraction" or reduction in which reality, composite and discrete, passes from potency to act. Or again: "God is the absolute quiddity of the world; the universe is its contracted quiddity." In this maximum contraction, or the universe, Nicholas shows the *explicatio* in the process of becoming rather than as completed. Like Plotinus, in fact, in his physics he tries to show that everything is still contained in everything: for instance, the four elements do not exist in a pure state, as in Aristotle; they are mixed, and fire itself contains a blend of the three other elements.

Knowledge, through which diversity is reduced in the soul to unity, is the reverse of the notion of *explicatio.* In Nicholas' theory of knowledge there is a basic confusion, noted by several historians, which is highly instructive. Like Aristotle, he assumes that the soul is in some way all things in the state of complication and that the knowledge it produces little by little is the "explication" of whatever is in it. Since the *explicatio* is a state of expansion and multiplicity, it is in principle inferior to the *complicatio.* Inversely, however, knowledge, or the actuation of the powers of the soul, is an enrichment. It would seem that Nicholas of Cusa was vaguely aware that knowledge depends on two opposite motions, analysis and synthesis, but that he calls them both *explicatio.*

How is dogma affected by his Platonism? His mind seems always to be torn between the Ockhamist principle that sets the truths of faith above human apprehension and the Platonic theses that describe the divine reality itself. Take this statement: "Since the universe was created by the highest being, and since in the case of the highest being to be, to do, and to create are one and the same thing, the act of creation simply means that God is everything."[5] Is creation identifiable here as a free, positive act of the divine will? Nicholas of Cusa does not assume, like Plotinus, that there is a necessary principle that forces the multiple to emerge from the one. It is forever impossible "to understand how diverse creatures participate variously in one infinite form,"[6] and the hope of any emanative metaphysics is abandoned. Here again we see that his approach is modern in that he tries to extract from Neo-Platonism not so much a metaphysics to provide a general explanation of the universe as a method and a spirit to enable him to attack concrete and limited problems.[7]

III *Platonism*

At many points Nicholas of Cusa surpassed by far the other thinkers whose Platonism we are now going to examine. The cardinal, overwhelmed by his duties, could devote only a little time to philosophical meditation, and his ideas were often vague; but he went beyond the mere discovery of a method in Platonism. By way of contrast the objective of Platonists after Marsilio Ficino had been to focus attention on the religious or poetic content of the master's doctrines. They searched not only for points of agreement between Platonism and Christianity to prove, contrary to the Paduan Averroists, that philosophy was Christian, but also for the unifying force of a religion common to all mankind: one which appears somewhat obscurely in the traditions of all nations and of which Christianity is probably but a momentary aspect. This notion brought the human-

[5] *Ibid*. ii. 24.
[6] *Ibid*. ii. 25.
[7] Nicholas had a French disciple in the person of Charles de Bouëlles (Bovillus), professor of theology at Saint-Quentin and author of *De nihilo* (1510); discussed by M. de Gandillac in *Revue d'Histoire de la philosophie* (1943), p. 43.

istic Platonists into conflicts with the Reformation and also, eventually, with the Counter Reformation.

The significance of the conflict between Aristotelianism and Platonism initiated by Pletho's pamphlet against Aristotle (Florence, 1440) is obvious. Like Cardinal Bessarion and his supporters, he intended to use Plato as a defense against fatalism and the negation of the immortality of the soul. The works of Marsilio Ficino, who translated Plotinus (1492) and wrote a commentary on Plato (the *Theologia platonica de immortalitate animorum*), are to be interpreted in the same light. He saw his philosophical investigations as a necessary complement to religious preaching, which was powerless to destroy the impiety of Averroes. What was needed was "a philosophical religion which philosophers will gladly hear and which, perhaps, will persuade them. With a few changes, Platonists would be Christians." [8] Ficino found in Plato God the Creator as well as souls endowed with a personal existence, freedom, and immortality. He was not an original thinker, but he was a skilled translator and commentator, whose books (published in Paris during the sixteenth century) remained the source of information concerning Plato and Plotinus throughout the Renaissance.

We find a kindred attitude but a more fertile imagination in Pico della Mirandola (1463–1494), who in his *Heptaplus* took up once again the common practice of interpreting the Mosaic writings allegorically. In his *Heptaplus* he rediscovered the complicated and dazzling metaphysics of the Cabala and the Zohar. His work contained nothing that had not been familiar since Philo of Alexandria, but it was notable in that it once again linked allegory and the idea of a universal religion.

The whole phantasmagoria of the Cabala reappeared in the sixteenth century in the metaphysical constructions of the German mystics. In their world, as in the world of Plotinus, everything is a symbol, everything is in everything, and science consists in identifying degrees of affinity which, when known, also enable us to under-

---

[8] *Theologiae platonicae procemium*, p. iv; quoted by Busson, *Sources*, p. 174.

stand how things act on each other. Such is the aim of the physician Paracelsus (1493–1541), all of whose works are but the discovery of presumed correspondences of this type between the things of nature.

We need not dwell on these oddities but should note their diffusion in the German-speaking countries. Notwithstanding the protestations of Lutheran orthodoxy, Paracelsus and Meister Eckhart, both writing in German, became the leaders of these mystical societies in which were incubated the ideas finally translated into the popular works of Valentin Weigel (1533–1588) and later of Jacob Boehme (1575–1624), initiates who went beyond the letter of Scripture, attaining to the mysteries of the divine life. Later we shall examine the outcome of this movement.

At the end of this chapter we shall see how Platonic spiritualism produced veritable philosophical systems. Here let us note briefly how it is linked, diffusely and unsystematically, to Christian beliefs. Plato's Christianity was becoming a favorite tenet of the humanists. Erasmus, in his book *In Praise of Folly* (published in Paris in 1511 and eminently successful), was quite happy to record that both Christianity and Platonism agreed that the human soul is chained to the body and prevented by matter from contemplating truth, and that the sages "who deplore the folly of those who mistake shadows for realities" are in agreement with the pious "who are wholly inclined to the contemplation of invisible things" (chap. xlvi). This eclecticism developed in France all during the sixteenth century: Amaury Bouchard, "clerk-counselor in the king's hostel," wrote a treatise (*ca.* 1530) *"De l'excellence et immortalité de l'âme,* drawn not only from Plato's *Timaeus* but also from a number of other Greek and Latin philosophers, from members of both the Pythagorean and the Platonic families." In other words, the quotations attributed to Pythagoras, Linus, and Orpheus were borrowed from Ficino's *Theologia Platonica.*[9] The *Encyclie des secrets de l'éternité,* a poem in eight cantos written around 1570 by Fèvre de la Boderie, is typical of the apologies of Christianity addressed "to

[9] Busson, *ibid.,* pp. 174–75

libertines and to those who have gone astray" and linked to Platonism: the immortal soul (the *Phaedrus*), the soul separated from the body and in possession of innate ideas (the *Phaedo*), and proof of the existence of God by virtue of the fact that the soul attains to Eternity. In the words of the poet:

> *Et puisqu'elle attaint bien jusqu' à l'Éternité,*
> *Il te faut confesser une Divinité:*
> *Car s'il n'en estoit point, ton âme tant isnelle*
> *Ne pourroit concevoir une Essence éternelle. . . .*

Here we have the elements of a Christian Platonism, the very elements that Descartes utilized seventy years later.[10]

One particular aspect of the influence of Plato compels attention, and this is the diffusion throughout literary and philosophical circles of the ideas on love found in the *Phaedrus* and in the *Symposium*: Platonic love (ἔρως) is quite different from the love of God (*caritas*), which according to the Gospel is the supreme virtue. The latter, whether it is considered by the Thomists as basically identical to the love of self or by the Victorines and the Franciscans as pure, disinterested love free from any attachment to natural impulses, is in either case an end.[11] Platonic love, the offspring of Resourcefulness and Poverty, is always a deficiency, a desire forever unsatisfied and deprived of the beauty that it seeks, a perpetual state of uneasiness. This doctrine expressed in the *Symposium* appears in books that were prevalent toward the middle of the sixteenth century. In *The Courtier* (1528), Baldassare Castiglione described all the stages through which love ascends from lower to higher beauties. But it was especially León Hebreo who, in his *Dialoghi di Amore* (1535), maintained that love and desire often coincide, that love is already expressed in the sublunary world by the desire for procreation, even though it is but an enfeebled image of the love that reigns in the

---

[10] Busson, *ibid.*, pp. 600–601.
[11] Cf. Rousselot, in *Beiträge zur Geschichte der Philosophie des Mittelalters*, Vol. VI.

world of intelligences.[12] In his *Solitaire premier* (1552), Pontus de Tyard, who translated León Hebreo's work into French, introduced the theory of amorous folly outlined in the *Phaedrus* and drew a parallel between the folly of love, or "the fervent desire of the soul to enjoy divine and eternal beauty," and prophetic and poetic inspiration. Finally, in his *Odes* (I, x) Ronsard followed Pontus de Tyard and asserted that "poetry comes from God, not from the resources of man." Thus love is no longer the end of a higher life but its starting point and its driving force.[13]

IV *The Paduans: Pomponazzi*

The University of Padua, dependent after 1405 on the Most Serene Republic of Venice which named and discharged masters without the intervention of the Church, remained a stronghold of intellectual freedom during the fifteenth and sixteenth centuries. The Inquisition itself and later the Jesuits who founded a college there saw their power annulled by the Venetian senate: there the secular state became the protector of philosophers.[14]

The most famous of the Paduan masters was Pomponazzi (1462–1525), who raised the following question: assuming that we possess no divine revelation, what idea are we to formulate concerning man and his place in the universe? He found an answer to his question in Aristotle and his commentators. In his *De immortalitate animae* (1516) he not only demonstrates that the intellectual soul, inseparable from the sensitive soul (since it cannot think without images), must be mortal like the body, but he also draws practical conclusions from his demonstration (chaps. xiii–xvi): man has no supernatural end and must take as his end humanity itself and his daily tasks; he must find in the love of virtue and the ignominy of evil a sufficient motive for action; he must know that it is "the legislator who, know-

---

[12] Cf. H. Pflaum, *Die Idee der Liebe Leone Ebreo* (1926), which nevertheless shows in detail (pp. 112–13) the influence of St. Bonaventure.

[13] Busson, *Sources,* pp. 399–400.

[14] Cf. R. Charbonnel, *La pensée italienne au XVIe siècle,* pp. 258–59.

ing man's penchant for evil and considering the common good, has decided that the soul is immortal, not through his concern for truth, but through his propriety and his desire to lead men to virtue."

Here is something not found in Siger of Brabant: a positive conception of human life not linked to supernatural destiny. The Stoic overtones are unmistakable, and we find the same Stoic inspiration in the *De fato, libero arbitrio et de praedestinatione,* written in 1520. The brunt of Pomponazzi's attack is leveled against attempts to bring about the reconciliation of free will, fate, and providence: "If we posit providence, we posit fate and destroy free will; if we posit free will, we destroy providence and fate." In his affirmation of the identity of providence and fate we recognize the Stoic spirit, and at the end of the book we find once again the complete Stoic theodicy (which is also that of Plotinus): all evils are justified because they fit into the plan of the universe, evil is inseparable from good, and the cycle of fortune metes out diverse fates to men. His is a conception of fate that bears no resemblance to the theory of scientific determinism in which facts determine facts; it is still the Stoic conception of the universe in which parts are defined by their relation to the whole.

Pomponazzi elaborated the consequences of his naturalistic conception of the universe in his *De naturalium effectuum admirandorum causis seu de incantationibus liber,* published in 1556. The theory of miracles that he expounds certainly owes more to the Stoic and Plotinian doctrine of the universe than to a true sense of scientific determinism. He is not willing simply to counter miracles by citing the postulate of scientific determinism. He acknowledges (as Plotinus does) that miraculous facts are exceptional facts pertaining to the establishment of religions, for example, and "do not conform to the common course of nature." Though they are still natural facts, they are to be explained by going beyond the depth ordinarily attained in the study of nature: one must learn about the occult powers of herbs, stones, and minerals, as Pliny the Elder described them; one must identify the sympathy that binds man the microcosm to the diverse parts of the world and subjects him to distant influences;[15] finally, one must know the power of the imagination, which is capable through suggestion of producing cures. The treatise as a whole was written for the purpose of substituting astrology for demonology: it represented a great step forward, though the advancement was social rather than speculative since it eliminated any pretext for witchcraft trials.

Even while proclaiming himself a faithful believer, Pomponazzi was disseminating a concept of man and the universe independent of dogma. Still, it should be noted that his view was alien to experience and to the positive sciences, and that it was based on very ancient conceptions of the universe. Indeed, the Aristotelians of Padua were far removed from the current that runs from Buridan to Kepler, Galileo, and Descartes: throughout the sixteenth century Italian Peripateticism countered the new dynamic with Aristotle's absurd theory of the motion of projectiles.[16]

It is obvious that Pomponazzi's conception of the universe owed more to Stoicism and Plotinus than to Aristotle. The famous discussions that took place between Alexandrians and Averroists, that is, between those who pretended to follow Alexander of Aphrodisias and those who pretended to follow Averroes in the interpretation of the Aristotelian theory of intelligence, did not penetrate to the heart of the matter. The Alexandrians (like Pomponazzi) held that the soul was mortal because the possible intellect on which the agent intellect acts was nothing but an arrangement of man's organs favoring such action; the Averroists held that the possible intellect, like the agent intellect, was eternal but also impersonal and conferred upon the human soul, to the extent that it participated in intellectual knowledge, an impersonal immortality. One of the most famous Averroists was Nifo, who took issue with Pomponazzi in his *De immortalitate* (1518), and whom Leo X encouraged in his struggle against Alexandrianism,[17] considered even more dangerous than

---

[15] Compare Plotinus *Enneads* iv. 4. 36–42.

[16] Cf. Duhem, *Bulletin italien* (1909).

[17] Charbonnel, *La pensée italienne au XVI° siècle*, p. 229.

Averroism. We should note that what was presumed to be the doctrine of Alexander of Aphrodisias actually reproduced the teaching of Aristocles, one of Alexander's masters, who was steeped in the Stoic doctrine: thus Stoicism reappeared once more in the interpretation of Aristotle. But we should also note that the debate implied that no progress had been made beyond a conception of the mechanism of intellectual knowledge, long since abandoned by the Ockhamists.

v *The Development of Averroism*

Geronimo Cardano (1501–1576), who studied in Pavia, then in Padua until 1525, and who achieved fame as a physician, was representative of Paduan naturalism: a Stoic and Plotinian conception of the world (Plotinus' theory of the world, isolated from his theory of hypostases, is very close to Stoicism) quite favorable to occultism and astrology. This incorrigible Bohemian, of whom Leibnitz said that "he was a great man in spite of all his faults and without them would have been incomparable," [18] stated in his confessions (*De vita propria*) that he was among other things "a disparager of religion, vindictive, envious, melancholic, hypocritical, perfidious, and a magician." His history of religions is indeed singular; in view of the grandeur and the decadence of religions and their distribution in diverse climates, he relates them to the influence of the conjunctions of the stars and matches their history with the great cosmic periods; he draws up the horoscope of Christ, born under the conjunction of Jupiter and the Sun, and relates the Judaic law to Saturn.[19] In his world, which is animated by a unique soul activated by heat and embracing all individual souls and in which all beings are living even though they may appear to be insensible, magical influences are propagated at will by those who know how to win control over them. His conception of the soul, sometimes called a

[18] *Théodicée*, sec. 251.
[19] Cf. Bayle, *Dictionnaire*, art. Cardan, *Remarque* P.

universal spirit, inclines Cardano to accept Averroism and to reject immortality.

The Paduan movement in Italy came to an end with Cremonini (1550–1631). A professor in Padua, he was brought to trial before a Roman court in 1611 and again in 1613. The doctrinal points that he was accused of having upheld in his *De caelo* are characteristic of Paduan Aristotelianism: the eternity and necessity of the heavens, which led him to deny creation; the close link between the soul and the body, which made him deny immortality; and the action of God as a simple final cause, which was not in keeping with the divine personality and divine providence. What impressed his contemporaries most was the fact that his propositions endangered Christian beliefs. It should also be noted that with the appearance of Copernicus, Kepler, and Galileo, Aristotle's concept of the eternal motion and finality of the heavenly bodies became nothing but an outmoded encumbrance. The Platonists, in contrast to the Paduans, were concerned with scientific progress.

It is therefore necessary to make a distinction in Paduan thought between trite obsolete formulations of dogma and moral and religious criticism whose influence was profound, especially in France. Because not translated into any rigid philosophical doctrine, such unhampered thought and criticism infiltrated literature and poetry in countless ways and became the hallmark of so-called libertines. There were many intellectual ties between France and Italy around 1540.[20] Calvin was well acquainted with the Italians and distrusted them. They are the ones, he wrote in 1539, who said "that religion was invented in ancient times by a few astute, subtle minds for the purpose of restraining the ignorant populace."[21] From 1542 to 1567 Vicomercato, at the request of Francis I, taught Averroism at the College of France. In France he had students like Jean Fernel who in the *De abditis rerum causis* (1548) sketched the portrait of a confirmed Alexandrian whom he calls Brutus.

[20] Busson, *Sources,* first part of Book I, chaps. iv and v.
[21] *Institution chrétienne,* ed. Lefranc, I, 5.

VI *The Scientific Movement: Leonardo da Vinci*

"A lie is so vile," wrote Leonardo da Vinci (1452–1519), "that even if it spoke well of divine things, it would detract from their charm; truth is of such excellence that it lends its nobility to the meanest things that it praises. Truth, even if it has to do with insignificant and inferior things, is infinitely superior to uncertain opinions concerning the most sublime and exalted problems. . . . But you who live on dreams, you find your pleasure in the sophisms concerning revealed, uncertain things rather than in certain, natural conclusions that do not rise to such heights." His opinion was diametrically opposed to that of the Paduans; Pomponazzi had stated that the nobility of a science derived from the nobility of its object rather than from the certainty of demonstration. Let us examine all the implications of this. In the centuries whose history we have been studying, the good was identified with God himself; the means of attaining to "truth," then, was either divine revelation through the Word, or reason; but truth itself was always beyond the means at the disposal of the human mind. If, on the contrary, truth is defined through certain, natural conclusions, it is for this very reason proportionate to the resources of the human mind; it can be defined without reference to a transcendent, external reality. But it is also true, and for the same reason, that truth is not revealed as a systematic and total vision of the universe (whether the vision is due to revelation, to reason, or to both revelation and reason), but is in some way dismembered into a multitude of propositions linked not by the unique truth that they express but by the method through which their certainty has been acquired.

As a scholar, Leonardo, though he did not accept the results of the dynamics of the Ockhamists, was nevertheless among the ranks of those who propagated its spirit. Criticizing the spider webs of the syllogism and looking upon alchemists and astrologers as "charlatans or fools," he allied himself with those who, like Tartaglia and Galileo, placed above all else the works of Archimedes and took up the questions of dynamics at the point where he left them. As a typical Italian of the Renaissance, however, Leonardo was a dynamist: in motion he sought the spiritual mover; in the human body he sought the action of a soul that has realized in the body its idea of the human form; and in the spirit, desire "which, with joyful impatience, always awaits the new spring, always the new summer . . . and this same desire is the inseparable quintessence of nature." Still, there is obviously a vast difference between this desire, an effusive production of forms that are forever changing, and the ancient Aristotelian form that imposes on things an order that is static and, to the degree that matter permits, eternal.

VII *Pyrrhonism: Montaigne*

It would be impossible to overemphasize the importance of the thinkers who looked with scorn on all systems, who spoke as men to other men and not as masters to their disciples, and who in the study of the human mind provided us with an example of sincerity like that provided by such men as Leonardo in the study of nature.

There were of course outspoken critics, freethinkers like Bonaventure des Périers, who in his *Cymbalum mundi* (1537), written in the style of Lucian, ridiculed the Gospel and its miracles.

We also find throughout the sixteenth century a current of Pyrrhonism and Skepticism which did not run counter to religion, which was often even in agreement with it, but which was directed against philosophy and the sciences. In his treatise *On the Uncertainty and Vanity of the Sciences and the Arts* (1527), Agrippa von Nettesheim recalled the old diatribes of the late Middle Ages against dialectic: the sciences (and by this he meant mathematics as well as the arts of divination, horsemanship, and the like) are uncertain and useless since religion alone shows us the road to happiness. Omer Talon, the author of the *Academia* (1548), stated that Aristotle was "the father of atheists and fanatics,"[22] and that by attacking him, he was attacking "the philosophy of the pagans and the

[22] Quoted by Busson, *Sources,* p. 287.

heathen." Thus Pyrrhonism, ridiculed by Rabelais (who borrowed
the formulations of Sextus Empiricus), is no way anti-Christian.[23]
Omer Talon viewed it not as a criticism of faith but as true philosophy "which has complete freedom in the appreciation and judgment that it brings to bear on things and is not chained to an
opinion or to an author." On basic points his book follows Cicero's
Academica.

Rabelais and Montaigne surpassed by far the authors of such
incidental writings. They were the creators of matchless literary
forms in which thought, liberated from the dialectical mold, penetrated to things and men. Though these moralists had hardly any
contact with the scientific movement of their time, they developed
a scrupulous intellectual integrity which was not easily compromised.
Rabelais' lucid raillery spared neither the debaters in the universities,
nor the workers of miracles, nor the authors of false decretals. Repudiating any theoretical construction, Montaigne strove to find in
himself and others the true nature of man, to view man in his intellectual and moral nakedness, apart from the deceptive appearances imparted to him by pretentious doctrines that define him
through his relation to the universe and to God.

In a passage from the *Apology for Raymond Sebond* (1580)
Montaigne drew up the balance sheet for science in his century:
"The heavens and the stars have been in motion for three thousand
years; everybody believed this to be true until about eighteen hundred years ago, when someone took it upon himself to maintain that
it was the earth that moved . . . and in our own time Copernicus
has established the doctrine so firmly that it is regularly applied to
all astrological consequences. . . . Before the principles of matter,
form, and privation introduced by Aristotle had won acceptance,
other principles found favor with human reason. . . . What cre-
dentials do the latter possess, what particular privilege causes the
course of our invention to end with them? . . . How long is it
that medicine has been in the world? It is said that a newcomer
named Paracelsus is changing and reversing the whole order of

---

[23] *Tiers livre de Pantagruel* (1546), chap. xxix.

the ancient rules. . . . And I have been told that in geometry (which is thought to have gained the highest point of certainty among the sciences) there are inevitable demonstrations that are subverting the truth of experience. For example, Jaques Peletier told me at my house that he had found two lines moving toward each other but had nevertheless verified that they could never touch each other even if extended to infinity. . . . A thousand years ago, anyone who cast doubt on the science of cosmography and universally accepted opinions would have been guilty of Pyrrhonism; to believe in antipodes was heresy. In our own century an infinite expanse of solid earth has just been discovered" (*Essais* ii. 12). No passage indicates more clearly that reflective men of the late sixteenth century were deeply conscious of the fragility of the medieval vision of the universe. The abandonment of geocentrism and criticism of the principles established by Aristotle, innovations in medicine, the discovery of asymptotes, the discovery of America—all were facts that showed, contrary to what had been believed, that reason could not attain to fixed and immutable principles on which might be founded a definitive science: mathematics, astronomy, medicine, philosophy, everything was at that moment undergoing change.

Was the old, ineffectual science to be replaced by another science, a definitive science? Montaigne was by no means convinced that it was: "Who knows," he said in speaking of Ptolemy and Copernicus, "but that a third opinion, a thousand years from now, may overturn the first two?" And in spite of Columbus' discovery, "the geographers of our day" are wrong "in assuring us that now everything has been discovered and seen." Change is not a provisional state; it is the continuous state of the human mind. But Pyrrhonism was not indifference and inertia either: dogmatism was inert; skepticism was an investigation, an unlimited inquiry conducted by an almost insatiable mind. Montaigne was not, like Omer Talon, an academician; he did not share in the "ordinary, bland opinion . . . introduced by docile people . . . that our self-sufficiency can lead us to the cognizance of other things, and that it has certain limitations beyond which it is foolhardy to put it to use." His skepticism could not accommodate the imposition of fixed boundaries on the human mind: "it is hard to ascribe bounds to our mind, for it is curious and avid. . . . Having proven through experience . . . that the sciences and the arts are not rigidly cast but evolve and take shape gradually as they are repeatedly wielded and polished, I do not cease probing and searching for whatever my strength cannot discover; and by re-examining and shaping the new matter, I provide my successor with some facility for deriving from it still more pleasure; so long as he does the same thing for a third person, my difficulty ought not to make me despair, nor should my lack of strength, for it is only my own."

The science that he repudiated was that which supposedly started from fixed principles. Concerning such a science he said: "If a man admits his ignorance of first causes and principles, let him not boldly unburden on me all the rest of his science; if the foundation is missing, his words are barren." Montaigne's criticism is not directed toward the positive results of the sciences but toward their presumed principles and the self-sufficiency of those who "proceed at a pace too imperiously magistral" (iii. 8).

The fact is that Montaigne's universe, if we can call it that, is just as diverse and varied as the traditional image of the world bequeathed by antiquity was unified and monotonous: nothing remains of the universal analogy that dominated the ancient conception of things. "The world is but variety and dissemblance" (ii. 2). "No quality is so universal in this image of things as diversity and variety. . . . Resemblance does not create oneness to the degree that difference creates otherness" (iii. 13). But this diversity must not be stated too categorically: experience shows that there are in the new Indies, among "nations who have never heard of us," customs and beliefs strikingly similar to those of the Christian nations (ii. 12). Is there then a common natural source? Certainly not! For here we are dealing with beliefs which, no matter how we approach them, "do not seem to belong to our natural discourse." Such resemblances are more astounding than reassuring: "The human mind is a great worker of miracles."

No unique, permanent nature at the heart of things. Human nature which the Stoics recommended that we follow is nothing that can be known; of course "it is reasonable to believe that there are some natural laws, as is seen in other creatures; but they are no longer to be found in us, for human reason boldly interferes in everything, dominating, commanding, muddling, and confounding the appearance of things in keeping with its vanity and inconstancy" (ii. 12).

Under such conditions, the doctrinal learning of men who are scholars by profession draws its rigidity not from knowledge of nature but from those who seek through it "to establish their fundamental self-sufficiency and worth." This does not prevent it from being "in its true usage the noblest and most powerful acquisition of men . . . a thing of very noble and very precious usage, which is not to be possessed at a mean price" (iii. 8). And this is probably Montaigne's authentic discovery: science by itself does not cause man to penetrate into a region that is divine and superior to mankind; it draws its value not from its object but from its usage; of little worth is the boasting of a surgeon who recounts his cures "unless he knows how to draw from his treatment something to shape his judgment." The worth of science derives from the worth of the man who dominates it and puts it to use. That is why Montaigne has for his perpetual subject, man—not evasive universal nature or man saved by the grace of God, but man as he finds him, "bereft of outside help, armed solely with his own arms and stripped of divine cognizance and grace" (ii. 12). Hence the undertaking of the *Essais,* whose methodical character becomes more definite as he writes: "I dare not only to speak of myself, but to speak only of myself" (iii. 8). "It is a thorny undertaking, more so than it would seem, to follow such a vagabond course as that of our mind, to penetrate the dark depths of its inner recesses, to choose and apprehend so many fleeting motions created by its agitations. . . . For several years I have been directing my thoughts only toward myself, examining and studying only myself; and if I study something, it is for the purpose of applying it to myself, or to put it more aptly, in myself. . . . No description compares in difficulty to the description of one's self, or surely in utility" (ii. 6). The object is neither to fall back upon what are presumed to be rational principles and to harden one's self against experience, nor to let one's self be borne along willy-nilly by universal change. Here, too, one must "choose and apprehend," and this involves not an intellect linked to a divine world but sincere, attentive, and prolonged self-examination.

The same active skepticism was put forward less brilliantly by the doctor Francisco Sanchez in his *Quod nihil scitur* (1581). By way of contrast, however, this breviary of skepticism in which he draws together the arguments against the existence of a perfect and complete science (things are so interlinked that complete knowledge of one of them would imply complete knowledge of the whole that is inaccessible to us) contains positive advice on how to know all that is accessible to man: "One must not turn to men and their writings, which is to forsake nature, but one must above all else make contact with things through experience."[24]

VIII *Moralists and Political Thinkers*

The conditions of development of the intellectual life brought about a rebirth of Stoicism in the sixteenth century. The ancient authors who were read most assiduously, Cicero, Seneca, and even Plutarch, were imbued with popular Stoicism of the type concerned more with moral guidance than with the exposition of a rational philosophical doctrine. Still, we can hardly speak of a rebirth since a nucleus of Stoic ideas, though somewhat neglected, had never disappeared during the whole medieval period. We need only recall the Stoicism of St. Ambrose, which preserved as the appropriate end a life of virtuous harmony between nature and self,[25] and the

[24] Quoted by G. Sortais, *La philosophie moderne*, p. 40.
[25] *De officiis* i. 135; i. 85.

extent to which handbooks of moral guidance such as those of Alcuin,[26] Hildebert of Lavardin,[27] and many others followed Seneca and Cicero in their definitions of virtues and vices and in their conception of honesty. Roger Bacon's moral philosophy was inspired from start to finish by Seneca. The moral philosophy of the Stoics could be put in juxtaposition with the truly Christian life, but Christianity could never absorb or supplant it; the Stoics of the Renaissance were conscious of the independence of their ethic even though they were not hostile to Christianity; indeed, their Neo-Stoicism represented a concerted attempt to reconcile the Stoic doctrine with the Christian life. Not without protestations, however, on the part of men like Calvin, who ardently defended the Christian doctrine against the reproach of Stoicism; he viewed with horror the confusion "maliciously" created by his enemies between predestination and Stoic "fate," the latter being "a necessity contained in nature by virtue of a perpetual conjunction of all things"; and there is a vast difference between the Christian who carries the Cross and the Stoic sage who seems "to be indifferent to everything and insensitive to pain." [28]

It was nonetheless true that in the second half of the sixteenth century especially, many men showed a predilection for the ethical works of Cicero and Marcus Aurelius, and an even larger number for the works of Seneca and Epictetus; all of their works were translated into French, studied, annotated, and imitated. These works, proceeding through metaphors and precepts which are impressed on the mind through a kind of immediate necessity, without demonstrations, and which satisfy a need for comfort or consolation, met with unprecedented success. They train the mind to discriminate between the supernatural end of our actions that can be known only through revelation and the effective guidance of our conduct. "M. T. Cicero and the other pagan Philosophers may have erred by mis-

---

[26] Migne, *Patrologia Latina,* CI, 613 ff.
[27] *Ibid.,* CLXXI, 1007.
[28] *Institution chrétienne,* I, viii, xvi; III, viii, ix.

interpreting the end of good works, but Christians can still learn from them and acquire from them profitable doctrines." [29]

But it was the complete Stoic doctrine, including metaphysics, that Justus Lipsius, the scholar from Louvain, took pains to disseminate. The excellent short works (*Manuductio ad Stoicam philosophiam* [1603] and *Physiologia Stoicorum*) in which he drew together and classified all that could be known in his time (mainly through Seneca, about the Stoics), were preceded by a preface in which the author was careful to warn us "that no one should follow the Stoics in seeking the ultimate good or happiness in nature unless nature is understood as God himself." We can say that it was thanks to Seneca's inspiration that he was able to deny everything in Stoicism that could shock the Christian mind: for instance, Seneca says that fate is but the will of God himself and that God is free "since he is himself his own necessity."

In the life and works of Guillaume Du Vair (1556–1621) we see fully the practical significance of Neo-Stoicism. Coming from a family of magistrates, he was at first under strong suspicion at the League, but with the arrival of Henry IV he became clerk-counselor of the *parlement* of Paris, and later first president of the *parlement* of Aix. His Stoicism, contrary to what seems to have been frequently true during this period, was not that of a submissive man who draws from his readings only the strength to accept the inevitable. He was ready for action (and this is the soul of Stoicism, the Stoicism of Epictetus). At the risk of his life he supported the cause of the legitimate king in his *Traité de la Constance et Consolation ès Calamitez publique,* written in 1590 during the siege of Paris by Henry of Navarre. The treatise was inspired by his desire to "serve his country," to cure France of all her ills—the luxury of the nobility, the simony of the Church, the perversion of justice.

Neo-Stoicism born of the desire for moral guidance was quite different (and here we find what might be called a paradox of history)

---

[29] Preface to *Les Offices de M. T. Cicéron,* trans. Belleforest (1583); quoted by Mlle Zanta, *La Renaissance du stoïcisme au XVIe siècle,* p. 131 (on translations, cf. all of chap. iii of the second part).

from the Stoic naturalism that nourished the minds of freethinkers such as the Paduans or the Platonists of the late Renaissance. The sentiment of spirituality that permeates the thinking of the Stoics whom we have been discussing is not linked to any particular conception of the universe; it concerns only the conscience of man and, far from being linked to any pantheistic vision of the world, readily blends with the Platonic spirituality whose role we have already indicated. It is interesting to note that Du Vair's *Constance* ends with the words spoken on his deathbed by de Thou, president of the *parlement* of Paris, concerning self-knowledge: "Discourse is necessary for knowing things whose forms are immersed in matter . . . but to try to understand the nature of our soul in this manner is to avoid learning anything about it. For as it is, it must enter the intellect naked and take up all the room; anything accessory thwarts it. . . . And for this reason the true means of acquiring knowledge of the nature of the soul is to raise it above the body and draw it back completely into one's self, so that self-reflection will lead to self-consciousness." [30] By asserting the independence of the self, such Stoicism borders on spiritualism, which asserts the autonomy of the mind with respect to the knowledge it has of itself.

Stoicism is responsible for the preservation of the tendency, even among the moralists who were not Stoics in the strict sense, to identify the source of our ills with defective judgment which it is up to us to reform. This idea from Epictetus, which we find expressed so perfectly in Du Vair ("for our will has the power to adjust our opinion in such a manner that it will give its assent only to that which is right . . . adhere to things that are manifestly true, forbear and delay in the case of doubtful things, and reject whatever is false"), is also at the heart of Pierre Charron's *Sagesse* (1603), notwithstanding the strength of Montaigne's influence on the book. [31] If Charron refrains from attributing to the word "wisdom" the "lofty and bombastic meaning of the theologians and philosophers who take pleasure in describing and depicting things that have not

[30] Ed. Flach, p. 221.
[31] *La Philosophie morale des Stoïques,* quoted by Zanta, p. 293.

yet been seen and elevating them to such a high degree of perfection that human nature is incapable of reaching them other than through the imagination" (Preface), it is nonetheless true that he requires as the conditions of wisdom "liberation from the errors and vices of the world and the passions," and "complete intellectual freedom with respect to judgment as well as will." [32] All this is pure Epictetus. We should add that his concept of freedom entails the precept "to obey and observe the laws, customs, and ceremonies of the land."

It follows that the moralist is inclined to study man as he is instead of trying to find some transcendent principle for his conduct. According to Charron, self-knowledge or knowledge of human foibles is an important element of wisdom, and the task of the moralist is therefore to depict passions and their causes.

Contemporaneously with humanistic moral philosophy there arose a realistic politics which rejected everything concerning the divine right of princes and contracts between princes and their subjects, which refused to see in society anything more than the play of human forces and the collision of passions. The prime example of the new politics is *The Prince,* the famous work by Niccolo Machiavelli (1469–1527), who gives us the fruits of the experience he acquired as a diplomatic agent of the Florentine Republic. Here are the aphorisms that justify the means through which the prince consolidated his authority: "The common people take delight in evil; a multitude without a leader is worthless." [33] Whether he is a prince by the will of the people who wish to use him against the powerful, or by the grace of the powerful, he must make everyone yield to his authority. The prince is not a legislator but a warrior: "war, its institutions, and its discipline are the only object to which the prince ought to give his thoughts and his application and which he ought to make his profession; for war is the true profession of one who governs." [34] Consequently a prince ought not to worry over

[32] Book II, chaps. i and ii.
[33] *Histoire,* II, 34; *Discours,* I, 44.
[34] *Prince,* chap. xiv, trans. in F. Franzoni, *La Pensée de N. Machiavel,* p. 173.

the charge of cruelty when he is exacting obedience from his subjects. True clemency consists in setting a few examples of harshness rather than in allowing the initiation of disturbances that will overturn the whole social order. Nor is the prince obliged to keep his word if such fidelity is hurtful. Here everything depends on the circumstances: a prince "must know how at the right moment to act like a beast or like a man"; he acts like a man when he fights with laws, but this way of fighting is not sufficient, and he must often act "like a beast"—that is, he must use violence.

Lessons in realism are indeed what men of the Renaissance found in Machiavelli, and a century later Francis Bacon could write: "We must thank Machiavelli and writers like him who say openly and without dissimulation what men are accustomed to do, not what they ought to do." [35]

It is the problem of the prince that Machiavelli poses at the beginning of the sixteenth century in Italy; it is the problem of the tyrant that Étienne de la Boétie (1530–1563) poses in his *Discours de la servitude volontaire,* which he wrote, according to his friend Montaigne, "not yet having attained the age of eighteen, in honor of liberty and against tyrants." How can an infinite number of persons allow themselves to be tyranized by one man? It is Machiavelli's problem, considered this time not from the viewpoint of the prince but from the viewpoint of the common people. The tyrant could do nothing if he did not find on the part of the people the will to be enslaved: "It is the people who cut their throats; who, having the choice of being serfs or freemen, forsake their freedom and take on the yoke; who consent to their misfortune, or rather pursue it." [36] If the people cease in this way to use their "natural right," it is because "the seeds of good that nature plants in us are so tiny and delicate that they cannot endure the slightest wound caused by improper nourishment; it is harder for them to subsist than to degenerate, to decrease, and to come to nothing." [37] Thus

---

[35] *De dignitate et augmentis scientiarum,* Book VII, chap. ii, sec. 10.
[36] Ed. Paul Bonnefon (1922), p. 56.
[37] *Ibid.,* p. 69.

the thought of La Boétie manifests a concern for the right of the people and a juridical idealism that set him completely apart from Machiavelli.

IX   An Adversary of Aristotle: Peter Ramus (*Pierre de la Ramée*)

On reading the elegant works of Peter Ramus (1515–1572) a modern reader may well be astounded by his fame in his time, by the tempests raised by his books, and by the tragic events that they initiated. The fact is that he was not primarily a speculative philosopher but rather a professional man who was disturbed by the sterility of the instruction offered in the Parisian schools, who wished to remedy the situation, and who encountered routine resistance at every turn. His tribulations are well known: born of a very poor family in Picardy, he won his degree of Master of Arts in 1536 by defending the thesis "Everything that Aristotle taught is false (*commenticia*)." In 1543 he published the *Aristotelicae animadversiones*; the Peripatetics had him brought before the *parlement;* the case was put before the king; Francis I, on account of his "concern" for "the growth and enrichment of his kingdom through all good letters and sciences," prohibited Ramus from teaching or publishing. The decree states that "because in his book on *Animadversions* he found fault with Aristotle, he obviously manifested and made known his ignorance, and he even showed bad faith by censuring strongly many things that are good and true." [38] The interdiction was lifted by Henry II in 1551, and for ten years Ramus had a brilliant career at the College of France, without departing from the old framework of the trivium and quadrivium, for his lessons dealt with grammar, rhetoric, dialectic, arithmetic, and geometry. Converted to Calvinism in 1562, he left Paris during the civil wars; he found a hearty welcome in Germany and Switzerland, where he taught from 1568 to 1570. He returned to Paris in 1570 and was assassinated two days after the massacre of St. Bartholomew, on

[38] Decree quoted by Waddington, *Ramus,* p. 50.

August 26, 1572. Charpentier, his colleague and implacable enemy, was accused of his murder.

A teacher before all else, he tried to bring to every subject taught a simplicity and clarity no longer prevalent. He was, as Bacon said not without irony, the "father of summations." His *Animadversiones* (1543) was supplemented by his brief *Dialectique* (1555) and by his *Advertissements sur la réformation de l'Université de Paris au Roy* (1562), in which he protested against the complexity of instruction. The heart of his criticism of Aristotle is probably stated in these lines: "He wanted to make two systems of logic, one for science and the other for opinion"; he wanted to separate live discussion, that practiced naturally by "poets, orators, philosophers and, in a word, by all excellent men," from a certain chaotic accumulation of useless rules that clutter the mind.[39] To sum up the thought of Ramus: logic or dialectic is a practical art based on nature. Some people start from doctrine and think that they are learning logic "to know how to reel off the rules in school."[40] One ought instead to start from nature and keep company for a long time with poets, orators, and philosophers.

It has been judiciously observed that Ramus' dialectic was modeled on the rhetoric of Cicero and Quintilian.[41] He divides dialectic into two parts: invention, which consists in finding arguments; and disposition or arrangement, which consists in putting them in order. These are the first two parts of rhetoric. Invention goes back to the topics, which indicate the general classes of arguments—causes, effects, and so forth. Disposition concerns both the formulation of arguments and the method of grouping them in the clearest possible order once they have been found. For Ramus order is distinct from the discovery of arguments. Method or order applies only to the resolution of problems such as this one: Having put each precept of grammar on a square of paper and jumbled the squares, how can we put them in order? Ramus has only to remark: "First, there will

[39] *La Dialectique*, p. 8.
[40] *La Dialectique* (1576 edition), p. 65.
[41] G. Sortais, *La phlosophie moderne*, p. 24, n. 3, and p. 39.

be no need for invention, for everything has already been discovered." He therefore has not the slightest presentiment of the intimate bond between order and invention that Descartes discovered not in orators and poets but in mathematics.

In some contemporaneous treatises we find a clearer presentiment of method. In 1558 Acontio published a *De methodo* that defined method as "a correct procedure that makes it possible, in addition to examining the truth (*citra veritatis examen*), to pursue knowledge of a thing and to teach in a proper fashion the method through which it has been acquired." [42] Thus his definition contains two parts: method of investigation and method of exposition. The method of investigation consists in going from the most familiar to the least familiar and the most familiar is to Acontio not only general ideas but also "innate notions which, when advanced, compel everyone to grant assent—for instance, the notion that the whole is greater than the part." But the method remains nothing more than an accessory that will not eliminate the need for examination of the thesis to which it leads.

Despite such real weaknesses, Ramism had a strong appeal until the middle of the seventeenth century, especially in Germany. Ramus clearly recognized and called attention to the exigency of clarity that characterized his era and that led him to forsake the schools and write in the vulgar language: "When I return from the Greek and Latin schools and desire, by way of imitating the example of good scholars, to deliver my lesson to my country . . . and to make known the fruit of my study through the medium of the vulgar language, I perceive several things repugnant to these principles—things that I was unable to perceive in school because of so many disputes." [43]

We should add that Ramus, the enemy of Aristotelianism, met along the way all the pupils of the Paduans. He attacked Aristotle not only as a logician but also as a freethinker and as the author of a theology that denies providence and creation as well as the author

[42] Quoted by G. Sortais, *La philosophie moderne de Bacon et Leibniz*, p. 46.
[43] Preface to the *Dialectique*, quoted by Waddington, *Ramus*, p. 405.

of a moral philosophy independent of religion. He therefore had as his opponents all the libertines of his time. Galland, the friend of the Paduan Peripatetic Vicomercato, in his reply to Ramus (*Pro schola parisiensi contra novam Academiam P. Rami,* 1551) confronted him with the indispensable character of an independent ethic, the one which "taught the pagans their domestic, public, and civil duties, and which teaches us to control our desires and our passions"; "at no price will I allow anyone to advocate piety and obedience to God while remaining silent about civic virtues." [44]

x *Platonism: Postel and Bodin*

The Platonic spirit had a pressing need for unity, a need not evidenced elsewhere. This search for unity characterized the great systems that brought to a close the period of the Renaissance.

First came Guillaume Postel's attempt, practical as well as theoretical in nature, to utilize his knowledge of oriental languages to realize the religious unity of the globe (*De orbis terrae concordia,* 1542). Postel thought that such unity was possible by virtue of the rational character of religious truths: hostile to Protestantism, which broke the unity of Christianity, no less than to authoritarian Catholicism, which established the Council of Trent, he saw salvation only in a return to the forgotten origin of all religions, which is reason. His main concern was to refute the Paduans by demonstrating creation *ex nihilo* and personal immortality, and he confronted them with Plato: "For to refute Plato's Ideas, the notion of separate substances, and everything implied by innate wisdom, they have gone so far as to deny God by representing him as being constrained to act." [45] We must add that Postel's *rational* religion remained that of a man of the Renaissance, that of a scholar who, like Marsilio Ficino and Pico della Mirandola, tried to relate it to a tradition whose echoes he found not only in Plato but also in the revelation of the sibyls, in the Jewish Cabala, and among the Etruscans to whom he

[44] Quoted by Busson, *Sources,* p. 225.
[45] *Ibid.,* p. 297.

devoted one book: a tradition that derives from Reason, here conceived no longer as a simple faculty of ratiocination but as the
Word, the Logos, the world soul that animates all beings and in-
spires the prophets.

The jurist Jean Bodin was the author of a *République* (1577),
in which he opposed Plato to Machiavelli and stated that the
authority of the state remains subject to natural law (for instance, it
cannot abolish private property), and that the state has no end other
than that of the highest human good. He introduced the com-
parative method in law with the intention of deducing from the
comparison a universal law. The fundamental idea of his *Hepta-
plomeres,* a colloquy between seven learned men—a Catholic, a
Lutheran, a Calvinist, a Jew, a renegade Moslem, a Theist, and a
Skeptic—was the same as that of Postel: to select from all existing
religions a common core that can become the universal religion
which "is simply the pure spirit's quest for God." But his religion
was still more simplified than Postel's, for it contained hardly anything except the affirmation of one God and of his worship through
the exercise of moral virtues; and in practice he arrived at a tolerant
attitude that caused him to recognize all religions "in order not to
be accused of being an atheist or a dissident capable of disturbing the
tranquility of the Republic." [46]

xi *Italian Platonism: Telesio*

Social preoccupations dominated the thought of Postel and of
Bodin. Quite different were the Italian thinkers to be discussed now:
those who believed in universal animism. Like the Paduans, they
subscribed to the theory of a living universe; they differed from
the Paduans in that, first, they were hostile to Aristotle and, second,
they offered their doctrine as a comprehensive view of reality, something wholly self-sufficient and not simply an adjunct to faith.

In the forefront was Telesio (1509–1588) who, according to Francis
Bacon, was the first of the moderns (*novorum hominum primum*).

[46] *Ibid.,* p. 168.

He revived Stoic animism, which he could have known through Diogenes Laertius, Seneca, and Cicero. He accepted dynamism with its two principles: an active force and completely inert and passive matter. But the moving force is divided into expansive force or heat and contractile force or cold. Expansion and contraction, through their diverse degrees, explain all the qualitative differences of living beings. The active force is a body, and the soul of the living being, which is a part of it, is also a body, a breath or pneuma, spread throughout the cerebral cavities and nerves. This conception of the soul, popularized in the prevalent theory of animal spirits, implies a thesis similar to that of the Stoics concerning the nature of knowledge: sensation is a contact wherein an object modifies the breath or spirit which reacts defensively in accordance with its own nature; its act of self-preservation (here Telesio follows the third book of Cicero's *De finibus*) accounts for the development of ethics, thanks to man's awareness of the interdependence of his welfare and that of others; and the principal social virtue (as in Cicero's *De officiis*) is mankind, whereas the inner virtue is the sublimity that finds goodness in virtue. Intellectual knowledge (memory and thought) consists in turn of preserving sensations and using them as a substitute for the senses when the latter are missing. Furthermore, sensation and consciousness are found not only among men and animals but also in all living beings whose harmonious whole constitutes the animate universe.

Telesio also firmly supported the thesis of an immaterial soul which is added to the other soul and which has to do with our supernatural destiny, but it is difficult to interpret this addition as anything but a prudent measure in view of the powers of the Church

XII *Italian Platonism: Giordano Bruno*

Giordano Bruno (1548–1600) often named among his Italian masters Francesco Patrizzi (1529–1597), professor at Ferrara and Padua, who had an important role in disseminating this esoteric type of Platonism that blends together the ideas in the dialogues, the mysticism of the Hermetic books, and the Chaldean oracles. The same syncretism appears in the works of Bruno.

"Only an ambitious and presumptuous man," wrote Bruno, "tries to persuade others that there is but one path that leads to knowledge of nature. . . . Even though we must always elect the surest and firmest, the most contemplative and distinct path and the loftiest mode of meditation, we have no right to censure another mode that yields good fruits even though they are not from the same tree. The Epicureans have said many good things even though they do not rise above the qualities of matter. Heraclitus says many excellent things even though he does not go beyond the soul. We can profit by reading Anaxagoras, who sets above the soul an intellect—the same intellect that Socrates, Plato, Trismegistus, and our theologians call God." [47]

No passage could better express Bruno's eclecticism and his dream of an all-encompassing philosophy. He had only one enemy—Aristotle—the man "injurious and ambitious, who wished to disparage the opinions of all other philosophers and their manner of philosophizing."

Such richness or rather such profusion of thoughts in a philosopher who, like Leibnitz at a later date, wished to lose no part of the speculations of his predecessors, has always been disconcerting to those who try to explain systematically the doctrine of Bruno. It contains a hierarchy of Plotinian hypostases—God, Intelligence, World Soul, and Matter; the heliocentrism of Copernicus and the infinity of worlds linked to it; Parmenides' Identity; and Democritus' atomistic theory, along with corpuscular physics. These are Bruno's principal theses, not ordinarily found together. We have seen Plotinism closely linked to geocentrism, which alone can provide a sensible image of unity; but Plotinus condemns any theory of atomism that would substitute mechanical composition for the continuity of life. Do we find in Bruno a series of successive systems? This seems impossible when we consider the works that

[47] *Della Causa* (ed. Gentile) i. 170.

he wrote over a period of ten years (1582–1592), between the age of 34 and 44. Or do we prefer to see a tissue of contradictions in the works written throughout a troubled lifetime by a man who abandoned the Dominican convent in 1576, aroused the suspicions of Lutherans and Calvinists alike, and languished for eight years in the prisons of the Inquisition, from which he was released in 1600 only to be burned at the stake? It is true that we find in his works many inconsistencies and even absurdities, such as his singular mathematical atomism which, composed of rows of points, seems to date from a period prior to Plato, before the discovery of irrationals. But he nevertheless managed to extricate Platonism from damaging solidarities: indeed, we recall that in the beginning Platonism, unlike the system of Aristotle, was not linked in any way to geocentrism; that Erigena and Nicholas of Cusa, two great Platonists whom Bruno particularly esteemed, favored the heliocentrism of the Pythagoreans; that in the *Timaeus* Plato himself, after speaking of the world as of a living being and of its soul, outlines a doctrine of atoms according to which the world is composed of corpuscles, regular solids inscribable in spheres. It is to Plato's doctrine of atoms (and not to that of Democritus) that Bruno refers in the following text: "To Pythagoras the first principles are monads and numbers; to Plato atoms, lines, and surfaces." [48] It is Plato, and not Epicurus, who suggested to him the idea of giving to all atoms a spherical shape.

Thus Bruno, a true exponent of intuition, broke away from secular associations of ideas. Vulgar Platonists did not go beyond the *contemplatio ordinis,* knowledge of the hierarchical order of things, but this is merely the fourth degree in a scale that includes nine degrees, the last two of which are "the transformation of one's self into the thing and the transformation of the thing into one's self." [49] Furthermore, Bruno sees the perfect interpenetration of every degree of knowledge: "It can be demonstrated," he writes, "that if intelligence participates in sense, then sense will be in-

[48] *De minimo* i. 10.
[49] *Sigillus sigillorum* i. 34.

telligence itself." This significant text contains no trace of the opposition between the senses and the intellect which is most hallowed
among the vulgar Platonists, and it clearly reveals Bruno's pattern
of thought: a continuous sliding (whether he is dealing with sense
and intellect or with the sensible and the intelligible) from par-
ticipation to identity.

This fact explains the principal traits of his vision of the world.
He reduces all hypostases—God, Intelligence, World Soul, Matter
—to one: the life of the universe, "the holy, sacred, and venerable
animal," which is at the same time one and multiple.[50] In particular,
he cannot postulate matter that is nothing more than non-being
and that does not already contain every seminal reason. Here he
differs from Plotinus less than is generally supposed, for a truly
divine reality is exactly what Plotinus meant by the term intelligible
matter. All individuals are to him only modes of a unique substance and are to the substance as numbers to unity, or rather as
the compound unities of numbers to the primitive unity to which
they owe their existence. God is the monad of monads, the entity
of beings, the substance of substances, or as it is expressed in *De
immenso*:

> . . . *Rerum facies dum tantum fluctuat extra,*
> *Intimius cunctis quam sint sibi quaeque, vigens est*
> *Entis principium, cunctarum fons spicierum,*
> *Mens, Deus, Ens, Unum, Verum, Fatum, Oratio, Ordo.*[51]

"Whereas the surface of things continues to fluctuate, he is more
essential to all things than they are to themselves, the living principle
of being, the source of all forms, Mind, God, Being, One, Truth,
Fate, Word, Order." In certain expositions Mind is broken up into
realities of different degrees: Mind superior to everything, or God;
Mind infused into all things, or Nature; and Mind that traverses
all things, or Reason.[52] In other expositions a unique reality is the

---

[50] *De immenso*, quoted by Charbonnel, *La Pensée italienne*, p. 455, n. 2.
[51] *De immenso* viii. 10. 1.
[52] *De minimo* (beginning).

focal point and such differences are of slight importance; they are of value only to those who seek to determine whether Bruno supports transcendence of immanence, which makes sense only when we accept God and nature as static and contiguous realities, not when we accept Bruno's dynamism with its stress on the active, animating principle.

That is the explanation of the thesis of the infinity of the universe, for divine infinity can be expressed only in a universe that is also infinite. That is the explanation, in spite of the apparent paradox, of his atomistic theory (which could more aptly be called monadology). The fact is that Bruno, like Leibnitz at a later date, makes simplicity the prime characteristic of substance: *Compositum porro nullum substantia vera est.*[53]

It is for this reason that he accepts atoms, but they are not the "impious elements" of Democritus.[54] Bruno's physics is not in any way mechanistic: surrounding atoms is the ether, "an immense region in which the world moves and lives," [55] a medium which fills the space, body, and soul of the world and in which atoms are constituted and combined; and in each individual is a soul that is like the nucleus around which atoms collect and fall into place. The result is that Bruno preserves both the Plotinian conception of the individual as the image of the whole and a microcosm, and the Democritean conception of the indivisible element as a constituent unit.

Through his system Bruno hoped, as Ficino did through Platonism, to achieve true religious unity, which he contrasted with the unity of the Reformers, misanthropic minds that sow discord everywhere; with the unity of fanatical, pessimistic Catholicism that is the enemy of nature; with the unity of Judaism and its jealous, bloodthirsty God;[56] with the unity that he associates with the "Egyptian religion," that is, with the religious Platonism of Hermes Trismegistus. His religion is a gnosis; it is knowledge on the part

[53] *De minimo* i. 3. 29.
[54] *De immenso* v. 8. 36.
[55] *De minimo* i. 2. 10.
[56] Cf. the texts in Charbonnel, *La Pensée italienne*, pp. 488–90.

of man that "God is near him, with him, and more essential to him than he can be to himself." [57]

The thought of Lucilio Vanini (1585–1619) falls far short of that of Bruno in precision and in breadth. He fled from one place to another seeking refuge from his persecutors and finally fell victim to the Inquisition, which had him burned as a heretic at Toulouse. He is remembered mainly as the disseminator and popularizer of the theses of the Paduans.

XIII Italian Platonism: Campanella

The animistic current culminated in the system of Tommaso Campanella, who was unquestionably a man of the Renaissance in spite of the period in which he lived (1568–1639). His most important work, *De sensu rerum et magia,* completed in 1604 and published in 1620, is described in the subtitle as "an admirable contribution to occult philosophy in which it is demonstrated that the world is the statue of the living, knowing God, and that all his parts and the parts of his parts are imbued with sense ranging from clarity to obscurity but sufficient for his preservation and for the preservation of the whole." In it scholars have identified the panpsychism of Bruno and of Telesio. Two of the main arguments to demonstrate that the world is a sentient being are of Stoic origin: that it is sentient because certain parts of it are sentient and whatever is in the parts is a fortiori in the whole; and that all its parts are sentient because they all have instincts or impulses that imply sensation. The first argument is that of Chrysippus in Cicero's *De natura deorum*; the second uses the theory of *De finibus,* but what the Stoics attributed only to animals is extended here to all living beings, following the example of Plotinus. Campanella no longer recognizes the hierarchy of animals, plants, and inanimate beings postulated by Aristotle and the Stoics. Like Plato and Plotinus he sees only degrees: the nutritive faculty presupposes the sentient faculty; intellect is identical to sense; animals think and are en-

---

[57] Quoted by Blanchet, *Campanella*, p. 452.

dowed with something that resembles discursive reasoning (*discursus universalis*). To this conception of the world is linked natural magic, conceived as Plotinus conceived it in the fourth *Ennead*: as a positive art of employing the occult forces that emanate from the stars or from the simple tension of the will.[58] The action of magic, which is typical of the action of nature, is diametrically opposed to mechanism, which was then on the verge of triumph.

On the naturalism of the Renaissance is erected a metaphysic that develops the principle of the Plotinian system: whatever is sympathy in the sensible world is intimate union and identity in the intelligible world. Sensible knowledge is but a contact between object and subject; it reveals to us nothing more about the object than the aspect through which the perceiver is identified with what is perceived. Typical of intellectual knowledge, however, is knowledge that the soul acquires independently of itself; all knowledge is in fact inseparable from just such self-consciousness. By acquiring knowledge of things, "the soul acquires knowledge of itself because it is what it is; it is other things at the moment when it feels itself changed into them. Yet the change is not knowledge but the cause or occasion of knowledge." According to the same principle, the common properties and similarities that bind things together provide the soul with an opportunity to contemplate Ideas; the assimilation of the known object to the knowing subject, imperfectly realized in our general concepts, is perfectly realized in the Idea. The soul and nature lead Campanella to a God who contains in his "primalities"—Power, Wisdom, and Love—the model of our soul and of all things: a universal analogy that allows this sensualist to ascend from the sensible to the intelligible.[59]

In 1599 Campanella took part in a conspiracy in Calabria where, according to the records of the trial instituted against him, he apparently represented himself as a new Messiah and tried to set up a theocratic republic similar to the one described later in *La Città*

---

[58] Cf. Blanchet, *Campanella*, p. 217.

[59] Gilson, "Le raisonnement par analogie chez T. Campanella," in *Études de philosophie médiévale*, p. 125.

del Sole, completed in 1602 and published in 1623. The dominant idea of his utopia is that of the regeneration of mankind on the basis of a more productive organization. He was deeply concerned with economic realities: "There are seventy thousand souls in Naples," he wrote, "and hardly ten or fifteen thousand workers are numbered among them. Thus the workers exhaust themselves and die for the sake of an employment that exceeds their strength. In the city of the Sun, the tasks are equally distributed, with the result that no one works for more than four hours each day." Still, the economic result was not the essential point: "A few men are spurred on to the discovery of the new world by the desire for riches, but God drives them there for a much more exalted purpose." This idea of a regenerated humanity that would attain its unity through a natural religion basically identical to Christianity, was the fundamental idea of those who brought about the revival of Platonism during the Renaissance.

XIV *Spanish Mysticism*

Just as the experimental method of Leonardo abandoned the metaphysical construction of the universe and saw in things momentary and changing equilibriums of forces rather than the realization of an ideal plan, so the contemporaneous mysticism of the Spaniards abandoned speculation on the structure of the divine reality. The sixteenth-century mystics practiced intellectual humility: "God," said St. John of the Cross (died in 1591), "does not wish us to give full credence (to our intimate and personal revelations) so long as they have not passed through the human channel of man's mouth." [60] Submission to the Church was total. The same St. John of the Cross rejected the idea that there was a rational procedure that could lead the spirit from the sensible world to God: "Nothing created or conceived can provide the intellect with an appropriate means of uniting with God. Everything that can be accomplished

[60] Miguel de Unamuno, *L'Essence de l'Espagne,* p. 215.

by the intellect is an obstacle rather than a means of approaching him." [61] Thus what the mystic seeks through union with God is not the revelation of the essence of things or an answer to a question, but above all else an inner freedom that liberates him from any restraints, an immediate knowledge not dependent on meditation or on a process of reasoning. According to the testimony of St. Theresa (1515–1582), the divine inner words which the mystic cannot fail to hear, which transform the soul, and which have such a force that nothing can efface them, are nevertheless produced in the soul at moments when the mystic is incapable of understanding them and are not prompted by a desire to hear them.[62] The Spanish mystic seeks the inner perfection of his soul and not, like Erigena or Eckhart, the revelation of the principles of the universe. The nature of the relation between the religious life and the history of intellectual thought, which had gone on for centuries, changed under the influence of such mysticism.

[61] Cf. J. Baruzi, *Saint-Jean de la Croix,* pp. 412–13.
[62] *Vie de sainte Thérèse* (trans. Bouix), chap. xxv, p. 323.

BIBLIOGRAPHY

I and II

Texts

Cassirer, E., Kristeller, P., and Randall, J., Jr. (eds.). *The Renaissance Philosophy of Man*. Chicago, 1948.
De Santillana, G. (ed.). *The Age of Adventure: The Renaissance Philosophers*. Boston, 1957.

Studies

Bouyer, L. *Christian Humanism*. Translated by A. V. Littledall. Westminster, Md., 1958.
Burckhardt, J. *The Civilization of the Renaissance in Italy*. Translated by S. G. Middlemore. New York, 1935. New edition, 1944.
Bush, D. *The Renaissance and English Humanism*. Toronto, 1939.
Collins, J. *A History of Modern European Philosophy*. Milwaukee, 1954. Pp. 13–50.
De Lagarde. *Le naissance de l'esprit láique au déclin du moyen âge*. 6 vols. Paris, 1948.
Ferguson, W. *The Renaissance in Historical Thought: Five Centuries of Interpretation*. Boston, 1948.
Gilbert, N. *Renaissance Concepts of Method*. New York, 1960.
Gilson, E. "Humanisme médiévale et Renaissance," in *Les idées et les lettres*. Paris, 1932.
Haydn, H. *The Counter-Renaissance*. New York, 1950.
Howell, W. *Logic and Rhetoric in England, 1500–1700*. Princeton, 1956.
Kristeller, P. *Renaissance Thought: The Classic, Scholastic and Humanist Strains*. New York, 1955.
———. *Studies in Renaissance Thought and Letters*. Rome, 1956.
Lucas, H. *The Renaissance and the Reformation*. New York, 1934.
Riedl, J. *A Catalogue of Renaissance Philosophers (1350–1650)*. Milwaukee, 1940.
Sellery, G. *The Renaissance: Its Nature and Origins*. Madison, Wisc., 1950.

259

III

Texts

Erasmus. *Opera omnia*. Lugduni Batavorum, 1703–1706.
———. *The Praise of Folly*. Translated by H. H. Hudson. Princeton, 1941.
León Hebreo. Critical edition of *Dialoghi di Amore*. Edited by C. Gebhardt. Heidelberg, 1929.
———. *The Philosophy of Love*. Translated by C. Roth. Soncino Jewish Publication Society. 1937.
Marsilio Ficino. *Opera omnia*. Paris, 1641.
———. *Five Questions concerning the Mind*. Translated by J. Burroughs, in E. Cassirer, *et al.*, *The Renaissance Philosophy of Man*. Pp. 193–214.
Nicholas of Cusa. *Opera omnia*. 7 vols. Edited by E. Hoffman and R. Klibansky. Leipzig, 1932–53.
———. *On Learned Ignorance*. Translated by G. Heron. London, 1954.
———. *The Vision of God*. Translated by E. Salter. New York, 1960.
Paracelsus. *Selected Writings*. Translated by N. Gutterman. New York, 1951.
Pico della Mirandola. *Opera*. Bologna, 1496.
———. *Oration on the Dignity of Man*. Translated by E. Forbes, in E. Cassirer, *et al.*, *The Renaissance Philosophy of Man*, pp. 223–54.

Studies

Bett, H. *Nicholas of Cusa*. London, 1932.
Cassirer, E. "Giovanni Pico Della Mirandola," *Journal of the History of Ideas,* III (1942), 123–44, 319–46.
Dulles, A. *Princeps concordiae: Pico della Mirandola and the Scholastic Tradition*. Cambridge, 1941.
Huizinga, J. *Erasmus of Rotterdam*. New York, 1952.
Kristeller, P. *The Philosophy of Marsilio Ficino*. New York, 1943.
———. "The Scholastic Background of Marsilio Ficino," *Traditio,* II (1944), 257–318.
Pachter, H. *Magic into Science: The Story of Paracelsus*. New York, 1951.
Phillips, M. *Erasmus and the Northern Renaissance*. London, 1949.
Robb, N. *Neoplatonism of the Italian Renaissance*. London, 1935.
Sigmund, P. *Nicholas of Cusa and Medieval Political Thought*. New Haven and Oxford, 1963.
Vansteenberghe, E. *Le Cardinal Nicolas de Cues*. 1920.

IV to VI

Texts

Leonardo da Vinci. *The Notebooks of Leonardo da Vinci.* Arranged and translated by E. MacCurdy. 2 vols. New York, 1938.

——. *Philosophical Diary.* Selections, translated by Wade Baskin. New York, 1959.

Petrarch. *Opera.* Venice, 1503.

——. *On His Own Ignorance and That of Many Others,* and other selections, in E. Cassirer, *et al., The Renaissance Philosophy of Man,* pp. 34–146.

Pomponazzi. *Opera.* Basel, 1567.

——. *On the Immortality of the Soul.* Translated by W. Hay, II. Revised by J. Randall, Jr., in E. Cassirer, *et al., The Renaissance Philosophy of Man,* pp. 280–384.

Studies

Douglas, A. *The Philosophy and Psychology of Pietro Pomponazzi.* New York, 1910.

Duhem, P. *Études sur Léonard de Vinci.* Paris, 1906–13.

Kristeller, P. "Augustine and the Early Renaissance," *Review of Religion,* VIII (1944), 339–58. On Petrarch.

——. "Ficino and Pomponazzi on the Place of Man in the Universe," *Journal of the History of Ideas,* V (1944), 220–26.

Mabilleau, L. *Cesare Cremonini: La philosophie de la renaissance en Italie.* Paris, 1881.

MacCurdy, E. *The Mind of Leonardo da Vinci.* New York, 1928.

Randall, J., Jr. "The Development of Scientific Method in the School of Padua," *Journal of the History of Ideas,* I (1940), 177–206.

Séailles, G. *Léonard de Vinci.* 4th ed. Paris, 1912.

Whitfield, J. *Petrarch and the Renascence.* Oxford, 1943.

——. *Machiavelli.* Oxford, 1947.

Wilkins, E. *Life of Petrarch.* Chicago, 1961.

Vidari. "G. Cardano," *Rivista italiana di filosofia,* VIII (1893).

VII to X

Texts

Guillaume du Vair. *The Moral Philosophie of the Stoicks,* written in French by Guillaume Du Vair. Translated by Thomas James. Edited by R. Kirk. New Brunswick, N. J., 1951.

Justus Lipsius. *Two Bookes of Constancie,* written in Latin by Justus Lipsius. Translated by Sir John Stradling. Edited by R. Kirk and C. Hall. New Brunswick, N. J., 1939.

Machiavelli, N. *Tutte le opere.* Edited by G. Mazzoni and M. Casella, Florence, 1929.

———. *The Prince and Other Works.* Translated by A. Gilbert. New York, 1941.

———. *The Discourses.* Translated by L. Walker. 2 vols. London, 1950.

Montaigne. *The Complete Works of Montaigne.* Translated by D. Frame. Stanford, 1957.

Pierre Charron. *Of Wisdom.* Translated by G. Stanhope. 3 vols. London, 1729.

Studies

Frame, D. *Montaigne's Discovery of Man.* New York, 1955.

Gilbert, A. *Machiavelli's Prince and Its Forerunners.* Durham, N. C., 1938.

Hale, J. *Machiavelli and Renaissance Italy.* New York and London, 1961.

Mauzey, J. *Montaigne's Philosophy of Human Nature.* Annandale-on-Hudson, N. Y., 1933.

Mesnard, P. *L'essor de la philosophie politique au XVIe siècle.* Paris, 1951.

Ong, W. *Ramus, Method, and the Decay of Dialogue.* Cambridge, 1958.

Popkin, R. *The History of Scepticism from Erasmus to Descartes.* Assen, 1960.

Ridolfi, *The Life of Niccolò Machiavelli.* Chicago, 1963.

Sabrié, J. *De l'humanisme au rationalisme: Pierre Charron.* Paris, 1913.

Saunders, J. L. *Justus Lipsius: The Philosophy of Renaissance Stoicism.* New York, 1955.

Strowski, F. *Montaigne.* Paris, 1931.

Whitfield, J. *Machiavelli.* Oxford, 1947.

Zanta, L. *La Renaissance du stoïcisme au XVIe siècle.* Paris, 1914.

XI to XV

Texts

Campanella. *Opera.* Vols. I, II, and IV. Paris, 1637.

Giordano Bruno. *Opere italiane.* Edited by G. Gentile. 3 vols. Bari, 1907–9.

———. *Opera latina conscripta.* Edited by F. Fiorentino, *et al.* 3 vols. Naples, 1879–91.

———. *On the Infinite Universe and Worlds.* Translated by D. Singer in *Giordano Bruno: His Life and Thought.* New York, 1950.

———. *Concerning the Cause, Principle and One.* Translated by A. Greenberg in *The Infinite in Giordano Bruno.* New York, 1940.

Guillaume Postel. *De orbis concordia.* Book IV. Basel, 1544.

Jean Bodin. *Les six livres de la République.* Lyons, 1579.

Jean Bodin. *The Six Book of a Commonweale*. Facsimile reprint of the English translation of 1606, edited by Kenneth Douglas McRae. New Haven and Oxford, 1962.

St. John of the Cross. *The Complete Works of St. John of the Cross*. Edited by E. Peers. London, 1934.

Studies

Baruzi, J. *Saint Jean de la Croix et le problème de l'expérience mystique*. Paris, 1924. New edition, 1931.

Blanchet, L. *Campanella*. Paris, 1920.

Bruno de Jésus-Marie. *Saint Jean de la Croix*. Paris, 1929.

DiNapoli, G. *Tommaso Campanella: Filosofo della restaurazione cattolica*. Padua, 1947.

Fiorentino, F. *Telesio, studii storici sull'idea della natura nel risorgimento italiano*. Naples, 1872–74.

Lefranc, A. "Communication sur Jean Bodin," *Académie des Inscriptions* (Session of January 6, 1928).

Mercati, A. *Il sommario del processo di Giordano Bruno*. Vatican City, 1942.

Mesnard, P. *L'essor de la philosophie politique au XVIe siècle*. Paris, 1936.

Moreau-Reibel, J. *Jean Bodin et le droit public comparé dans ses rapports avec la philosophie de l'histoire*. Paris, 1933.

Namer, E. *Les aspects de Dieu dans la philosophie de G. Bruno*. Paris, 1926.

Nelson, J. *Renaissance Theory of Love: The Context of Giordano Bruno's "Eroici Furiori."* New York, 1958.

Peers, E. *Spanish Mysticism: A Preliminary Survey*. London, 1926.

———. *Studies of the Spanish Mystics*. New York and Toronto, 1927.

Troilo, E. *La filosofia di Giordano Bruno*. Turin, 1907.

Yates, F. *Giordano Bruno and the Hermetic Tradition*. Chicago, 1964.

INDEX

PHOENIX BOOKS
in Philosophy

PHOENIX BOOKS
in Religion

PHOENIX BOOKS
in History

PHOENIX BOOKS
in Political Science and Law